FROM *Chantre* TO *Djak*

Cantorial Traditions
in Canada

Compiled and edited by
Robert B. Klymasz

Mercury Series
Canadian Centre for Folk Culture Studies
Paper 73

Published by Canadian Museum of Civilization

CANADIAN CATALOGUING IN PUBLICATION DATA

Main entry under title :

From chantre to djak : cantorial traditions in
Canada

(Mercury series)
(Paper / Canadian Museum of Civilization. Canadian
Centre for Folk Culture Studies; CCFCS73)
Includes prefatory material and articles in French.
Includes bibliographical references.
ISBN 0-660-17834-6

1. Church musicians — Canada.
2. Synagogue music — Canada.
3. Cantors (Judaism) — Canada.
4. Cantors (Church music) — Canada.
I. Klymasz, Robert B. (Robert Bogdan), 1936– .
II. Canadian Museum of Civilization.
Canadian Centre for Folk Culture Studies.
III. Series.
IV. Series: Paper (Canadian Museum of Civilization.
Canadian Centre for Folk Culture Studies);
CCFCS73.

ML3795.K59 2000   782.2'92'0971   C00-980000-X

PRINTED IN CANADA

Published by
Canadian Museum of Civilization
100 Laurier Street
P.O. Box 3100, Station B
Hull, Quebec
J8X 4H2

Senior production officer: Deborah Brownrigg

Cover design: Expression Communications Inc.

Front cover: Cantor (*djak*) George Danyleshko,
east central Alberta, May 1973 (still from *Luchak's
Easter*, 16-mm colour film produced by the Canadian
Centre for Folk Culture Studies, National Museum
of Man, National Museums of Canada, 1975).
CMC slide S73-1047.

Canada

OBJECT OF THE MERCURY SERIES

The Mercury Series is designed to permit the rapid
dissemination of information pertaining to the disciplines in which the Canadian Museum of Civilization
is active. Considered an important reference by the
scientific community, the Mercury Series comprises
over three hundred specialized publications on
Canada's history and prehistory.

Because of its specialized audience, the series
consists largely of monographs published in the
language of the author.

In the interest of making information available
quickly, normal production procedures have been
abbreviated. As a result, grammatical and typograph-
ical errors may occur. Your indulgence is requested.

Titles in the Mercury Series can be obtained
by calling 1-800-555-5621;
by e-mail to <publications@civilization.ca>;
by internet to <cyberboutique.civilization.ca>;
or by writing to:

Mail Order Services
Canadian Museum of Civilization
100 Laurier Street
P.O. Box 3100, Station B
Hull, Quebec
J8X 4H2

BUT DE LA COLLECTION

La collection Mercure vise à diffuser rapidement
le résultat de travaux dans les disciplines qui
relèvent des sphères d'activités du Musée canadien
des civilisations. Considérée comme un apport
important dans la communauté scientifique,
la collection Mercure présente plus de trois cents
publications spécialisées portant sur l'héritage
canadien préhistorique et historique.

Comme la collection s'adresse à un public
spécialisé, celle-ci est constituée essentiellement de
monographies publiées dans la langue des auteurs.

Pour assurer la prompte distribution des exemplaires imprimés, les étapes de l'édition ont été
abrégées. En conséquence, certaines coquilles ou
fautes de grammaire peuvent subsister : c'est
pourquoi nous réclamons votre indulgence.

Vous pouvez vous procurer les titres parus dans
la collection Mercure par téléphone, en appelant
au 1-800-555-5621, par courriel, en adressant votre
demande à <publications@civilisations.ca>,
par internet à <cyberboutique.civilisations.ca>
ou par la poste, en écrivant au :

Service des commandes postales
Musée canadien des civilisations
100, rue Laurier
C.P. 3100, succursale B
Hull (Québec)
J8X 4H2

Abstract

The performance of sacred song often relies on the talents and dedication of cantors or other persons who perform similar roles. In many cultures, these individuals also act as intermediaries serving to bridge two worlds: the religious and the secular.

In order to illuminate the importance of this phenomenon, this volume documents and analyzes many aspects of cantorial practice. Although the text gives prominence to East European cantorial traditions as manifested in Canada, other traditions are explored as well. An annotated bibliography supplements these findings and suggests a variety of areas for further research.

Résumé

L'exécution des chants sacrés dépend souvent des talents et du dévouement des chantres et d'autres personnes qui jouent un rôle semblable. Dans de nombreuses cultures, ces personnes servent également d'intermédiaires entre deux univers : le monde religieux et le monde laïque.

De manière à souligner l'importance de ce phénomène, cet ouvrage présente et analyse de nombreux aspects de la pratique des chantres. Bien que les traditions d'Europe de l'Est, telles qu'elles se manifestent au Canada, y occupent une place prépondérante, on y explore également d'autres traditions. Une bibliographie analytique complète ces travaux et propose divers domaines où pousser les recherches plus avant.

I am completely lost in this ocean of Eimos, Sedalions, Theotokions, Troparions, Kontakions, etc. first and secondary ones, and sometimes I feel I am going off my head. When I asked Father Alexander again how his cantor manages when he sings the canon with the stichiras and how he does know what he has to read and sing (for the church has extremely exact rules about what to sing and read on particular days, in what mode and how many times); he answered: 'I don't know, before each service he looks something up in the book.' If the clergy don't know, what am I, a sinner to do?

Piortr Ilyich Tchaikovsky (June 24, 1881)

He who sings the liturgy, prays twice over.

Metropolitan Andrej Sheptyc'kyj
("To the Cantors", 1939)

The rabbi, the deacon, the butcher, the cantor,
All the sacred attendants are dancing!
Shout then all of you, with all your might!

Yiddish ditty, Montreal, 1955

CONTENTS

AVANT-PROPOS

La fonction essentielle du chant sacré, c'est l'adoration et la louange de Dieu. Mais ce qui fait l'objet de ce livre ce n'est pas tant la relation particulière que chacun entretien avec le sacré que la recherche, dans l'histoire sociale et dans les récits de vie de quelques chantres, du sens donné à la vie par la pratique de la musique et du chant sacrés.

Les auteurs de cet ouvrage nous livrent une réflexion sur divers aspects de ces traditions musicales et nous montrent que la musique sacrée, loin d'être un phénomène isolé, fait partie des pratiques sociales qui se rapportent à notre époque. Sous forme de récits, d'observations ou d'analyse, ils abordent des sujets aussi variés que l'esthétique musicale, le pouvoir thérapeutique de la musique et la stratégie utilisée pour captiver une assemblée de fidèles.

Tout en mettant en évidence la tradition du chantre ukrainien *djakivstvo* et quelques autres traditions de l'Est de l'Europe, les auteurs abordent également certains aspects de la vie de chantre au Canada, dans l'Église anglicane, juive et catholique. Pour mémoire, rappelons l'origine commune de la tradition du chant liturgique qui remonte aux premiers chantres chrétiens, venus du judaïsme, tout comme le répertoire littéraire du grégorien en usage dans l'église chrétienne. Différenciés par leur contexte culturel et religieux, le chantre, le *cantor*, le *djak*, le *khazan* occupent des fonctions similaires dans la pratique.

Comme le souligne l'éditeur de ce livre, peu de recherches ont été faites sur la tradition de chantre au Canada. La Division des études culturelles du Musée canadien des civilisations dont le mandat est d'étudier l'expression culturelle des Canadiens contribue par cette publication à faire découvrir un domaine jusqu'ici négligé par la recherche et souhaite encourager l'intérêt des ethnologues et des ethnomusicologues pour l'étude d'une pratique de notre temps et d'une tradition qui fait partie de la mémoire collective des Canadiens.

Carmelle Bégin

INTRODUCTION

by
Robert B. Klymasz

The Icon in Canada published by the Canadian Museum of Civilization in 1996 may properly lay claim to instigating this compilation of research materials on Canada's cantorial traditions. Like sacred art, music in religious worship manifests itself in many ways. And in many cases, the vitality of this particular connection often depends on a class of practitioners identified as "cantors." Besides singing, performing and leading others, these carriers of religious song frequently serve as intermediaries on various levels of study, both musical and non-musical in nature. Though marginal to the concerns of most studies on religious music, the important roles and functions of the cantor highlighted here can not be passed over or ignored: as pivotal agents of continuity and change they warrant serious attention.

The goal here is to help document our cantorial traditions and to suggest avenues for future research into this rich yet neglected aspect of musical creativity. As such, this assemblange of findings represents the fruition of a lingering concern that I first identified three decades ago in my *Bibliography of Ukrainian Foklore, 1902-1964* (Ottawa: National Museum of Canada Anthropology Paper No. 21, p. 4).

Largely a collaborative effort, the present work owes much to the talents of numerous scholars and enthusiasts. The "Preface" by Natalie Kononenko draws upon her expertise in the field of Ukrainian minstrelsy to explore the cantorial tradition as a sphere of verbal creativity. Part One features an autobiographical account by Joseph Roll and two papers that use contrasting approaches in their study of individual cantors. In his explosive investigation of a cantor from Manitoba (Gary Robertson), Michael Owen Jones favours the behavioral perspective, while Anne-Marie Poulin, on the other hand, offers a meticulous study that treats the career of her dedicated *chantre* (Claude Gosselin of Quebec) in a more diachronic fashion. Part Two offers an ethnomusicological analysis by Claudette Berthiaume-Zavada, Bohdan Medwidsky's investigation of cantors and godparents as saints and sinners in Ukrainian folklore, Shelley Posen's study of cantors in Ottawa's Jewish community, and Marcia Ostashewski's report on her interview with Toronto's eminent Anglican cantor, Albert Mahon. Part Three provides documentary material in the form of two excerpts from authoritative handbooks that offer directives for cantors to follow, and an annotated bibliography.

As in the past, the present publication owes much to the support of the Research Division of the Canadian Museum of Civilization and its publication production unit. My thanks to all who helped and participated in this project!

PREFACE

by
Natalie Kononenko

In the beginning, there was the Word. And the word has always been a special offering to God. Perhaps because speech distinguishes human beings from other creatures, words have been the way that people reach out to God. God has been addressed in prayer, in hymns, in the liturgy. While God will accept any speech, the special word, the one with an artistic element, with rhyme, with rhythm, the word that can be chanted -- that is the word we feel to be especially meaningful, especially suited as a divine offering. This is the word that heals human souls if they are troubled or in pain. This is the province of the cantor. He or she can pray for us or lead us in prayer. The cantor is the person with the beautiful voice, with the knowledge of music. But as important as the musical element of the cantor's art may be, it is the words that dominate. Often, only the words are written down and the music is either learned or left to improvisation. The music must be there, but it must always be appropriate to the words, must never obscure them, or detract from them, just serve as a vehicle for communicating the words more effectively, for influencing people in the best possible way.

Minstrels have been extensively studied and some of the information we have about them can be used to understand the art of the cantor. Ukrainian minstrels, for example, the *kobzari* and *lirnyky*, are linked to cantors in many ways. Describing Ukrainian material closely related to chant, the recitative of Ukrainian minstrels, the musicologist Filaret Kolessa (1871-1947) noted the dominance of words over music and speculated that most performers sing to one, or at most two, melodies.(1) During the period from which we have the most information, the middle of the nineteenth century through the first quarter of this one, minstrels were organized into church-affiliated guilds, performed a repertory dominated by religious song, and used a style resembling church chant, the recitative mentioned above. It is likely that in the past, the ties between minstrels and the church were closer still and minstrel guild members lived on church grounds, interacting with seminarians, men studying for the priesthood or, more likely, to become *diaky*, the deacon/cantors of the Ukrainian church.

Everything we know about minstrelsy speaks to the preeminence of words. This is true of the period of apprenticeship and of the techniques minstrels use to acquire new material after their apprenticeships are complete. Learning words was the key to becoming a *kobzar* or *lirnyk*. Ukrainian minstrels had to be blind, and when a blind child went to study with a master, he or she first learned the basics of survival: how to compensate for blindness, even how to travel on one's own. After that came training in the rudiments of begging: how to approach a home or draw attention to oneself at a fair or religious festival, how to perform the begging song or *zhebranka*, a ritualized request for alms, how to thank the patron by singing a song of gratitude. Acquiring this knowledge insured survival, even for a blind person who never went beyond this level, and he or she could leave training at this point and become a guild-affiliated beggar. A true minstrel, however, went on to the next stage: learning the words of songs. This was the heart of the apprenticeship and considered the most difficult part of training, the one that took the most time and effort. During this stage, the apprentice learned the words to religious songs, satirical songs, historical songs, and *dumy* -- the epic songs for which Ukrainian minstrels were most widely known. From what we can tell, most masters taught the words to the songs alone, without the musical accompaniment, teaching the playing of the musical instrument, the *lira* or the *bandura*, only in the next phase of training, one that was considered less difficult and less time-consuming. It was only then that youngsters studying the minstrel's craft put words and music together.(2)

As words were the key to learning songs during apprenticeship, so a mature performer acquiring new material could pick it up from the words alone. Ivan Kravchenko-Kriukovs'kyi, an outstanding performer from the second half of the nineteenth century, stated that the source of the majority of songs he mastered after apprenticeship was a man so old, he could no longer sing. This man was willing to dictate, however, and from his words Kravchenko-Kriukovs'kyi picked up a wealth of material.(3) Scholars working with minstrels would sometimes read texts to them and these spoken words alone were enough for the performers. Words seemed to "dictate" the music and a mature *kobzar* or *lirnyk* needed only the words to sense how they should be sung.(4) Similarly, cantors speak of the dominance of words over music, stressing that the words determine how they are to be performed.

Even in traditions that allow a more elaborate melody or a more ornate style, words take precedence over music. The Jewish tradition, for example, allows the use of popular music for at least certain texts. Jewish cantors, however, underscore that it is not the popularity of a particular tune that determines its choice. Rather, the words of a text, and the appropriateness of the popular melody to those words, govern usage.

Improvisation is integral to the cantor's art. With the dominance of words over music, there is a certain flexibility in music choice. Sometimes cantors are aware of improvisation, and the Jewish cantors interviewed by I. Sheldon Posen for the article published here speak of consciously using a new melody for a text they plan to perform. Sometimes improvisation is spontaneous or unconscious, and particular words seem to demand one melody in the mind of one performer and a different melody in the eyes of another. Kolessa felt that minstrels used the one melody they knew for any text that crossed their paths rather than trying to reproduce the music they had heard. Similarly, some cantors may have one and only one chanting style which they use for all of their pieces. Conversely, some cantors and other performers change melodies over time, feeling that the way they had sung a particular text in the past was no longer appropriate.

It would be simplistic, however, to say that flexibility in music is responsible for the improvisation characteristic of cantorial chant. Improvisation is a more elemental feature. *The New Catholic Encyclopedia* tells us that the "role of cantor ... came to achieve official recognition in the Christian liturgy also, but not until the 4th century, and then somewhat obscurely." As the history of Catholic cantors is obscure, so, in many traditions, the position of the cantor is ambiguous. The cantor can be the same as the deacon, as in the Ukrainian Uniate Catholic and Orthodox churches. The cantor can hold a recognized church office and be entitled to a prebend, or a cantor can be someone in training for the priesthood. There are solo cantors and records of organized *scholae cantorum*, or cantors' groups. In the articles presented in this book we see a wide range of possible cantors. Thus, the cantor himself or herself seems subject to improvisation. This is the crux of the matter and reveals the essence of most cantorial traditions: the cantor is an intermediary between the clergy and the people, adapting and changing as the needs of the congregation change.

The role of the cantor as intermediary puts him or her much closer to the people and may explain the many and varied ties of cantorial traditions to folklore. Cantors are supposed to make the liturgy more accessible, to help the congregation have a meaningful spiritual experience. They are charged with leading others in prayer and guiding them in other ways, such as by setting patterns of righteous behavior. One of the many results of these efforts is the development of folk group after folk group patterned on cantors. Cantorial traditions seem to generate secondary intermediaries who are extensions of cantors or take the place of cantors when these are not available.

Kobzari and *lirnyky*, the minstrels considered emblematic of Ukrainian folk creativity, are an extension of the cantorial function, as suggested earlier in this preface.(5) During the Soviet period official state policy considered religion the opiate of the people and actively sought to discourage religious expression, including the work of the cantor. This work was so important, however, and the role of the cantor so flexible, so amenable to improvisation, that it was easily assumed by folk practitioners. The reading of the Psalter over the body of the deceased is considered necessary for the repose of the soul and this is typically the work of the *diak*, so much so that it is attested in folktales, folk legends, and the stories of Nikolai Gogol (Mykola Hohol in Ukrainian). But when village deacons ceased to exist during Soviet times, the reading of the Psalter was taken over by pious elder women, women who had previously been called in to wash and dress the body and to maintain a vigil over the deceased while the corpse lay in the household. They perform this function now in the many villages that have yet to be assigned a deacon or a priest and, in those villages where some sort of church has been established, they have formed the nucleus of the choir, chanting many of the songs that had been led by the deacon. When I was collecting data in the summer and fall of 1998 on rituals of marriage, birth, and death, the best sources of information, especially on the words that were supposed to accompany the various rites, were the women who had assumed the role of cantor. (6)

Because the cantor is an intermediary between the clergy and the congregation, he or she is more like the people and more subject to human frailties and foibles. Thus the cantor is a stock comic figure and used as such, not just in the folklore and literature of Ukraine and other European countries, but in the literature of Canada, as the bibliography to this volume shows. The cantor appears in serious literature and folklore also, especially in frightening stories where his shortcomings almost lead to his demise. Thus there are plentiful Ukrainian folk narratives of the supernatural, supposedly true stories, where the *diak*/cantor plays a major role. In one such story, a two-timing *diak* dates two women, both of whom happen to be witches. His duplicity is discovered and one of the women tricks the man into killing her rival. As *diak*, the man is obliged to read the Psalter over his victim, who uses her fearsome supernatural powers to try and exact revenge. Fortunately, the witch/girlfriend who prompted the murder is savvy enough to give her lover the means to survive the Psalter ordeal and even the legions of witches that the dead woman summons to her aid. In the end, the couple marries and lives happily ever after. (7) In Gogol's story *Vii*, a young seminarian with a weakness for food, drink, and other pleasures of the flesh inadvertently kills the daughter of a rich man. This woman, too, turns out to be a witch and attacks the hero as he reads the Psalter over her body at night. Here the young man does not survive the experience. Curiosity gets the better of him and he yields to the temptation to gaze into the eyes of one of the demons the dead woman rouses from beneath the earth.

Apparently many real-life cantors were less-than-perfect individuals. An extraordinary autobiography of an eighteenth-century cantor named Turchynovs'kyi was published in *Kievskaia starina*.(8) In it we learn of a man who was quite quarrelsome, yet managed to succeed as a *diak*, rising to higher and higher posts, singing in better and better churches, arranging plays, and other performances, in spite of his disagreeable nature. The autobiography begins with man's coming into conflict with two traveling companions, only to be rescued by a friend of his father's and offered the position of scribe. Turchynovs'kyi soon left this man's employ and became a student in a city called Mohilev, where he attracted the attention of an Orthodox bishop with his singing and was asked to join the church choir. While working in the choir, he quarreled with the choir master and was bodily thrown over the railing of the church balcony, escaping death only by falling on the heads of the congregation below and mortally injuring one of its elder members. The autobiography continues in a like vein. We learn of Turchynovs'kyi's barely escaping death again and again. He quarrels with clergy and parishioners, is imprisoned, is forced to leave town because he offended prominent citizens. All in all, we see a man who does not strike the reader as godly, or even pious. Yet Turchynovs'kyi tells us that he wrote his autobiography to instruct his children and grandchildren and, assumably, the behavior he describes was acceptable in a seminarian and a *diak*.

Since the *diak*/cantor is the intermediary between the human and the divine whom most people experience directly, he is sometimes assigned extraordinary supernatural powers. There are a number of stories where the deceased over whom a *diak* must read the Psalter is accursed in some way: he or she was a sorcerer, a witch, a vampire; he or she was in alliance with the unclean force, and is possessed by that force after death. The unclean force tries to thwart the attempts of the *diak* to save the soul, making the body rise up from the coffin, trying to frighten the *diak*, or even physically attacking him. Although in some stories and legends the *diak* is frightened, sometimes even unto death, in many such narratives he overcomes fearsome evil and is able to win eternal repose for the unquiet soul.(9) Working in the archives of the Ukrainian Academy of Sciences, I found a song which was kept secret from the general populace and performed by minstrels only in the company of other minstrels and possibly clergy. In it, a *diak*, by reciting holy secrets, is able to control the devil himself. This song contains a numerology of sorts: the singer has to recite what is one in religious belief, which is God, what is two, and so forth, on up to fifteen. We know that this powerful knowledge is attributed to a cantor from the marginalia, where the *kobzar* / minstrel reports to the collector that, by chanting this song from beginning to end without stopping, a *diak* was able to keep the devil at bay. And now, according to the minstrel, anyone who sings the song can ward off the evil one.(10)

The knowledge and artistry of the cantor were considered not only powerful, but very valuable. We know from various Ukrainian accounts that seminarians and cantors of the past sold their knowledge to support themselves. They would hire themselves out as tutors to the children of the wealthy and would serve as the scribes of Cossack regiments. Similarly, in the North America of today, Joseph Roll (see his autobiographical narrative in this volume) worked and still works in education. Ukrainian cantors composed poems, wrote and staged plays, whatever the public demanded. In many senses, their stock in trade was art per se. If priests were theologians, then *diaky*/cantors were the ones who provided the artistic rendering of things religious. Their primary forms were verbal and musical expression, but many seem to have been people with a strong aesthetic sensibility which attracted them to all of the arts. Thus we hear of *diaky* from the past working in the representational arts, painting icons, portraits - just as some of the cantors described in this book are painters, collectors, builders, people trying to create an aesthetic environment, to express themselves in a variety of ways (see, for example, the paper by Michael Owen Jones).

Art satisfies the spirit, and providing artistic services was much in keeping with the function of the cantor. Often, cantors were driven as much by their own spiritual cravings as by a desire to serve the congregation. Modern studies emphasize biographical and autobiographical material and many of the chapters here show how cantors use art for their own spiritual fulfillment, as well as to satisfy the needs of others. Even in the past, when self-expression was not a prevalent concept, we see *diaky*/cantors motivated by a love of art. Turchynovs'kyi, the wayward eighteenth-century *diak* cited earlier, stayed in the church and kept on singing because he had a thirst for religious knowledge and was powerfully attracted to the beauty of church music. Sometimes Turchynovs'kyi appears cynical and mercenary, yet surely the desire for money and power was not what kept him working in the church, singing, and staging plays. He would probably have done better, and found an outlet for his pugilistic tendencies, if he had followed in the footsteps of his military and civil official father, but he chose not to do so. Likely the same artistic talent that earned him forgiveness for his quarrelsome ways drove him to insist on a profession where he could chant, sing, and practise the dramatic arts, where he could find an outlet for his talents. Some of our modern cantors are difficult men, with abusive childhoods, who need art with a religious component to maintain their equilibrium. Even those men who are not psychologically distressed and who could probably have done well in professions that had nothing to do with art and faith, still speak of their strong attraction to both religion and the beauty of chant.

The cantor, then, is an artist guided by faith. He or she seeks to meet spiritual needs, his own and those of others. The cantor does not seek to provoke or to make a social statement. He or she does not want the pressure for novelty and inventiveness that we often associate with artistic creativity. For the cantor, innovation is secondary to improvisation and the improvisation exists, not for the sake of newness, but as a way to adjust for effective expression. Although the cantor finds his or her art deeply satisfying personally, the drive to perform is always other-oriented; the cantor seeks to respond to the religious dictates and the needs of the audience. Faith is very important, and spiritual concerns lead the cantor to religious art rather than to secular music, poetry, or other forms of expression. Yet the cantor chooses not to be a rabbi or a priest, but to seek spirituality through artistic means, finding, perhaps, a more immediate form of expression than the clergyman, one more suited to the congregation's needs.

Many years ago I came across the autobiography of a Turkish *asik* named Sabit Yilmaz, who took the performer name Mudami. *Asik* means lover of God and, although these minstrels are now secular performers, Mudami's biography encapsulates many of the traits of a cantor's life. Sabit's father was an imam, a Muslim cleric who lost his wife and took care of his young son the best way he knew how: by forcing him to read verses from the Koran at a very young age. Try as Sabit might, he just could not do what his father wanted. One day the boy tossed aside his reading assignment and went to play with the other children, only to be caught by his father. The father was furious and beat his son to the point that he bled from the nose and mouth and fell into a deep sleep that lasted twenty-four hours. During this sleep, Sabit saw a magical initiatory dream which, he believes, made him an *asik* and conferred musical and verbal ability. Because the *asik* was a secular performer, Mudami hid his activity as a minstrel from his father. Although he feared his father's disapproval, Mudami wanted him to know what he was doing and to accept his career choice. The climactic scene of the autobiography, told some fifty years after the fact, describes how the father discovered his son singing a verse about divine love and was moved to tears. Mudami, like many cantors, was strongly attracted to spiritual, religious material, but needed something beyond scripture. He needed art. He wanted to be able to sing and to perform. He wanted flexibility, the opportunity to improvise. Yet he did not want total freedom and chose an established tradition. His actions were governed by his own needs, yet the approval of others was very important and he wanted his art to satisfy the spiritual needs of his audience. He wanted to offer up the artistic word and he wanted this to be a divine offering on his own behalf and on behalf of his people.(11)

The complexity of Mudami's experience is the complexity of cantorial traditions. We see flexibility and rigidity: improvised oral composition and adherence to Scripture. We see the canonical combined with the folk, the personal with the traditional. But most of all we see faith combined with art: words, music and other forms of artistic expression.

NOTES

1. Filaret Kolessa, *Melodii ukraiins'kykh narodnykh dum*; first printed as volumes XII and XIV of *Materialy do ukraiins'koi etnolohii*. L'viv: Etnohrafichna komisiia naukovoho tovarystva im. Shevchenka, 1910-13; reprinted separately in one volume, ed. by S.I. Hrytsa, Kyiv,1969, pp. 50- 59.

2. See my *Ukrainian Minstrels: And the Blind Shall Sing*, Armonk, New York and London, England: M.E. Sharpe, 1998.

3. Vasyl' P. Horlenko (Vasilii Gorlenko), "Bandurist Ivan Kriukovskii (tekst deviati dum s biograficheskoi zametkoi)," *Kievskaia starina*, 1882, vol. 12, pp. 483-84.

4. *Ukrainian Minstrels*, pp. 114-17.

5. The preeminent champion of church/minstrel ties is Pavlo Zhytets'kyi (Pavel Zhitetskii), *Mysli o narodnykh malorusskikh dumakh*, Kyiv: Kievskaia starina, 1893.

6. I thank Halyna Kornienko of the Cherkas'kyi kraeznavchyi muzei for her help with collecting.

7. "Vid'my-diakovi kokhanky" recorded in July 1911 from Ivan Lutsyk in the village of Daleshev, Horodenkyi region, by Ivan Volosyns'kyi and published in Volodymyr Hnatiuk, *Znadoby do ukraiins'koii demonologiii* (volume XXXIV of *Etnografichnyi zbirnyk naukovoho tovarystva imeni Shevchenka*), L'viv, 1912, pp. 149-53.

8. "Avtobiografiia Iuzhno-russkogo sviashchenika 1-oi poloviny VXIII st.," *Kievskaia starina*, 1885, vol. II, pp. 318-32.

9. Hnatiuk, *Znadoby*, pp. 20-22, 205.

10. *Ukrainian Minstrels*, pp. 273-81.

11. Natalie K. Moyle, *The Turkish Minstrel Tale Tradition.* Garland Publishing, New York and London, 1990.

At the moment, it's more of a hobby of mine, but I would very much like to study to be a "diak" (cantor). Not so much to hold the position, but to know the meaning of all the elements in the liturgical dialogue between the priest and the choir. To learn the meanings of all the icons in the church.

Roman Hurko, Toronto, 1996 (*The Ukrainian Weekly*, Jersey City, N.J., Nov. 24,1996)

BECOMING A CANTOR

by
Joseph Roll

I was born on June 13, 1949. I always felt comfortable in church, i.e., in the church building of my childhood. It was an extension of my home, another room to explore. Since my father and mother owned a 'mom and pop' grocery store to which our house was attached, it wasn't unusual to have various rooms to play in besides the more typical kitchen, bedroom, and living room. The aisles and shelves of the store, and the 'backroom' (my dad's office and storage space for unpacked groceries) were familiar and welcoming. The church was equally interesting and inviting. We usually left through the front door of the store to go to church on Sunday mornings. There was another church directly across the street. Almost every Sunday, just as we were leaving, its big bell would begin to ring. It was almost as if it were watching us. It was scary. It even vibrated the big pane glass windows of the store. Sometimes it made me cry. But then, it was the bell of the Methodist church, not our church.

We always would walk the three blocks to our church, even in the rain or snow. Sometimes my dad and I would go to the early service, and my mom and brother would go to the later one since she sang in the choir. They thought the choir-sung Liturgy would be too long for me. They thought I would get fidgety. Most often our cantor (*djak*), Mr. Kost Rudy, rather than the choir, would lead the singing when I was in church for the earlier service. I recall slouching in the pew. I always liked to sit at the end so I could play with the woodcarving on the outside of its frame by tracing my fingers on the maze that formed a cross there. I would also stare at the lights of the chandelier or count the bricabrac on the *iconostas* (the wall of pictures) separating the people from our priest, Fr. John Bilanych, as he stood at the altar. I think that's the way I learned how to count, or at least practiced at it. There were always things for me to do in church while the grownups were doing whatever they did. They didn't seem to mind if I sat while they stood, as long as I was relatively quiet. They didn't even mind my humming along with them in their vocalizations. Many of them seemed to be humming along with Mr. Rudy much the same way that I was.

I also remember the times when all my family went to church together. Sometimes we would wait for my brother after the church service ended and almost everyone else had left. He was completing his altar boy 'serving' responsibilities behind the *iconostas* after the Liturgy. I could only glimpse what was behind it. I was envious of my brother. There were probably interesting things there to explore. I thought that when I was bigger, I would become an altar boy too; but first I had to go to school. It would be some time before I would be in the first grade.

I actually didn't become an altar boy until I was in the second grade. Even then, it was because my brother was already serving that Fr. Bilanych and the nuns at school allowed me to serve at the altar. Usually altar boys had to be at least in the fourth grade. My brother was in the fifth, and they thought he was responsible enough to look after me and show me the ropes. Servers usually had duty for an eight-day week. They would begin with 8 o'clock Liturgy on Sunday morning, continue each weekday morning with 7 o'clock 'Low Mass' (hardly any singing), serve any other seasonal services that might occur during the week, and finish with the 10:30 service sung by the choir the following Sunday.

Altar boys had important things to do even before the services started -- light the candles, clean the ashes out from the censer and light a new charcoal in it, and determine what color vestments to wear. Sometimes they even put out the vestments for the priest, filled the cruets with water and wine, turned on lights, and opened or closed windows (depending on the season). There were many more responsibilities during and after the liturgical services as well. Going to church during the week was different than on Sundays. Typically, altar boys would arrive at about 6:40 a.m. Mr. Rudy was often there already. It was still dark at this time of the morning during several months of the year. I can't remember the church ever being locked when I was young.

One particular cold morning, when I was in the second grade, is as clear in my mind today as though it happened yesterday. I was seven years old. It had snowed cold, dry, small flakes all night. My mom awoke my brother and me at 6 a.m. My brother was sick with a bad cold. She decided he shouldn't go to serve. She also said it was too nasty outside for me to go alone. I really wanted to go. After all, I had to show that I was responsible to be an altar boy even though I was only in the second grade. Otherwise the nuns or Fr. Bilanych might say I should wait until the fourth grade as most other boys had to. Besides there would be two other servers coming. They were older and knew what to do. I shouldn't stay home because my *brother* was sick. She let me go.

It was dark outside, but the sky had that eerie glow of yellow-gray that happens when it snows. It was also very windy. I walked the three blocks to the church. The snow was deep. It was well over my boots except where it drifted away to bare the pavement in some places. When I arrived at the church, the door was unlocked, but the lights were out and nobody was there. The votive candles in front of the *iconostas* gave the only light. Thanks to my brother, I knew where the light switch was in the vestibule. It lighted the back of the church, but the front, near the *iconostas*, was still only illuminated by the candles. It was dark and spooky walking down the aisle. I knew if I made it through the right door of the *iconostas*, I could find the sacristy and turn on the light in it. I knew where that switch was, too, thanks to my brother. After doing this, I felt less trepidation. I took off my gloves, coat, and boots. The other altar boys or Father or Mr. Rudy would probably be coming soon.

I waited for what seemed to be a long time, but no one else arrived. I was getting nervous again. I never lit candles or the censer before. I didn't even know where the rest of the light switches were. I opened the closet and put on a black cassock. It was too long, so I tried on another. "Let's see," I thought, "are we supposed to wear a purple or a black dalmatic?" I put on a black one over the cassock, but it felt tight and uncomfortable. I didn't understand why. There were only two sizes, and as usual, I put on the small one. I was beginning to worry. The church was still dark and empty. I struck a match to light the taper at the end of the long pole used to light the huge altar candles. It went out. I didn't pull the taper out far enough. I tried again. Once I lit it, I went to light the altar candles. It was impossible. The candlesticks on the altar were so tall, I couldn't even see up to their tops, let alone find the center of the candles in them that needed to be lit. I went back to the sacristy and started to cry. I heard the front door of the church open and close. Someone was coming in, and I didn't have anything ready. At the same time the door leading to the priest's sacristy opened. Fr. Bilanych was coming in, too. As soon as he saw me, he came around to the altar boys' sacristy and realized what I was trying to do. He didn't yell. Instead, he smiled and even laughed a little. Mr. Rudy then came in through the side door of the *iconostas*. He came over to me. He took off my dalmatic. (I had put my head through one of the sleeve openings by mistake. That's why it felt funny.) While he helped me to put it on correctly, he said, "Don't worry, sonny, I fix for you." Father went back to his sacristy to put on his vestments. Mr. Rudy lit the candles and prepared the rest. For the entire service he stood next to me, rather than in his usual place in the first pew. He gave all the responses. He put his hand on my shoulder and led me around the altar for the processions. It was as if he were serving with me rather than for me. Fr. Bilanych, Mr. Rudy, and I were only ones in church that morning. When I returned home, I discovered that school was canceled because of the snow. It was great! At the time, it made what recently happened in church seem trivial. Too bad for my brother, though -- to be sick on a day when there wasn't any school.

I attended SS. Cyril and Methodius Ukrainian Catholic School from grades one through eight. In many ways, the school was an extension of my church (also SS. Cyril and Methodius). The faculty consisted of only three nuns from the

Basilian order who taught religion and all the other subjects to each of the eight grades. There were multiple grades of about 30 students in only three classrooms. Since our church and school were Catholic, much of the religion we learned was similar to what was taught at the other two larger Catholic schools in town. However, since we were *Ukrainian* Catholic, much was different. We followed a different ritual, observed a different calendar, and used Church Slavonic rather than Latin in our church services. On the one hand, it was important to the nuns that we understood we were *Catholic*, like the children who went to St. Joseph's or St. Mary's schools; on the other hand, it was also important that we be proud of our *own* customs. Our religion was closely associated with our heritage and nationality. For this reason, the sisters spent much of the day teaching us the language and music of church rituals. It was also the reason our small parish of 300 families found it important to maintain its own school. This was the case with most other Ukrainian Catholic communities in the many small towns of rural Pennsylvania besides Berwick, my hometown.

We had twenty-one holy days throughout the year. (The Roman Catholics had only five.) Whenever a holy day would occur on a school day, we would go to church and attend Liturgy cantored by Mr. Rudy before marching two-by-two the five blocks to school. Sometimes we would sing devotional hymns in Ukrainian along the way. Attending church on these days was very interesting. I was happy when others were called to serve as altar boys, for I preferred singing in the congregation with Mr. Rudy. Since holy days usually fell on workdays, most of the people attending, in addition to the nuns and students, were women and elderly men. They sang differently than the choir. They were noisier and more spontaneous. There were usually a few older men standing near Mr. Rudy who tried to follow him when he led from the choir loft. Their voices weren't very good, but they sang loudly and enthusiastically. Many people tried to sing harmony. Sometimes this made us children laugh. A sister would turn around and give us dirty looks. Sometimes she would take a giggling student or two from the pew and make him or her sit next to her. We were all encouraged to sing, but warned that it wasn't supposed to be funny.

We always sang in Church Slavonic, which is similar to Ukrainian. We never sang in English. The sisters and the old people in church knew how to speak Ukrainian, but we students only knew how to say the sounds, I learned how to read and sing the church language very thoroughly without really knowing what I was reading or singing. I was also encouraged to harmonize, especially by Sister Ignatius, when I was in the fourth grade. Sometimes she made me sit next to her not because I was misbehaving, but to teach me how to sing a second or third voice to the responses. She also taught me to follow closely the parts of the text that changed from holy day to holy day. I enjoyed it very much.

At age nine, after I had some experience with singing, Fr. Bilanych suggested to my parents that I, rather than Mr. Rudy, sing the creed solo in church. It was either for the coming Christmas or Easter holiday, I can't remember which. The service was to be aired on the local radio station. This happened very rarely in our town. My parents would tell all the people coming in our store to be sure to tune their radios to the live broadcast. People who didn't even go to our church would hear me sing. As the broadcast day approached, I became more and more jittery. I enjoyed the attention, and was practicing the chant used for the creed at home and in school...but thinking about singing in front of all those people and on the radio was getting scary. What if I forget the words, or had to sneeze or cough? It was also decided that I was to serve as an altar boy. At the appropriate time, I was to exit through the side door of the *iconostas* and proceed to the center of the church. From there I would sing the creed surrounded by representatives of the congregation holding candles. What if I tripped on my cassock or came too close to the candle flames?

None of this happened. Instead, all the tension that was building in me, especially the 'butterflies' that crescendoed in my stomach as I marched to the center of the church, left as soon as I started to sing. When I finished chanting the creed, I collected the candles that were given to the others who surrounded me, and processed back to the altar. I have never felt nervous about singing in church since then, although there have been times since that day when I *did* sneeze, cough, forget the words, or trip in the procession. These imperfections are not uncommon among cantors. Cantors do not 'perform' as in a concert. They often sing one text while they are looking for the next, or have other liturgical responsibilities that need to be done (like distribute and collect candles) while they are singing. Cantors know how the liturgical services are structured. They try to keep a level head, have a good sense of timing, and are prepared for what happens next. They are even prepared to cover what is supposed to happen next when it doesn't happen. Most people in the church congregation are willing to overlook a cantor's voice failing owing to illness or old age because of these talents. I didn't learn this on that day while singing the creed. However, I did learn not to be scared, and to think on my feet. That was a very important step in learning how to cantor.

Throughout grammar school, I routinely served all the types of church services celebrated in our parish - weddings, christenings, vespers, Lent, holy week and other seasonal services. I was especially fond of serving at funerals. It meant a morning off from school, a hot meal rather than a cold sandwich for lunch, and maybe even a dollar from the funeral director if he decided to pay the altar boys a stipend. I also enjoyed serving outside the church building by assisting Fr. Bilanych in blessing the homes of parishioners on the feast of the Epiphany, and singing the requiem service at the cemetery on Memorial Day or Pentecost.

Mr. Rudy had retired in 1957 after cantoring steadily for 36 years. Mr. Peter Gelety, who wasn't much younger than Mr. Rudy, started as the 'new' cantor. He was one of the men who sang along with Mr. Rudy who caused some pupils a pinched ear and/or a seat next to one of the nuns during the church services. His voice certainly wasn't as clear as Mr. Rudy's. He often sang several lines by memory even before he even found his place in the text. (This is the case with many other cantors.) He learned the skill by years of watching and osmosis. Unlike Mr. Rudy, who attended classes in cantoring in the early 1920s, Mr. Gelety had no formal training. He was hard of hearing and his eyes were failing. But he could think on his feet. He and I got along very well. If I was not serving as altar boy, I often stood next to him singing harmony. I would also give him the cues to start the responses of the less familiar services because of his poor hearing and sight. Before his problem was addressed, there were occasional 'shouting matches' between the priest and the cantor. Fr. Bilanych would sing as loudly as possible so Mr. Gelety could hear him. At the same time, Mr. Gelety, *still* unable to hear the priest, sang on because he thought Fr. Bilanych missed *his* cue or lost *his* place. I later found out that Mr. Gelety often could hear quite well. He was annoyed that the priest was altering the services to shorten them. His singing out was a way of protest. I learned the structure of the services somewhat from this 'competition', as well as realized that priests and cantors do not always interpret what is appropriate in a particular situation in the same way. The format of liturgical services is not permanently fixed nor strictly followed. Mr. Gelety and Fr. Bilanych remained good friends. Each tried to keep the other on his toes by competing to win points over the other in a rather cacophonous but friendly 'contest.' Many in church thought this routine was actually part of the ritual, or at least expected it and didn't find it very upsetting. I later found that some priest-cantor relationships are not quite so noisy, but hardly as good-natured either. Mr. Gelety would retire from cantoring at the age of 92 in 1987.

By the time I was about to finish grammar school, I realized that my interest in church was hardly typical. There was something inside me that felt a little embarrassed about this interest because it was so unusual. However, with the encouragement of my parents, the priest, the cantor, and the nuns, I decided to enter the seminary with the expectations of perhaps becoming a priest. I spent the next six years (four of high school and two of college) at St. Basil's Ukrainian Catholic Seminary in Stamford, Connecticut. My experiences at this institution greatly augmented my interest in cantoring. I was to learn the material for the first time in primarily a technical rather than parochial context. The fact that this could even be done was a revelation to me. It may seem strange, but up to this point, I never considered the music of my church to be 'legitimate' music at all. I never heard what was sung there anywhere else in the public 'real' world. Some music of other church denominations (or ethnic groups) is known or occasionally heard by people outside of those groups. I felt my church's music was deficient because it had no such recognition. There may be others even today who feel this same inferiority as I did up to that point. I was amazed to find at St. Basil's that there really was a rationale to the music. Like me, there were also others who wanted to learn it, and teachers who could explain it analytically. I stopped being apologetic in finding the music beautiful. I stopped being defensive about my interest in it.

There were several people responsible for cantoring at St. Basil's. There were students in the college and the high school divisions who routinely led the singing of the various liturgical services. They also set the order of the parts of the services that changed from day to day. These chapel leaders earned their positions and were respected by their peers as well as the seminary administrators. They had positions of authority. Stephen Zinski, a high-school senior, was the cantor in the lower division when I came to the seminary. He knew so much more about cantoring than was apparent to me from my limited parish experience. He knew more devotional hymns, the structure of more services, and especially the 'tones,' i.e., the chant melodies used for texts that changed from day to day and from feast to feast. I was familiar with some of these from listening to Mr. Rudy and Mr. Gelety, but I never realized their variety, intricacy, or logical sequencing. Steve Zinski could also read Old Slavonic in its own alphabet rather than only in the Ukrainian alphabet (as I could). More importantly he could *understand* Ukrainian and even some Church Slavonic. He was only three years older than I was. I had so much to learn! In the college division, the student cantors, Conrad Dachuk and Charles Mezzomo, knew and did even more. They were actually writing and arranging music. (They are now Ukrainian Catholic priests.) Other students who were not the official seminary cantors contributed as well.

Professor Ivan Zadorozny was the primary music instructor at St. Basil's. He was a student at the theological academy in Lviv, Ukraine before World War II. He was the first of only a few people I've known to be 'real' professional musicians as well as cantors. He knew music theory very well, could sing, play several musical instruments, spontaneously transpose from key to key, arrange, compose, and conduct. He knew liturgical structure and applied all these skills to cantoring. In fact, he felt that this was his primary musical vocation. He was an outstanding teacher. He was tall and slender with rather long, wavy hair. He looked like a musical director. He was a choir director as well as a cantor. This is very important. Often, church choir directors are good musicians without the latter talent. This deficiency affects the rationality, flow and timing of liturgical celebrations.

All seminarians attended weekly music classes that covered the basic melodies and structures of the liturgical services. In addition, there were courses in music theory and appreciation taught in the higher grades. There were also *a cappella* choirs, in both the high-school and college divisions. Sometimes the two choirs were combined for liturgical celebrations. It was especially impressive when we would sing four-part harmony to the chant melodies of the 'tones' by following only the words of a text. Cantors must be able to do this routinely. However, since cantors often interpret the phrases and cadenzas differently, two or three of them singing together often leads to 'contests' of interpretation. These are boisterous, disorderly, and hardly celebratory. Yet under the direction of Prof. Zadorozny, the combined choirs of 60 voices were synchronized while singing chants not even written under music notation.

Prof. Zadorozny had a stroke one evening when he was driving home after conducting a practice of the Dumka choir in New York City. His slurred speech and stumbling gait led the police to believe he was drunk. This postponed treatment for several critical hours. As a result, he became totally paralyzed. After several months, he regained his voice and the use of his right arm and hand. However, he never recovered beyond this point. I was at St. Basil's less than a year when this happened.

Prof. Zadorozny's tragedy was a blessing in disguise to me. God works in mysterious ways. Students would often visit him after his partial recovery. His family's apartment was just a few blocks away from the school. At first, the visits were short and formal. We went out of a sense of duty and felt quite uncomfortable seeing a man once so vital in his debilitated condition. As his infirmity extended over the year, fewer students visited. Those of us who continued spent more time and were more relaxed with him. As time passed, we talked and argued politics. (I remember laughing when he said in 1966 that Ronald Reagan would be president some day.) We talked religious affairs, especially the effect the Vatican Council would have on our Church. We especially talked music. He was still teaching, even from his bed. Since I had some training in music before I came to the seminary (my brother, who became an accomplished pianist, taught me to play the piano), he encouraged me to become one of the school's cantors. I really didn't need any encouragement. I had wanted this position from the day I had entered the seminary. He quizzed me on my knowledge of the tonal melodies and corrected my arrangements and compositions. He showed me how to read the old style 'diamond' notation of earlier chant manuscripts, and taught me the basics of choral conducting. In his absence, I conducted the combined seminary choir for the first time when I was in my third year of high school. I continued cantoring and directing the seminary choirs for the next four years. Prof. Zadorozny died eight years after his stroke in 1972; yet he lives on as a source of inspiration to his students.

Prof. Alexander Bernyk, who occasionally came to the seminary to teach instrumental music before Prof. Zadorozny's stroke, became the seminary's next full-time music instructor. Prof. Bernyk was a highly skilled professional musician. He also became the director of the Dumka choir in New York succeeding Prof. Zadorozny. He, like Prof. Zadorozny, had a formidable presence in the Ukrainian community and was a tenured music professor at Hunter College in Brooklyn. However, he wasn't a cantor. This was also a blessing in disguise for my education. Prof. Bernyk always relied on the seminary student cantors to set most of the agenda for liturgical music. The college cantors, Dachuk and Mezzemo, would often do this by transcribing musical arrangements to wax stencils and mimeographing them. I watched them and learned a great deal about printing, a skill essential to cantors today given the variety of texts and translations available.

Prof. Bernyk always directed the choir's concerts, but allowed the student-cantors to direct most liturgical services in the seminary and even outside its walls when we would go on tour. Sometimes we would conduct together. He would direct the occasional elaborately composed choral pieces they contained, and let the students conduct the shorter dialogue responses or tonal chant melodies. Both he and Prof. Zadorozny taught by allowing students to be prominent, active and relatively independent. I have found many other choir directors and cantors to be less secure in their own talents, less willing to share responsibilities and teach. Often cantors seem threatened by the would-be apprentices of the next generation. This is perhaps one reason the number of cantors is dwindling.

Prof. Bernyk was also part of a group of teachers at the seminary who produced theatrical performances. There were always plays, concerts, and musicals in the seminary. Teachers often wrote the scripts. Students were not only encouraged to act, but to build scenery, stage-manage, and write scripts as well. I felt very comfortable on and behind the stage. I helped in writing a few skits in high school, and a two-act play in college. This skill is also quite traditional with cantors. I acted in plays even in grammar school. However, I didn't realize until later that before the nuns started my hometown parochial school in 1948, the church choir director, Mr. Theodore Motichok, (who retired before I was born), had produced and directed parish plays and musicals for several years. Children, adolescents, and adults all participated in these productions. It was genuine community theater. The experiences I gained in the seminary with printing and theater would later help me to fulfill my tangent cantoring responsibilities more adequately.

An important contributing factor shaping my growth and interest in cantoring was the Second Vatican Council and Pope John XXIII's call to "open the windows" (*aggiornamento*) of the church. The years of the council (and its immediate effects) corresponded to my stay at St. Basil's. It focused many seminarians' attention, including my own, on the history and current status of the Ukrainian Catholic Church and its relationship to other Christian communities. As far as a cantor is concerned, this addresses a need to re-examine the types of rituals that are appropriate, to consider ways of increasing congregational participation, and to find or prepare the texts of the worship services in good vernacular translations. Differing interpretations of many priests and cantors responding to these needs were divisive thirty years ago, when I was in the seminary. They are still divisive today. They often lead to confrontations more boisterous than the 'contests' that I used to referee between Mr. Gelety and Fr. Bilanych. Guidance given by the church hierarchy concerning these needs is often ambiguous or incomplete. Priests and cantors today must think on their feet much more so than when I was a child. They often find that they are not walking in step together, or may even be walking in opposite directions from each other. The confusion of ritual and/or language has discouraged many from pursuing a career in cantoring. For some reason, I personally found it more challenging than discouraging, hoping to establish amelioration and common ground rather than to contribute to the controversy.

While I was attending the seminary, the church building of my childhood was replaced by a new larger edifice, which lacked most of the appointments of the old one, save but a few iconographic mosaics. It took nearly twenty years until the *iconostas* was added to the new building. I had (and still have) the opinion that this and other architectural features are integral to worship and ritual, not merely decorative ornamentation. Fr. Bilanych and I disagreed about this. He and I also interpreted how to increase participation in church services differently. He advocated simplification of the basic rituals and elimination of the less familiar services. I thought education rather than elimination to be the key. (I still do.) I had an ally in my view - Mr. Gelety. My studies in liturgics at the seminary also reinforced my position. Because of these differences, I began to take an interest in other churches, which share the same Byzantine ritual, but are not Ukrainian Catholic. While home for summer vacation between the last year of high school and the first year of college at St. Basil's, I went to the local Orthodox Church (only a block away from my own) to attend a Saturday vespers service for the first time. When he heard about this, Fr. Bilanych was quite upset. We had eliminated vespers as a weekly ritual in our parish, and I explained to him that I missed its celebration.

When I first stepped inside Holy Annunciation Russian Orthodox Greek Catholic Church (now under the jurisdiction of the Orthodox Church of America), I discovered the interior to be similar to my congregation's former building. It was appointed in much the same way. (I still enjoy visiting it as one of the closest reminders I have of my childhood.) Mr. John Yevich was the cantor of Holy Annunciation. He held the position for a total of 56 years. He had more formal training than Mr. Rudy or Mr. Gelety. A bishop ordained him to the clerical order of *chtets'-pivets'* (lector-cantor) when he was still in Europe. I didn't meet Mr. Yevich during that first visit. I stayed in a pew near the middle of the church, not wanting to be conspicuous. This didn't work very well since there were only a few people in church and none as young as I was. After the service, a few parishioners thanked me for coming. Some knew who I was, and that I was in the seminary. (Small towns have few secrets.) They also said that I was welcome anytime, and that they hoped to see me again.

When I returned armed with my vespers prayer book the following Saturday, having discovered in my previous visit that the service structure was virtually the same as the one I knew, Mr. Yevich invited me to join him at his cantor's stand in the front of the church. I told him the chants I knew were different from his. He said in broken English, "You sing *Halychky*, I sing *Carpat'sky*, but that no matter. When I lead, you follow, when you lead, I follow." He then took a music book that used diamond notation from the bottom of his stand. He said, "This is music from your church." The receptivity with which Mr. Yevich welcomed me remains unparalleled, especially since many cantors are suspicious and even rude to strangers. They often attempt to protect their trade from innovators, whom they see as threats to their authority. Perhaps I was no stranger to him, and Mr. Yevich knew more about me than I suspected. Nevertheless, I was very gratified. I have been fortunate that Mr. Rudy, Mr. Gelety, and Mr. Yevich treated me so well. I often returned to Holy Annunciation during the holiday breaks from the seminary. There were occasions when student colleagues who were visiting me joined in the singing services with Mr. Yevich. I learned several *Carpat'sky* chants by this experience. I also discovered there were other Byzantine ritual churches in the region that used *Kievan* (or *Synodal*) chant. Now that I had my driver's license, 'church hopping' from town to town became a favorite vacation pastime. I had never attended a non-Catholic church before going to Holy Annunciation. (I rarely attended the local Roman Catholic churches either.) In finally doing so, I felt I was simply following the dictates of the Second

Vatican Council. I was 'opening the window.' Two years later I would open it even wider and stick my head outside of it. That's when I decided to leave the seminary.

I had spent a little more than six years at St. Basil's, exiting nearly two years before completing the college-level program. Leaving was a very difficult decision, but I felt I had outgrown the institution. It was not a statement of protest or disinterest in the Ukrainian Catholic Church or its priesthood. Rather, I was caught up in the turbulence of the late sixties in much the same way as many other young people were. I wasn't 'dropping out.' Instead (for better or worse), I was attempting to find seemingly better ways to address critical issues that I felt the 'establishment' (the seminary in particular, the church in general) wasn't handling very well. Many of my seminarian colleagues thought and did the same.

Returning home to Berwick after leaving the seminary was only a stopgap in my determination to continue studying for the priesthood elsewhere. I wanted to go to Catholic University in Washington, D.C. However, I had to wait to be accepted there. Catholic University was also the site of the major Ukrainian Catholic Seminary (the theologate) for the United States. Since I left one Ukrainian Seminary, it would be unlikely that I would be accepted into another. So if I were to attend Catholic University, I would not be able to stay in the traditional Ukrainian study house. Since I no longer had a seminarian deferment, there was also a possibility of being drafted into military service for the Vietnam War, which I strongly opposed. These were obstacles that I would overcome, perhaps by determination, but perhaps more so by Divine Providence.

At home, I worked the midnight to 8 a.m. shift in a food factory and took a few courses at a local college. This schedule allowed me the time to be involved in cantoring and other church affairs. I needed to show that I was still serious about my vocation. Fr. Bilanych was not in complete agreement with my decision or views. However, he was empathetic about the need to better serve the Ukrainian community. He and I spent countless hours talking about church affairs, our concerns and visions. I am grateful that he never treated me with condescension because of my youth and inexperience. His objection to my occasional attendance at the local Orthodox Church was primarily due to its not being a *Ukrainian* Orthodox Church. Although he saw the need to use English in our parish, it was still very important to him that we maintain our cultural nationalism. In his view, the neighboring Orthodox Church was a threat compromising this position, because both churches had initially started as a joint community in our town years ago. We agreed to disagree on this and other matters. He thought in particular that I should accept not being in the seminary more definitively. I should get on with other things. He was very appreciative of my desire to cantor, especially since we had begun to sing services in English, and Mr. Gelety was unable to do so. The director of the choir, Mrs. Catherine Kalanick, also allowed me to teach the choir new pieces of music, some of which were English translations that I had adapted from what I had learned in the seminary. It was fortunate that language was never a heritage issue in our parish. (I have witnessed situations when it has been such an issue, wherein priest, cantor, or choir director *refuses* to use either Ukrainian or English, or occasionally even both, insisting on maintaining the use of Church Slavonic.)

The parochial school had been closed for a few years because of declining enrollment and the availability of fewer nuns to teach. During the year in which I waited to matriculate at Catholic University, I organized some of the parish youth to help in church activities and taught a weekly catechism class to help fill part of the vacuum left by the nuns. I directed a St. Nicholas play and concert with the younger children, continuing the tradition that the nuns (and earlier Mr. Motichok) had started. I even helped to print the parish bulletin and did some bookkeeping. These are all typical duties that some cantors have in addition to singing. (The one responsibility that I never took on was that of a janitor. There are cantors who do this as well.) Working the midnight shift at the factory allowed me the time for these responsibilities. Fr. Bilanych often gave me some money for my services on holidays, and the funeral director still paid me a dollar for each funeral, but these were tips rather than a salary. My determination to show that I was still involved in priestly formation rather than financial remuneration gave me my motivation.

To my knowledge, cantors (and choir directors) in Ukrainian churches have always been underpaid. Mr. Rudy became the parish cantor in the 1920s when his older sons were old enough to become the primary breadwinners of his family. He himself only worked at the foundry on a part-time basis, allowing him ample time to cantor most services. Working part-time was not unusual for Eastern European immigrants then. Employment, if they could get it, was not steady. His daughter recently told me that he had initially received a monthly salary of five, later ten, finally fifteen dollars a month from the church before his retirement in 1957. Mr. Gelety, who worked more steadily in the foundry and had retired from it before he became cantor, probably received a higher salary. (He never talked about it, nor was it published in the parish's annual financial statements.) He also had a small foundry pension to supplement his retirement income. Some parishes provide their cantors with living quarters in addition to salary, stipends, and tips. This was not the case in Berwick. I have never known money to be the primary motivation of any cantor, even in large parishes. The motivation I felt to be involved in the church was about to lead me on an adventure away from my small town and parish. Other than to visit, I was about to leave home for good.

I had visited Washington and Catholic University in the spring of 1970 before beginning classes there in the autumn of the same year. I had stayed at St. Josaphat's, the Ukrainian Catholic theologate houses. Because I was *persona non grata* with the seminary establishment, some students I knew from St. Basil's now residing there had smuggled me in. I slept in an empty room in the attic. It was a wonderful cloak and dagger experience! The rector, Msgr. Basil Makuch, was not amused when he discovered me some days later. He allowed me to stay the night, but insisted that I leave the following morning. I had been there long enough to establish a 'feel' for the university. I would be entering the Bachelor of Arts program in philosophy, completing the two years that I had missed at St. Basil's. Seminarians also advised me to try to re-establish my seminary status through Bishop Isidore Borecky in the Ukrainian Catholic Eparchy (Diocese) of Toronto. Bishop Isidore had already helped American seminarians, who desired to continue their priestly studies, but no longer were in the ordinary established programs at St. Basil's and St. Josaphat's. A few weeks after my visit to Washington, I flew to Toronto. It was the first of many times I would be in Canada.

Bishop Isidore, addressing the Vatican Council's call to 'open the windows,' had actually opened the door to many seminarians. He was allowing those intending to marry before becoming priests to study in his eparchy. There is a long-standing tradition of married priests in the Ukrainian Catholic Church. He was challenging the *de facto* policy of celibacy recently enacted upon it. Although celibacy was not the issue that drew me to him, he sympathized with my interests and concerns for the continuance and preservation of ritual and the chant system of music. He gave me his blessing and the necessary documentation to continue my studies as a seminarian at Catholic University. (This documentation also eliminated my military draft concern.) He suggested that once I completed the philosophy program, I might take a closer look at the parishes of his eparchy to find a suitable place to offer assistance or gain experience. He offered the suggestion as an invitation, not as a *quid pro quo* mandate. I was very impressed with his charity, his vision, and his concern. I kept the window opened to Toronto.

My years at Catholic University were full of new educational experiences. Attending a major university in a university town was exciting. I grew very fond of philosophy, joined the CU concert chorus, and actively participated in anti-war politics. However, there was still room for my first love. In addition to students residing at St. Josaphat's, there were others like me living outside its walls pursuing the same curriculum as those inside. I took up residency with three of them. We had all been formerly at St. Basil's. The others had actually stayed at St. Josaphat's (not in the attic) for a time. We lived in an old building owned by the Atonement Friars together with many other university students who found the cheaper (if less extravagant) accommodations more appealing than the traditional dorms or fraternity houses. We arranged a basement room into a chapel, constructing an *iconostas* from the shelves of an abandoned library in the house. There was little difficulty in finding priests at Catholic University who understood and were willing to celebrate the Byzantine ritual. We had services regularly. Some from the university not familiar with the Byzantine format also attended. They found the celebrations and music more appealing than the typical guitar or coffee table Masses popular in the university at the time. Msgr. Makuch, aware of who and where we were, and what we were doing, commented that our liturgical services were often better attended than those at the seminary.

I worked part-time in one of the print shops at the university during the academic year and full-time during the summers. Since no students were residing at St. Josaphat's during the summer, and I knew Msgr. Makuch traveled to parishes without resident priests in Virginia on the weekends, I decided to ask him if I might accompany him and help by cantoring. This could be an opportunity to ameliorate our relationship given the circumstances of our initial encounter. He reluctantly agreed. After a few weeks of traveling with him, one Sunday upon our return, he asked me to stay for dinner at the seminary. He offered me a vintage of wine he said he kept for when the archbishop visited. I had won him over.

The trips south of Washington were very enlightening. The parishes we visited were small. The one in Manassas, Virginia, was directly across the road from a cow pasture. The cantor had died, and the community never had a choir. The singing, without any formal leadership for years, was purely congregational. It cut some corners, but it was lovely. The few times I cantored there, I led the singing as much as I followed it. It was strange hearing southern accents singing in Ukrainian chorused by the mooing of cows. It was unique. It also impressed me that the chant melodies I knew were ubiquitous in the Ukrainian Catholic Church. Even though they were sung with local nuances, they were the same basic *Halychky* chants I had heard in all the Ukrainian Catholic churches I had visited while in St. Basil's seminary, as well as when I was 'church hopping' at home. After graduation from Catholic University, that realization would become further confirmed. I was about to become a typical full-time parish cantor with all the usual responsibilities in spite of my age. I was twenty-three.

There are several Ukrainian Catholic parishes in the anthracite coal region of eastern Pennsylvania. Although not a coal town, my hometown borders this region. Many Ukrainian immigrants, including both my grandfathers, worked in the mines when they first came to the United States. Through 'church hopping' I had befriended Fr. Adam Polischak, the pastor of Holy Trinity Ukrainian Catholic Church in St. Clair, Pennsylvania. St. Clair is a coal town of five thousand people and twenty-one churches. (It made the *Guiness Book of World Records* for this statistic.) Five of these churches are categorized as 'Greek Catholic'. Locally (and elsewhere) that term refers to Slavic churches in both Catholic and Orthodox jurisdictions that follow the Byzantine ritual. Two of these churches in St. Clair are Ukrainian Catholic. Two are Orthodox (Orthodox Church of America). The other is (non-Ukrainian) Byzantine Catholic. They separated years ago. Each was (and still is) intact, desiring to maintain its own character and independence. Although exaggerated in St. Clair, this kind of fragmentation permeates the 'Greek Catholic' world in the United States and Canada. Sometimes disputes occur over matters of faith, but often they occur over national origins, property, calendar, ritual, language, or married priests issues. The opinions of cantors are frequently very local. They are often at the center of controversies. Fr. Polischak wanted to stop a controversy before it started. That was in part the reason he hired me.

St. Nicholas Church was the other Ukrainian Catholic parish in St. Clair. Its pastor had recently died. The archbishop decided that Fr. Polischak should look after both parishes since there was a shortage of available priests. Many members of both parishes saw this as a possible threat. Each community thought that sharing the same pastor was the first step in eliminating its own independent existence. The two parishes wanted to remain good neighbors, but no more than that. The cantor at St. Nicholas (in his 90s) had also very recently retired. The parishioners of Holy Trinity had been singing without a cantor for a few years, having been taught music by visiting Sister Servants of Mary Immaculate. Fr. Polischak's plan was to present me as the cantor of St. Nicholas. I would reside in its empty rectory (formerly occupied by the family of its late priest). I would merely 'assist' at Holy Trinity. Fr. Polischak would remain the pastor of Holy Trinity (continuing to reside in its rectory), and merely 'assist' at St. Nicholas. The plan worked. There was continued peace and cooperation. One parish had a resident priest, the other a resident cantor. It is significant that the parishioners considered the personnel of priest and cantor to be on the same echelon. In time, both Fr. Polischak and I respectively were accepted as the pastor and cantor of both parishes equally. In the years establishing the first generation of Ukrainian churches in the United States and Canada, parishes without resident cantors were rarer than parishes without resident priests. This might mean that cantors were more fundamental in starting a parish community, or perhaps merely more available than priests. This is not the case today. Currently, there is a shortage of priests, but an even greater shortage of cantors.

Mr. Harry Zubar, the retired cantor of St. Nicholas Church, who went to church with a top hat and cane, seemed to give me a qualified nod the first time he heard me sing. He said, "Boy, you sing pretty good, *ale treba vipite*." Roughly translated it means, "You should have a drink before you sing." I thought his comment as well as his appearance was somewhat odd. It took me some time to decipher them, but I think I finally did.

In St. Clair, members of one Ukrainian parish began to frequent services at the other Ukrainian parish. Fr. Polischak attempted to divided the liturgical services equally between the two churches. People sang them enthusiastically following the music of the host parish. When I sang in one, I eventually learned to follow its style and version; when I sang in the other, I learned in turn to follow the alternative style and version. At first, I sang 'by the book' without adhering to any of the differences in an attempt to correct and unify the nuances and disparities of the two. This resulted in periods of relative silence and disapproving glances. I found that the local variations to the chants are subtle marks of a parish's unique identity and history that parishioners often have struggled to establish and maintain. I disagree with those who attempt to eliminate the local differences thinking that such variations destroy the integrity of the chant system. I believe the differences are inevitable. They reinforce the vitality of chant by making it a personal statement of identity as well as a prayer. A cantor with significant knowledge of chant will sing alone unless he (or she) listens to and incorporates the local variations. I'm fairly certain that is what Mr. Zubar meant by his advice to me when he first heard me sing. He wasn't telling me to take a drink; he was telling me to loosen up and listen.

Fr. Polischak also made arrangements for me to work in a Roman Catholic parochial school in a nearby town. He was a friend of the pastor of one of the parishes that supported the school. Having this position allowed me time off for funerals or other cantoring responsibilities without jeopardizing the job. Because of my musical talents, I was responsible for teaching the students the music used in some services of their Roman Catholic rituals. I became especially acquainted with the Forty Hours devotion, first Friday Mass, devotional hymns, and the Confirmation ceremony. By combining the role of cantor with teacher, I was becoming known outside my immediate parish communities as many others cantors do. I joined the "Byzantine Male Choir," a local area chorus whose members consisted of cantors and other men who sang in their own particular 'Greek Catholic' church choirs. I also cantored the frequent outings of the Holy Name Society, which routinely visited virtually all the area's Ukrainian Catholic parishes in the course of a year. These experiences increased my familiarity with the *Carpat'sky* and *Kievan* chants and gave me opportunities to practice and learn the local nuances of *Halychky* chants.

At Holy Trinity and St. Nicholas, I started a youth club for high-school age students of both parishes. At the request of the young people, we made no distinction between parish affiliations. One of them wrote a Christmas comedy that questioned the practice of blindly following nostalgic traditions. The play alluded to the division of the community into the two parishes that happened years ago. We performed the play on the stage in Holy Trinity's church hall. From St. Nicholas parish, we asked the man who often played the part of St. Nicholas to present gifts to the children after the play. We hoped this would equalize the two parishes' participation in the production. It worked. People from both parishes attended. Given the personal theme of the production, Fr. Polischak and I weren't sure if we would be run out of town or patted on the back for re-instituting the tradition of the Christmas play. The audience was joyously tearful after the performance. Their children brought them together on a level of cooperation they hadn't experience in years. It reminded them of the 'old days' when *Professor* Zubar used to organize parish plays. The parishes' youth also went door to door caroling to the homes of parishioners of both churches. I taught a number of people, young and old alike, to sing many hymns, carols, and the basic liturgical responses in English. (Several people whom I had instructed would take on leadership roles in liturgical singing after I left St. Clair.) Using English was becoming increasingly necessary to sustain participation. Fr. Polischak and I prepared many texts of the seasonal services in formats that were easy to follow. These texts began to circulate to many of the parishes in the area. I didn't wear a top hat and carry a cane, but after a while, people in the area started calling me *Professor* Roll. A perk of a cantor once accepted into the community is respect and admiration. This is sustained even if cantors become less productive. Parishioners are grateful and have very long memories. Cantors must be cautious not to abuse this position. Cantors may not be well paid, but they are often pampered. Likewise, they live in glass houses. People who have prominent public roles often do. In St. Clair at least, cantors are numbered among them.

It was in St. Clair that I realized a cantor has an actual vocation, and that it is separate from a priest's. I was finding fulfillment in this vocation without merely viewing it as a step towards the priesthood. Although a priest may be more effective with a cantor's knowledge, he may not have the musical (or dramatic) talent associated with a cantor. At the same time, a cantor will be more effective if he or she has the spiritual foundation of theology associated with priestly studies. I felt a need to pursue this -- not to become a priest (as I had previously intended), but to become a better cantor. The temptation to stay in St. Clair was great. However, I could not overlook the invitation of Bishop Isidore Borecky. I wanted to continue my education in Toronto. (My decision confirms that many cantors start as seminarians preparing for the priesthood.)

I came to Toronto in September of 1974 with all my wordly possessions packed in my car. I had enrolled in August in a graduate program in philosophy at the University of Toronto. It was my intention to continue with a full-time academic career while I would 'explore' some of the parishes in Bishop Isidore's eparchy. I soon realized that I could not do both. My stay at U of T was short. After a few months, I was asked to become the full-time cantor of St. Demetrius Ukrainian Catholic Church in Etobicoke (the west end of Toronto), a parish only twenty years old. Having such an opportunity as this was very surprising to me. How could it be that a young man from rural eastern Pennsylvania could be given such a prestigious position in such a large prominent urban parish in Toronto, a city recognized as a cultural center of the Ukrainian Catholic Church?

Fr. John Tataryn, the founder and pastor of St. Demetrius Church, had a vision for his parish. He wanted to present the traditions of the Ukrainian ethnic community, including its Eastern Christian spirituality and rituals, to those who felt that these traditions were losing relevancy in their cosmopolitan, fragmented, fast-paced lives. Many of St. Demetrius's parishioners, who originally came from numerous remote western Canadian farming communities, felt the same way. They had a strong sense of heritage as Ukrainian Canadians. However, they also believed that this heritage was being lost to the next generation (in practice if not in name), since the demographics of their former cohesive communities on the prairies had so radically changed in Toronto. Ironically, their Ukrainian identity was greater than what I had experienced in Pennsylvania, yet its expression didn't include the component of many viable rituals the small, tightly knit 'Greek Catholic' communities regularly celebrated there. Since I came from one of these communities, was familiar with most rituals in both Ukrainian and English, had experience with formatting and printing texts, and believed in encouraging participation in services, Fr. Tataryn offered me the position of cantor. I was given a salary, an apartment next door to the church, and generous stipends. It was enough money to live on, if not enough to plan retirement. But then again, cantors usually don't 'retire' in the normal sense of the world.

I discovered Fr. Tataryn had a view that the cohesive effect ritual has in smaller parishes could serve as a model in larger ones. Since bigger parishes have greater numbers of faithful, only a small percentage of parishioners have active liturgical responsibilities. To promote more active participation and responsibility by more parishioners, and to make the rituals more comprehensible require careful planning. As cantor at St. Demetrius, I was to be part of a core group who would attempt to promote these twin goals. I met regularly every few weeks with priests, deacons, and the choir director to plan each service for very specific celebrations. We also attempted to avoid any possible conflicts of time or space. Knowing, e.g., that the Boy Scouts would attend the first Liturgy on the third Sunday of Lent and have a communion breakfast after it affected my choice of hymns and preparation of a Scout to read the epistle. Since that particular Sunday honored the Holy Cross, we encouraged them to carve crosses that would be blessed and then distributed among the congregation. The event would also change the timing of when the parking lot would be emptied between the first and second Sunday services and the theme and length of the sermons. Planning and preparation of the endless array of such events, given the great number of organizations associated with the parish, took care and creativity. However, it also made for a smoother operation, provided opportunities for more people to become involved and understand the liturgical ritual, and enhanced a greater community spirit. It became the routine at St. Demetrius as it should be in all parishes desiring to familiarize and involve parishioners with ritual.

My activities in the parish were much the same as those I had in St. Clair, but on a grander scale. It was a full-time job with several chrismations and funerals each week, and a significant number of weddings each weekend from April through September. In addition to cantoring these, I often would explain the rituals to the congregation before they took place and occasionally provide commentary during them as well. I usually arranged for others related to the principals to take active roles in the ceremonies. Deaconal candidates and interested parishioners attended cantoring classes that I conducted weekly. There were also weekly rehearsals of a women's folk choir that I directed and a youth organization that I led as its president for two years. I also wrote and directed a musical production about the circumstances under which Ukrainians came to Toronto (both from the Canadian prairies and from Europe). The show was performed 18 times and was seen by 26,000 people during "Caravan," the Toronto folk festival in 1976. In addition to leading the congregational singing at most of the parish's services, I wrote and printed many bilingual texts of the seasonal liturgical services following 'reformed' rituals used in the parish suggested by its clergy. These texts were structured to promote participation. They were also sensitive to time constraints. I was more comfortable with 'streamlining' rituals according to these formats rather than those that Fr. Bilanych had advocated years ago in my hometown. However, I was uncomfortable because St. Demetrius parish had such a high profile. Its texts were interpreted by some to advocate final versions rather than only experimentation with liturgical rituals. This inference promoted debate among the clergy and cantors of the Toronto Ukrainian Catholic community. Fr. Tataryn was pleased that it was being discussed because he felt that ritual isn't dead if it is a topic of interest and debate. I couldn't agree more.

Fr. Tataryn's vision went beyond his own parish's boundaries and broadened my own.

Many priests and cantors of other Ukrainian Catholic parishes in Toronto, who had originally found the 'innovations' at St. Demetrius to be a threat, came to appreciate the goals of the parish, if not the means of achieving them. Cantors in the other churches also began to accept me as a colleague, although they frequently still tested me when I had occasion to sing in their churches. I was fortunate to have learned the more traditional cantoring style in the seminary and in Pennsylvania besides the style I was using at St. Demetrius. I was very happy to demonstrate my knowledge of the former to them and correct their misconception of my role at St. Demetrius as being more akin to a master of ceremonies than to a cantor. Cantors usually have to know more than they ordinarily show to win the confidence of their peers.

Bishop Isidore Borecky ordained me *chtets'-pivets'* (lector-cantor) on the feast of St. Demetrius in October of 1977. He jokingly asked me during the ordination ceremony whether he should continue with the ritual that includes the order of subdiaconate. I smiled and said, "No thank you, Excellency." However, his question gave me some reassurance of his confidence in me. I had begun a master's degree in theology that summer in New York at the John XXIII Center for Eastern Christian Studies which had students from both Catholic and Orthodox jurisdictions. Several of the clergy at St. Demetrius had already attended. Encouraged by Bishop Isidore and Fr. Tataryn, I was pursuing the theological base that would deepen my vocation.

I received a phone call near the end of my fourth year as cantor at St. Demetrius from the Most Rev. Basil Losten, bishop of the Stamford diocese. He informed me that Professor Bernyk, still teaching at St. Basil's Seminary, was planning to retire at the end of the current academic year. Prof. Bernyk had worked at St. Basil's for 16 years. Bishop Losten was offering me his position. Once again, the decision I was to make in leaving another parish was not easy. However, the opportunity to return to my *alma mater* and to continue the work of Professors Bernyk and Zadorozny was overwhelming. It was also very challenging. The footsteps they left were large, and their trail was lengthy. However, I returned to St. Basil's happily in 1978 and have remained there (minus a brief hiatus) ever since.

There were fewer seminarians attending the institution than when I had left ten years earlier, but the program was much the same. Unlike my predecessors, my teaching responsibilities included more than music and cantoring instruction. I also taught courses in religion, philosophy, and Latin. Falling enrollment and less financial support meant fewer teachers having broader assignments. There were also fewer priests available to teach than before. The shrinking support for the institution was caused in part by the same demographic issues eroding the cohesiveness of parishes identified by Fr. Tataryn. Regardless of these strains, St. Basil's remained viable. The seminary choir toured several parishes each year and produced two recordings. One featured the *Halychky* chants used for the liturgical services of Great Lent; the other offered liturgical arrangements and original compositions of the several music instructors who taught at St. Basil's from the time of its inception in 1933. There were seminarians who readily took on the responsibilities of student cantors. They were fewer in number, but no less enthusiastic or responsible than when I was a student. Nevertheless, enrollment continued to fall. By the mid-eighties, the high-school division no longer had resident students coming from the Ukrainian Catholic parishes throughout the United States. It opened only as a day school. This exacerbated the enrollment decline in the college division. In 1990, St. Basil Prep closed and St. Basil College became dormant. I sought employment for the first time in my life totally outside of the Ukrainian Catholic community as a Latin teacher at Greens Farms Academy, a private school in a neighboring town.

I believe that the decline of cantors in parishes supporting St. Basil's had contributed to its fate. Cantors, unlike priests, traditionally remain part of a parish on an almost permanent basis. A cantor is a visible sign coming *from* a parish of its affiliation, attachment, and participation in a larger ecclesiastical community. The communal expression of liturgy, music, and ritual comes through the local congregation. A cantor is both a member of the congregation and a leading instrument of this expression. Without a cantor (or the realization that one is needed), a parish loses a vital link that more fully identifies and involves it as a member of a larger community - a Church. Kost Rudy, Peter Gelety, John Yevich, Harry Zubar, and an entire generation of cantors that preceded me attest to the longevity of a cantor's exclusive parochial membership and involvement. In this sense, I have never been a 'real' cantor. If I were, I would still be in my hometown (or perhaps St. Clair or Toronto). Parishes need to regain (or continue) the security a cantor provides in connecting them through music and ritual to a larger community. Sustaining the institutions of that larger community (such as seminaries) requires that parish cantors also need to be sustained.

I wanted to address this issue when I returned to St. Basil's and soon realized the strains under which I was operating. I proposed to Bishop Losten that we establish a Cantors Institute at the seminary. We would invite seasoned cantors to come for a few weeks to the seminary over the summer months to update and enhance their skills. We would offer texts according to the new translations of services in vernacular languages and provide an opportunity for a new generation of musically talented people to become cantors in their own parishes where former cantors had retired or were deceased. This service was very important since so few new cantors were learning the trade through apprenticeship, as Mr. Gelety did. We would also allow participants to vent their frustrations, as well as network and brainstorm their ideas. The project was ambitious. It demanded that I prepare texts as well as establish mailing lists. Bishop Losten gave me the green light. I worked furiously over the spring and early summer of 1979, and to my delight the first Cantors Institute was held in August of that year. Bishop Losten suggested we call it a success if fifteen people attended. Much to his and my surprise, forty-two people enrolled from as far away as Winnipeg and St. Louis. Some were veterans; some were novices.

The institutes have continued annually since then with only one interruption in 1990 when the seminary temporarily closed. They were first held in Stamford, then in other major centers with Ukrainian populations such as Philadelphia, Newark, and Chicago in the United States; Winnipeg, Saskatoon, Yorkton, and Vancouver in Canada. Some years as many as sixty-five, some years as few as a dozen have attended. Some participants actually learned their cantoring skills in Ukrainian communities in South America, Australia or Western Europe before moving to North America. In every instance, I have been inspired by the enthusiasm of the novices as well as by the experience of the veterans. I continue to expand my familiarity with more chants, having become aware of the variations used by more than a hundred Ukrainian Catholic parishes. Many cantors participating in these institutes (as well as those who haven't) have anecdotes of their experiences and careers that both reflect and go beyond my own personal story. The institutes have slowed the decline of cantorless parishes, but have not stopped or reversed it.

The challenges to continue the cantoring tradition and maintain cohesion in it are great. In addition to changing demographics, several versions of texts now exist in multiple English and Ukrainian translations. Liturgists still debate how best to deconstruct the layers of the services to make their presentation more comprehensible. Resolution of these divisive problems is not readily apparent. However, one unifying factor still remains. The Galician (*Halychy*) Chant tradition catalogued by Fr. Isidore Dolnitsky late in the last century *can* and *has* survived changing languages and ritual presentations. It has demonstrated spiritual inspiration, aesthetic appreciation, and malleability to those who are familiar with it. Virtually only the Ukrainian Catholic Church uses this chant system. Perhaps this may give impetus to the parishes of that Church to preserve its use as an identifying characteristic and living symbol of its now worldwide community. That is my hope. It has also been the vision of those who have continued to organize and support the Cantors Institutes. Computer technology and internet access suggest the possibility of an even wider horizon.

St. Basil's College re-opened in 1992 with only a handful of seminarians. I once again began to work there (in addition to Greens Farms Academy). It continues to grow with a student body coming mainly from Ukraine. The Ukrainian Catholic seminaries there are filled beyond capacity after the collapse of the Soviet Union. The current enrollment at St. Basil's, an overflow of these institutions, is predicted to rival the highest numbers the college has ever had. If successful, many students will return to become priests in Ukraine. I feel honored to be able to re-transmit to them a musical tradition that was given to me by our mutual forefathers. A circle has been completed, and I'm not yet fifty years old...the age when 'real' cantors often plan how best to settle into a parish to begin their cantoring careers in earnest. I don't know if that will be the case with me. However, if God has designed my life to continue, it is more than likely that it will.

March 4, 1998

I am willing to concede bias; my insistence that the cantor's status in a faith community uniquely manifests the latter's attitude towards matter, humanity and God has certainly been conditioned by my personal history. With a father and two brothers serving as cantors, a grandmother whose maiden name was *Diakovych* (the English equivalent would be "Cantorson") and myself having been co-opted into the profession at the tender age of eleven, my regard for the cantor is bound to be exalted. Personal history aside, however, I would insist that anyone chosen to stand before a community to give voice to its faith in melody is bound to be an enfleshment of its fundamental convictions.

Peter Galadza (Kule Family Professor of
Eastern Christian Liturgy, St. Paul
University, Ottawa), March 1999

"HOW I QUIT BEING CANTOR": CHANTING, AESTHETICS AND "MOOD AFFECT"

by
Michael Owen Jones

> "If one attends one of our Orthodox services and follows it
> closely. . .it is impossible not to be moved. I also dearly
> love the All-night Vigil. To set off on a Saturday for some
> ancient little church, to stand in the half-light filled with the
> fumes of incense, to become absorbed in oneself, seeking there
> answers to the eternal questions: why, when, whither, for what. .
> .--oh! How tremendously I love it all! It is one of the greatest
> pleasures of my life!" -- Piotr Ilyich Tchaikovsky, 1887

The central issue in this presentation is: What is the relationship between music and "mood affect"? That is, how are chanting, singing and listening to music used to establish mood, evoke reflection, stimulate an aesthetic response, control emotions, reduce stress or achieve other goals in an individual's everyday life? Exploring the question of how music and mood are related requires data on real-life experiences reported in an individual's own words rather than laboratory experiments, for it is in the context of a person's life, everyday activities and emotional and physical concerns as well as interpretations of them that we can most clearly see music at work.

The subject of this study is a 60-year old man living alone with his dog on a farm east of Winnipeg, Manitoba (Jones 1996a, 1997a). Although the information about Gary Robertson presented here is necessarily personal, he urges the sharing of it with others who may learn from his attempts to deal with family trauma, stress and anxiety. At his request, therefore, I identify him by name even though some of his experiences have been difficult and his memories of them painful. The information is derived from taped audio and video interviews with Gary in 1995, 1996 and 1998 as well as his letters, daily logs and hundreds of pages of memorabilia and autobiographical commentary that he compiled recently. To understand the role of music in his life and his having been a cantor in a local Ukrainian church for more than a decade, it is necessary to consider not only ethnic and religious identity but also childhood experiences, emotional states, physical ailments and even diet as well as various art forms in which he participates.

I begin the chapter with general background on Gary Robertson, provide increasingly greater detail about events that left an indelible impression upon his psyche, review studies of music and mood affect and then explore the importance of chanting, prayer and aesthetics in his life, health and daily endeavors. The overall perspective is behavioral (Georges and Jones1995; Jones 1975, 1987, 1991, 1993, 1994b, 1997b), not cultural (Geertz 1966, 1973). Details that the study's ethnographic methods uncover have implications for numerous areas of research including vernacular religion, creativity in everyday life, identity discourses and alternative medicine.

Gary Robertson praying before cross and grotto on his riverbank property, near Elma, Manitoba. Photo (1998): Michael Owen Jones.

Living as a Lay Monk

Of Polish and Ukrainian descent on the side of his mother, who married a Scottish immigrant, Gary Robertson was born 22 April 1939. He worked as a shipping clerk for a department store in Winnipeg for many years, then briefly as a postman in East Selkirk. Despairing of city life entirely, he bought a farm 60 miles east on the Whitemouth River in 1975, where he attempts to live a monastic life of prayer, music and iconography.

It took Gary Robertson 20 years to complete his home, constructing it from two abandoned cabins in the area that he disassembled, numbering each log. He built a wooden dome on one, an observation tower on the other and a bell tower between the two (on religious architecture, see Goa 1989). He obtained windows, siding and stained glass from old churches, halls and other buildings. He covered the roof in sheet metal, much of it salvaged. He left the logs exposed inside the house but covered them with insulation and vertical boards outside. The second story contains bedroom, display area and loft overlooking a dining room downstairs. On the ground floor are the kitchen, dining room living room and solarium (but no indoor plumbing). Also on the first floor is a 16' x 16' chapel furnished with two dozen icons that he painted. On Sunday, 27 September 1994, on the Feast Day or "name day" traditionally celebrated with Exaltation of the Holy Cross, the local Ukrainian Catholic parish marked the day with a visit to the cemetery, special mass, outdoor procession and, in conclusion, a tour of Gary's newly completed home and chapel and a potluck dinner served in a tent on the grounds.

Gary's style in painting, architecture and interior design is visually dense and highly textured, every surface covered with designs and images just as his chanting richly integrates Latin, Polish, Russian and Old Slavonic with English. His house features antique furniture and equipment as well as meticulously arranged, eye-catching displays of medicine bottles, tobacco cans, beverage bottles, dishes and tea boxes. He has adorned walls with his own paintings and textile pieces. A triptych fills one corner of the living room; it depicts the Black Madonna as well as the Prophet Elijah, St. John Padrom and St. George (Gary's favorites). Near it hangs an embroidered piece, begun by Gary in his youth and finished only recently, that he worked on when emotionally troubled. Above it is an icon of St. Mamas, the hermit saint. "Twenty years ago when I came here that's what the farmers nicknamed me: 'Oh, that's that old hermit lives down by the river.'"

Potted plants sit on tables, and vines climb the walls. He chiseled Polish and Ukrainian designs on wood beams. Above windows, hanging from the ceiling, nailed to the walls and resting in many nooks and crannies are old tools, equipment and utensils. Gary says he feels comfortable with old objects and salvaged building materials, for they have a spirit, a history, a meaning. It's like an old church whose walls are permeated with prayers and the petitions of the people, he says.

Gary's mother and her brother rejected the ethnic language, customs and Orthodox religion of their parents. Largely neglected by his mother, Gary lived with his grandparents off and on during his childhood and youth, learning a bit of their household dialect as well as several Ukrainian traditions from his grandfather, such as religious rituals, Easter egg dyeing and the making of such garments as the vest or *huppl* and the riding coat or *zupan* (which Gary has worn on church holidays). He painted his first icon when he was 15, a gift for his grandmother based on a printed household icon of Our Lady of Czestochowa.

He remarked several times that he is self-taught as a builder and icon painter as well as cantor. Many of his icons derive from images in calendars, newspaper clippings and books as well as visits to churches in Manitoba. They represent different countries, cultures, eras and styles. Some are his own combination of elements. He paints mostly in oil (often on Masonite), but sometimes uses acrylic or house paint. "I don't have access to a lot of paint," he said. He is vague about canons and procedures. "With no schooling I guess I just paint by my own method" (on icons, see Barasch 1992; Barida 1977; Bilash 1994; Hordynsky 1988; Keleher 1989; Quenot 1991; Schlieper 1986; Stepovyk 1991).

Talking about his way of doing things, such as the red floor in one room, fuchsia in another and a mixture of Native American and Oriental rugs throughout, he said, "I'm a little outlandish in my colors." But it seems to work, colors and textures complementing each other. As we talked about the design of his house, Gary said, "Balance is important, I guess. Like what a window will look like on the inside, it's got to look good outside: at night, with lights on. Everything has got to have a sense of balance."

When I noted that the house has a tactile quality, Gary replied, "This is not just a house or a home, this is my own exterior from inside, my soul's exteriorizing with the building. Other people, I go in their houses, they have these new chipboard walls, I can't stand them, I'm totally uncomfortable in it. I could live in a 10 x 20 log shack. The fact that it's wood, it's logs, it's natural. Touching. So I guess when I'm sitting in the room everything is touching me, because in a sense everything in it is from within. Like some people, say, gee, like I've got so much clutter on the walls, but I can't stand bare walls. When I look at something, I might have the TV on but God knows where my mind is. So I need all these interesting things to look at."

Why construct the house, build the chapel, paint icons? "A hard question to answer," replied Gary. After a pause he said, "I feel directed to have done this. That's the only way to describe it. . . . It's just something I had to do."

His art consists not so much of the icons he painted but the lifestyle and environment he has created--the house he built and the way he furnishes it including chapel, altar in the dining room, plants and assemblages of found and salvaged objects. "I collect and preserve the antiquities of the neighborhood regardless of ethnicity."

Everywhere you see rich colors and textures, religious statuary and antiques treated as sculptural forms. The logs of walls and ceilings are exposed, their earth tones a warm background for the reds, blues and gold that dominate his icons. The green, carefully tended plants throughout the house add accent. A storage area in one corner above the wood stove and the old electric stove in the kitchen holds crockery pots, a huge copper tub and tea kettles, all resting on a beam into which he incised Polish designs in 1985. "I had no schooling" in artistic endeavors, he says. "Just came out naturally. My old aunt says, 'You live the way people used to live'" (on the personal uses of tradition, see Georges and Jones 1995:269-312; Jones 1975, 1989, 1995a).

Gary Robertson has created a sanctuary, a refuge from the noise, pollution and sources of stress and tension of city life of which he despairs. "Man wasn't meant to live that way. . . . I hated it. I couldn't, I wanted to get back to the land." Looking out the window on a quiet, restful scene he said, "You need quiet to develop spiritually."

"The Home Church"

Collecting antiquities, living as people did in a bygone era and attempting to develop spiritually are frequent themes in conversation. So too are allusions to the "home church," the basis for Gary Robertson's knowledge of Orthodoxy and one of the sources on which he drew as cantor.

When asked how he learned to be a cantor Gary replied, "I guess it started at home without realizing it because when I was in grade school, all the prayers were said at home, and Grandma was teaching me to pray in Polish, but every day we sang 'The Angel of the Lord Declared unto Mary' in Polish. So that meant singing the 'Hail Mary' and everything. But the way she did it, in retrospect, she was Roman Catholic, but because they lived in a village [in Western Ukraine] that was basically all Orthodox and they went to the Orthodox Church, and their [Roman Catholic] church was like 13 kilometers away, my grandmother is Orthodox. And her spirituality and way of thinking. I didn't know this as a kid, but this was my first experience."

Gary Robertson beside religious triptych he constructed in 1994. Photo (1998): Michael Owen Jones.

The prayers, icons and songs in his grandparents' everyday activities constituted a vernacular religion (Primiano 1995), a lived experience that would inspire their grandson years later. Gary calls this "the home church," distinct from "organized," "official" or institutional religion (Danielson 1986; Yoder 1965/66, 1974): "Just how your parents teach you their faith at home, how they transmit it to you. So the home church has a real impact. Because I had 11 years of schooling by nuns and priests as a Roman Catholic, and in the end I still turned out to be Orthodox. Because what they didn't have in the Roman church in the school was the spirituality." His grandparents, as evident in their daily behavior at home, "had Eastern spirituality, much different from the Western concept. I learned that so well. To me it's richer."

Wasyl (Bill) Polak (Pollack) was born 1 April 1894, and Maria Adelina Sagal on 22 September 1895 in the village of Kozivka in Western Ukraine (Galicia). He was baptized in a Greek Catholic church in Kozivka, she in a Roman Catholic church at Baworów. Bill died 18 December 1967, and Maria passed away on 15 March 1969. They were Gary Robertson's Ukrainian grandfather, a tailor, and his Polish grandmother, a seamstress. They wed in 1917 at the St. Olga and Vladimir Cathedral in Winnipeg. "I thank both of them for instilling in me their spirituality and Eastern Catholic, Orthodox faith," writes Gary in one of four books of memorabilia and autobiographical accounts that he compiled during the winters of 1997 and 1998*. "Prayer was a cure for problems and worries of life." In another volume he wrote a few days after Christmas 1997, "The death of the two people that had meaning for Christ's birth to me died over 30 years ago now today," which "makes December a very depressing month and am glad it is over for another year."

Continuing on the subject of the home church, Gary said, "There was the children's choir in grade school I belonged to, we sang hymns because it was a Catholic parochial school. . . and then when I'd come home during grade school, that would have been the first hymn I learned in the Polish language. . . . It's called 'The Angelus.' They used to ring the church bell three times a day and people would, you'd recite this morning, noon and evening. . . . So that was a long prayer before you start your lunch! Then you say your grace [laughs]."

Gary's mother (Krolova, or Didi) married a Scotsman (William Robertson) who was either Baptist or Presbyterian. "Because the Ukrainian Catholic church in the district used all Ukrainian and he was English speaking, the compromise was that they'd go to the Roman Catholic church, 'cause Grandma was Roman Catholic anyway, so he took instructions and became a convert. But then later when I was growing up, this must be shortly before he died [at age 49 on 18 December 1961], he said 'The only reason I did that was to marry your mother,' he didn't believe anything. He was an atheist. He just went through the whole thing just to marry her. If you can imagine! But love's blind or something. Plus my mother was ashamed of her background so my grandparents were given specific instructions that I was to be raised as an Anglo-Saxon."

When Gary lived with his grandparents as a teen, his grandmother "was teaching me to pray in Polish and to sing in Polish, it was totally what my mother didn't want. And she used to take me once in a while to the Polish church. So from an early youth I sang in English, Polish and Latin. Ukrainian I was barely exposed to because that was really forbidden to go to the local Ukrainian church. So it was to funerals--and grandpa took me to the odd service, regardless of what my mother said. . . . From only small exposure at home or wherever, but I already had in my head the basis of how the Byzantine chant went. A lot of my friends were Ukrainian so that's probably where I picked it up. . . . So I must have been exposed to a lot of it anyway subconsciously. The choir used to come to the house [of his grandparents] every year and sing, and the Ukrainian priest used to come to bless the house, and people spoke because they're [his grandparents] a dressmaker, tailor, if people came over they didn't speak English or they were comfortable with their own language, so they spoke Polish and Ukrainian in the house and I was addressed in English but by hearing it I guess I was picking things up."

When Gary was about 20 he joined a Polish organization for a year "so I learned to dance and sing in the Polish language, and how to dance Polish folk dances. . . . From about 16 to 21, that's when I made an extreme effort to absorb the culture. 'Cause when I was 16 years old that was the time I told Mother, 'Go to hell.' She came in once, Grandpa was showing me a dance or something like this in Ukrainian, she got all upset about it, so I said, 'I'll learn what I want, why don't you just F off? Get out of my life! Had enough of you!' From then on I did exactly what I wanted, and then my grandparents did too, once I stood up for myself and told her to get lost. But before that they wouldn't. Whatever they taught me, I guess they didn't realize that they were teaching me on the sly, in secret sort of."

The need to be surreptitious was so great, said Gary, that when he was about 10 his grandmother "used to take me to Camp Morton, it was a church camp run by the Roman Catholic Church, up north of Gimli. And there was a church in the camp and down the road about a half mile walk to the railway station there was an ethnic Polish church there, Roman Catholic, because there was Polish Germans settled, but mostly Polish, in that area. And some Ukrainians. So she used to take me, leave me in the church, because it was Latin and English, and she'd disappear. One Sunday I followed her and then she used to walk to this other church because it was in Latin but the rest of the service was in Polish. In order to take part in her own ethnic service, that's how bad it was, she'd leave me at the English-speaking church and she'd walk half a mile to the Polish church without telling me where she was going! And then after that I think she must have started taking me, once I found out what she was doing. . . . So after that I think she opened up, but it was still secret, because they always had to avoid my mother. 'Oh here she comes,' and they'd speak English, or whatever."

Learning to be a Cantor

The knowledge on which Gary drew initially to be a cantor was what he had absorbed in childhood and later learned more purposefully from his grandparents. "So you can see what I mean by the home church. That was the home church. It was strong. It was really powerful. . . .When I was small, it was taught to me in English, the culture, because the language was forbidden. And by reading I started figuring things out. . . . They taught me the culture but in the English language, basically."

For several years Gary distanced himself from institutional religion, owing in part to changes made as a result of Vatican II. "So then it's not that I stopped believing in God, I still practiced the home church. Like the way I was brought up. So I had my icons, communion at home, all the prayers and stuff, I did all this even before I was a cantor. But I didn't go to church any longer. . . . I purged everything Roman Catholic out of my life. . . . I converted on my own. The icons had a lot to do with it. The painting of the icons, and praying. . . . I said, 'This is my background, that's what I have. I'm Orthodox, I'm not Catholic.' And that's amazing, after being taught by nuns and priests for 11 years, having Roman Catholicism droned into my head, but the home church was so strong because my grandparents lived it day in and day out, regardless of their arguments or their family problems. Their religious beliefs came first."

Within three years of moving to his farm east of Winnipeg, Gary had begun visiting local churches, including one presided over by Rev. Semen Izyk. Called The Exultation of the Holy Cross Ukrainian Catholic Church, it is Greek Catholic following Orthodox rituals and Catholic dogma. Not long after Gary first attended monthly services, a man sitting next to him suggested he go upstairs to join the choir because he had been answering some of the responses. Nick, a former Polish Army officer who had immigrated to Canada in 1926, as well as his brother, Andrew, "used to come up and stand right next to me and try to get me to get the melody right. So all these old guys are helping me to sing."

Because "everything was Ukrainian," which only the older immigrants could understand, "and there was no young people hardly, I approached Father Izyk with a bit of backing about having two services, one in English and one in Ukrainian. To have two services a month instead of one. He walked away angry, he didn't like the idea. But then he come back and he said, 'Okay, we'll have this, this, this and that in English, and Robertson will lead it, and Robertson will sing the Epistle, you ask him what to do.' That's how I became the English cantor in the church. So I had to improvise on all my knowledge of Polish and Roman Catholic singing and what I'd learned at home, and I had to literally make tunes up for the Creed to sing it in the church because I knew nothing about it. Father says, 'Here it is, you're the cantor in English, you sing it.' I had absolutely no one to show me, I had to just make it up. At that time I had few records in Ukrainian or Russian. . . . But I dived into it. . . . I made melodies up, based on when I was altar boy for 10 years in the Roman Catholic church. . .and plus my grandma sometimes took me to the Polish church, so I knew some singing from the Polish church."

Gary combined Latin and Polish based on childhood experiences, Ukrainian or Russian recordings, published transliterations and also mentoring from others. As he writes in one of his journals, "It was difficult. I had to make up melodies for the Creed etc. based on what Nick taught me, my 10 years in a Roman Catholic choir and Polish R. C. church and recordings of Orthodox liturgies at home." Nick became Gary's godfather. "I used to go to his house and ask about the singing [which was in Ukrainian], or just things I wanted to know. . . . He was humble, he was patient with me, I could go to his house and he'd try to explain things." Gary also learned from a subsequent *djak*, Eva (who emigrated from Ukraine after World War II). "She would show me things, but it had to be her way or else. . . . She wasn't like Nick. . . . She was nothing but trouble. Her and a few other bags contributed to wrecking my health. But anyway I did learn from her but then her and I got in a big dispute."

The upshot is that Gary first sang in the choir with informal tutoring, then led a service mainly in English but with some phrasing, passages or whole songs in other languages learned through his grandparents and in Roman Catholic school and church, composed melodies himself, sought help from Ukrainian speakers in the local church and finally became the principal cantor following Nick and then Eva as *djak*. He served as cantor for a decade, until he had a falling out three years ago with the new circuit priest, Father Izyk's successor, who rejected Orthodox chanting and imposed Catholic ritual. The situation too closely resembled aspects of Gary's conflicted childhood and youth.

Between Two Worlds

In conversation and his books, Gary Robertson often refers to the persecution of the Ukrainian church and its clergy in the Soviet Union, the preoccupation with assimilation in Canada during his youth and family problems. "I'm sure all this has something to do with my formation and the singing. Even subconsciously wanting to be cantor, I suppose to preserve my heritage because I was brought up in a time when it was denied to me personally, and in the Old Country it was denied to the people. We were a persecuted people."

Many pages in his historical and biographical compilations concern all three themes; remarks about assimilation pressures and family problems are particularly poignant. Writing on 6 March 1998 regarding "religious and racial prejudice," Gary notes that "the pressure to assimilate, that is to be white Anglo-Saxon Protestant, was pushed on you from all sides." He includes a photo of himself in Polish costume receiving an award on 2 May 1970 on the 300th anniversary of the Hudson's Bay in Canada. He writes that "As part of the celebration they wanted employees to dress up in period clothing so I wore my ethnic folk dress for 1 week. This opened the eyes of some of the bigots. In the earliest years of the Portage Ave. store they would not wait on women in babushkas as this store was for the upper class of Winnipeg, not Bohonks. How things change. Here I am winning an award for best-dressed male (portable black-and-white T.V.) in my Bohonk outfit." On the next page he writes that "where I really was exposed to profanity and racial slurs was when I started to work at 16 years old at the Hudson's Bay Company. My mom chose to be Anglo-Saxon & hide her Slavic origin. For a lot a people this was what they chose."

Most of the preceding 90 pages in this volume, and many subsequent pages, concern Gary's family relationships. He describes arguments, abusive behavior, his parents' drunkenness and sexual promiscuity, his mother's rejection of him as well as control over him. On page 9, written 10 January 1998, Gary notes that his mother's labor lasted three days, a priest standing by to administer the last rites at one point. Finally Gary was delivered by Caesarian section. "Grama said I was all bruised and head deformed. I was coming out the wrong way. My mother up til about 10 years ago--she's now 80 years old--keeps throwing it in my face how I deformed her beautiful body by having to give birth to me."

A couple of lines later he writes that when he was nine months old "my grandfather went in their house and took me from the crib and my mother chasing him down the street with a butcher knife. He told her she wasn't fit to raise a child." A few lines later under the heading "about 1942-1943, 3-4 years old," he writes that "I can remember sitting on the floor in the kitchen and playing with blocks and my mom and dad fighting, throwing things." Below that, for "1943-1945, 4-6 years old," Gary writes that "I remember my mom and dad fighting and drinking. I was lying in the bed. He didn't want the little bastard and neither did she. Their solution was to put me in a home. I was upset and crying & screaming. When I got up my dad was standing over my mother, piss and blood on the floor & a butcher knife. No doubt she had hacked him and he punched her out. . . . From here on in I was a loner and turned inward to my own thoughts to survive and am still this way at 58 years old."

Other experiences with his parents contributed to Gary's sense of rejection. Writing a few pages later and referring again to when he was three to four years old, he notes that his father's idea of babysitting was to pick up two police officers on the beat, "drive out of town and drink beer and bull shit. Or picking up a couple of women and drive out to some abandoned farm. There were a lot of them because this place was hard hit in the 1930s by drought. One would keep me busy showing me things in the abandoned buildings while he screwed the other." He recalled at age six his mother taking him to a movie, then standing waiting for a streetcar. "There was a soldier at the stop. Mom said when he comes over if he asks who I am I am her kid brother. Wonder if she got banged that night. Later in life when I told her I look at her as an older sister that left home she didn't like it. Not a mother. She didn't like it. Too bad you can't have your cake and eat it too." On the next page he writes about an incident a year later when his father took another man and Gary fishing and wound up at a hotel in Winnipeg: "Two beds, a sink, a long narrow room as I remember. They both got drunk and were naked and taking a piss in the sink. I was in one bed and they were on the other naked and drinking. Whether they made out or not I can't remember or maybe I don't want to. If my dad was bi-sexual this doesn't bother me even now. But he should not have exposed his seven-year-old son to this."

Yet other entries detail arguments between his mother and her parents, illustrate her vindictiveness and dwell on the conflicts within the family that often concerned his mother's drinking and promiscuity, unsuitability to raise Gary and control that she sought to exert over him through his grandparents. When Gary was in second grade, 1946-1947, "my grandfather finally got fed up with my mother's slutting around. One Sunday morning I woke to a big fight. Grampa must of stayed up and packed her stuff and put it outside when she come home 6 a.m. from partying etc. He won't let her in. Told her to phone a cab and get lost. He was tired of her coming home at all hours. Because she had custody of me she got room & board in a house in Arlington Ave. area. Then to be a bitch she took me to live there." On page 67 under the heading "1955-56, grade 8," Gary writes that he was living with his mother and stepfather while attending St. Alphonsus. "I had a hell of a time adjusting to living with them. They were both drinkers. Once when I come from high school no one answered the door. I looked in the window and Mom was on the floor. I thought she died. I broke in and she was just dead drunk and I put her to bed and poured the booze down the drain which she bitched about. There was a hell of a lot more going on toward the end of my grade 9 term. I talked to Father Toreky, my history teacher. I told him how I felt. I was ready to break down. He advised me to go back to my grandparents. I did. . .and arrived at Grama's. She didn't know what to do as Mom always had custody, and she was scared. . . . Grama gave in. . . ." Gary had a collection of items from another boy a few years older (old cowboy cards, scout hat, real spurs, Classic Comics "and other neat stuff") that Gary kept in a trunk brought by his paternal grandmother from Scotland in 1910. "When I asked for the trunk of my personal things I had collected all my life. . .there was a sheep skin there she said was mothie so she had George [her second husband] dump everything into the garbage. She did this on purpose to spite me (know what kinda bitch she can be) so I had nothing from a kid to 15 years old. I am still very upset about this. She went down to the school and reamed out the priest in public for advising me against her. This was all very embarrassing for me. Who in their right mind forces a 15 year old away from the people that raised him [i.e., his grandparents]. I cried bitterly over the separation. My grandfather cried the last time I left the house. This was the first time I seen him cry in my life. I knelt down on the doorstep. He put his hands on my head and blessed me as I left his home. The fact I returned [a year later] was good for us. I went home to Grama & Grampa. I weep now as I write this. You forgive but the pain never goes away."

Gary Robertson with his maternal grandmother at Lake Winnipeg, circa 1942.

Stress, Illness and Diet

In another volume of memoirs concerning dreams and illnesses (among other topics), Gary writes that "All my life I have had rheumatism-arthritis, colitis, hypoglycemia, headaches and two hernias in the groin & curvature of the spine as one leg is shorter than the other and the frame curved to compensate." He has suffered sinusitis, hemorrhoids, physical debilities and sometimes depression since youth. A few years ago he thought he had a stress-related ulcer. More recently he has added to the list of ailments enlarged prostate and increased severity of rheumatoid arthritis that leaves him in constant pain. Colitis has plagued him all his life.

"Of course this colitis goes back to when I was a kid, " said Gary, "I had this trouble in school with the stomach, but I didn't know what it was. But because of the turmoil with the break of the family, parents fighting—I used to crawl under the bed when I was small I was so terrified. Wait till you read that stuff. So I was sick all my life. I was sick when I come here. That's why I retired early from my job. When I was 26 I was on three Valium a day. I was ready for a nervous breakdown. It wasn't from the job so much, it was from family stress." His memoirs echo these statements, for he writes that "after a rotten childhood, a mother who was self-centered, spoiled and got her way regardless who got hurt, constant fighting in the family, years of hard work and pressure of the job (by 26 years old I was on 3 Valium a day because of family), when I came here my health was broken in 1975."

Singing helped. "Because when I worked here, building the house, I remember Reinhard's sister coming here sometimes, the kids would sneak up, they want to see what you're doing. They'd kind of laugh because they didn't understand--I'd be working here building the foundation or something, singing [he sings a few words in Polish about a rooster and an old woman]. I was just singing some folk songs in Polish and working."

Over the years, however, his health worsened. According to his written accounts on 8 April 1995 he sought medical help for a suspected ulcer. A doctor put him on antacid and a prescription for bacterial infection. "At the end I had horrible hives and diarrhea for 3 weeks. Even water would not stay down. About 1994 I really started going downhill: 55th birthday April 22, gaining weight. . . . My poverty was chronic and I did without proper food. . . . The arthritis had been getting worse and every other ailment with age setting in. . . . Here I was about to turn 56 and my whole system collapsed. I was between 190-195 after the 3 week Diarrhea and some time after [that] I weighed myself, I was 145 lbs."

Gary began reading books on herbs and dieting for health, querying a dietician and doctor at Beausejour, reviewing what he knew about folk remedies (he devotes more than a dozen pages of one volume of memoirs to traditional therapies used by his grandparents some of which he employed), purchasing commercial herbal preparations and growing herbs or harvesting them in the wild. He compiled data sheets on foods and teas, listing their known properties and effects, and he experimented with different combinations. Since 17 November 1995 he has kept a daily journal of what he has eaten, at what time of day, the supplements he has taken and any illness that he has suffered. On 4 December 1995, for instance, he records having had at 8:25 a.m. sweet potato, vitamins A and C, a pot of fennel tea, warm water and yeast; at 9:10 wheat germ plus butter, vitamins B and C, Winter Easy and alfalfa pills; at 1:30 p.m. a salad and yoghurt as well as vitamin E; at 1:40 p.m. papaya pills, vitamin A, chicken and peanut butter; at 4:35 roasted squash and carrots, soya, sunflower seeds and later bee pollen as well as strawberry tea and flax tea; at 7:40 canned pineapple and papaya pills; and from 9:00 to midnight cinnamon buns, tacos, chocolate, black tea and milk as well as a garlic pills. He also notes "stomach upset."

Eventually he eliminated sugar as well as most meat from his diet, stopped smoking and quit making and drinking berry wine or other alcoholic beverages. He developed a schedule of six to eight meals a day, drinking only herbal tea which he took between meals rather than with them (he alternates about 10 teas, several of which he makes from wild plants or herbs in his garden). He separates foods into alkaline and acidic, reducing his consumption of the latter and not mixing the two at any one meal. He distinguishes such categories as meat, starch foods, dairy, fruit, vegetables, juices and teas, consuming only one category at a sitting. He avoids eating or drinking anything hot or cold. He committed the essence of his dietary regime to one page in a notebook:

This diet has no sugar or salt even in bought products. Especially sugar.
And no dairy products except as mentioned in diet ["V" stands for vitamins or commercial dietary supplements, and "?" means "sometimes when needed"]:
1. Rinse mouth with warm water. V: Echinacia, Eye Bright, ? Herbal Nerve
2. Juice and warm water (apple or grape--blue or white)
3. Yoghurt with cumin or buttermilk warm. V: ? papaya
4. Wheat germ & bran & yeast or corn meal, buckwheat & millet or rice or barley
5. A cooked veggie (peas, beans, asparagus--one group, acid) and (pumpkin, carrots, turnips, celery, spinach, beets--alkaline, plus supplement)
6. Fresh cantaloupe, lettuce, celery, cucumber (red and green sweet peppers sparingly), apples and other non acid fruits; avocado, kiwi, bean sprouts, alfalfa sprouts
Or 6. Dry stewed fruit, canned peach or pear without sugar, pineapple crushed
Or 6. Sweet potatoes, potatoes, parsnips, bananas (must be followed by protein), no bread [at same time] or [will get] upset stomach
7. Fish: fresh or salmon or sardines in can; heart, liver, tongue, kidneys, chicken, tofu, cottage cheese and [on] rare occasion ham on the bone baked on cookie sheet
or for 7 or 7 & 8 plain perogies or bag of tacos plain, as I eat till bed time
8. Bread & a little margarine; bread with no sugar or lard (different supplements are taken: kelp, alfalfa, E, zinc, bee pollen, etc.)
Every day a pot of plain herb tea of my making
9. Occasionally late in evening Ovaltine in a glass of water

Below this entry Gary writes, "My stomach was raw and still is. I eat 6 to 8 times a day one item at a time and separate food groups (meat, veggies, fruits & salad, starch; dairy, yoghurt and buttermilk only; juices, tea from herbs only)." He tries to reduce the swelling in arthritic joints by avoiding acidic foods as well as by taking a commercial dietary supplement called Devil's Claw twice a day, along with other herbs, although the pain persists. He takes St. John's wort to combat depression. While he has been free of colds and flu for three years and his bouts with colitis have diminished, he notes that he still suffers headaches almost daily making it difficult to concentrate on reading, meditating, writing and painting. Further, "Any stress at all sets my stomach off and makes headaches worse." He provides three examples in his autobiographical accounts. One occurred on 9 and

10 March 1998 at about the time he committed his diet to writing. It involved a series of phone calls to and from four other people that night and throughout the next day regarding a young friend's wanting to buy a house in Elma and move it to Gary's farm. "That night I can barely sleep and have mild diarrhea and grumbling stomach and sour (raw), and headaches," writes Gary. "As you can see I can take absolutely no stress. I quit church because of certain people and the present priest. Why do people always have to make life stressful for others? Jesus I don't know. You tell me."

One of the most anxiety-ridden events in recent years involved Gary in conflict at the local church. The former priest of 30 years, who had allowed Gary to hold an English-language service once a month and eventually to become the cantor, retired. His successor insisted that Gary not sing the responses, only read them. He put plastic statues of Jesus and Roman Catholic pamphlets for sale on the tetrapod interfering with the veneration of icons, instituted a low mass on Saturday afternoon, dispensed Catholic doctrine and made other changes (on liturgical song in Orthodox worship, see Drillock 1997; on Byzantine aesthetics, see Matthew 1963). Gary quit the church once in 1995 a few weeks before I met him and again a year and a half later. The first time that he stalked out was during a communion for his godchildren, Christopher and Susan. On both occasions the issue was his chanting.

"The first Sunday I was there," said Gary, the priest insisted that he read rather than sing the responses. "I says, 'Father, I can't do that.' He says, 'You're real Byzantine!' And I says, 'That's right!'. . . . There's something wrong with this priest, believe me. And he kept telling me to read the Epistle for this Sunday--I says, 'That's not the right one,' I says, 'We're still on the old calendar.' So. . . .it was like a pulling thing, this service. . . . So it was like a battle between us! . . . So who the hell does he think he is! . . . He knows absolutely nothing about the singing --all he knows about singing he learned from his mother. He's Ukrainian. He went to Roman Catholic seminary, he was ordained by a Ukrainian Catholic bishop, and a Ukrainian priest took him around to the churches and said 'This is how you do it.' And that's it. So all his theology is Roman Catholic, the only singing he knows is like I learned, from home or in the congregation. . . . I'm a little overexcited about talking about this stuff. . . . Oh it was still Easter, and he's in the sanctuary with the Deacon, and he says to me--I'm going back to the first time I quit--'Oh, read this Epistle! It's for Pentecost!' And I says, 'This is still Easter!' And he went out to do something and he come back in and I says to him, 'You know what? You don't know what the hell you're doing!' He says, 'I don't know what I'm doing?' I said, 'You're Goddamn right you don't! You take your church and shove it up your ass!' And I folded up my books and walked out and it was my godchildren's first communion, I missed the whole thing, and there was other people in the church. And he bitched and complained about some couple that wanted to get married outside or something--well, they joined the Lutheran church! But this is leading up to something. And then my two godchildren--they quit going to church too. These kids weren't raised in church. It's hard to get them interested."

Gary continued: "Then we come to the second time after I went back to church after a year and a half. The next service, he didn't say anything, I did it just the way I always did, and then the last part we read it because after the first half he'd just give up, 'Oh we sang enough.' And he skips things, doesn't even know what page he's on--page 58!--You know? So anyway there was a general church meeting after public meeting, so in front of all the people he says to me, 'If you're going to drag the singing way out, from my experience, you're going to scare all the young people away from this church.' And so Harry said, 'There's nothing wrong with the singing,' and I kept my mouth shut. I thought, F you! I didn't say anything. He scared all the young people, he did all of the damage ahead of time. So, you old son of a bitch, I'll never go to this church as long as I live! And that's why now I've got nothing to do with the Ukrainian Catholic church!"

In sum, "That's how I quit being cantor," said Gary. "That was a pretty low-handed, rotten thing, in front of the whole congregation. . . . I've got nothing against him as a person, I'd go for coffee with him, but as far as church, I want nothing to do with him. . . . Quickie service: 'Let's get out of here.' So I got too upset. I said, 'There's no use, I'll just stay home and sing.'" October 1996 was the last time he sang the Divine Liturgy in church, according to his autobiography. But chanting in church was not the last, or his only, use of music.

Music and Mood

Gary Robertson, like many people, selects music to fit a mood he is in, to put himself into a particular frame of mind or to accompany an activity. If he differs from others it is in the importance he attaches to ethnicity and spirituality in musical selection, and the regard he holds for chanting.

Many studies in recent years consider the effects of music on mood, as diversional intervention in medical treatment and even in altering perceptions of others (in the 1960s experiments were also carried out on the effects of prayer and music on plant germination and growth; see Klymasz 1978). McCraty et al. (1998) report on their study of music's effect on mood, tension and mental clarity. Subjects who listened to grunge rock music showed significant increases in hostility, sadness, tension and fatigue. In contrast, those listening to "designer" music (music designed to have specific effects on the listener) had significant increases in caring, relaxation, mental clarity and vigor (results for New Age and classical music were mixed). In a review essay, Marion Good (1996) finds that most of research, despite between-study differences in experimental techniques, sample size and controls, supports the effectiveness of relaxation and patient-selected music to reduce postoperative pain (see also Buckwalter, Hartsock and Gaffney 1985; Cook 1981; Schwartz 1993; Vedantam 1995). Ezzone et al. (1998) detected significant differences between controls and a music intervention group in regard to reducing nausea and vomiting among patients undergoing bone-marrow transplants. Bouhuys, Bloem and Groothuis (1995) report experiments inducing depressed and elated mood by music and the resulting effects on perceptions of facial emotional expressions. In one study 30 healthy subjects judged 12 faces with respect to the emotions expressed (fear, happiness, anger, sadness, disgust, surprise, rejection and invitation). The researchers found that a particular face could reflect various emotions. In a cross-over design, 24 individuals judged the faces after listening to depressing or elating music. The faces were divided into six "ambiguous' ones (expressing similar amounts of positive and negative emotions) and six "clear" faces (those showing a preponderance of positive or negative emotions). The experimenters discovered that, when feeling more depressed, the subjects perceived more rejection or sadness in ambiguous faces and less invitation or happiness in clear faces. Moreover, the subjects saw more fear in clear faces.

Other research exploring the neurobiology of music suggests that music stimulates specific regions of the brain responsible for memory, motor control, timing and language; that different parts of the brain involved in emotion are activated depending on whether the music is pleasant or dissonant; and that music is often a useful therapeutic tool in helping to rehabilitate stroke patients, controlling pain, affecting mood and even overcoming emotional illness (Benson 1975, 1984; Hesser 1995; Hotz 1998; Lofaro 1995; Redmond 1997). For instance, hypnotist Sean Kelly (1993) reports several cases in which he suggested to patients under trance that they think of a particular kind of music when confronted in waking life with a troubling situation. One case involves a young man who had a long history of abuse as a child at the hands of his mother that left him "with a marked sense of guilt and an inability to defend himself, which went with a rather masochistic style of relating" (Kelly 1993:87). While using real and fictional stories about victimization in therapy, the man began to employ the Lone Ranger as a metaphor for himself (in the original story, a man shot from ambush by outlaws and left for dead is nursed back to health by Indians and becomes a protector of others). While under trance the patient was instructed to imagine the bugle notes of the opening of the William Tell Overture (the theme music for the televised series *The Lone Ranger*) simultaneously concentrating on his growing feelings of strength and self-reliance, so that one would bring to mind the other even out of hypnosis. "To hear the bugle was to recall emotionally a panorama of ideas and feelings, not just a simple phrase or thought such as 'It was not your fault.' It gave him a powerful way of reminding himself of the lessons he had learned in therapy" (Kelly 1993:88).

Through his own initiative, Gary Roberts has used music as a means of generating or sustaining moods, reducing anxiety and coping with interpersonal problems. One set of activities in which music plays a role is physical labor and chores. Earlier I mentioned his singing Polish folk songs while constructing his house. "For washing dishes I like folk music, something really lively to keep me going. 'Cause that's one thing I hate doing. I save my dishes til I'm nearly out, and I say, 'Okay dog, move over, I'm gonna have to use your dish or do these dishes.' 'Cause I got better things to do than dishes! So music, I guess you get something out of it, but I know what I want to listen to, so I must be in some kind of a mood to listen to that. It just enhances the mood I'm in. If I'm in a solitary mood that's what I want to be in. If I want to be in a gay, jovial mood maybe I'll listen to one of Lawrence's acid rock tapes! I even listen to some of that stuff."

Painting icons requires another kind of music. "I listen to Byzantine chant mostly or quiet classical music. I like Chopin, I don't play much piano music because it's a little too jarring, and I found some of this New Age music, and I like it, it's quiet and it's good for the writing and stuff like that. I like it, it's soothing. . . . I like either classical music or chanting in the background when I paint icons. That is maybe my way of praying and painting at the same time. Just doing the verbalization puts me in a spiritual mood, I guess that's what's happening [Vladyshevskaia writes, 1991:15, that "the icon and the prayer sounding before it formed the pulse of ancient Russian culture, defining the spiritual character of Rus"]. Because I don't like any other type of music. For other things it's okay."

Most of his comments about music, however, dwelt on chanting and praying. "The liturgy is like a trance. Even in the Roman Church years ago, which they probably don't do anymore, we had the 40 hours' devotion and we sang the whole litany of the saints in Latin, and we went up and down all the aisles of the church with the Blessed Sacrament, this constant repetition of [he chants in Latin]. It almost puts you in a hypnotic trance in a way. It fixated you on the Blessed Sacrament, this repetitious singing. I think that's good." In regard to what chanting can do for a person, "if I had a problem with the boy [a young man he has taken care of who has sometimes been in trouble with the law,], trying to tell him something, and once I get in that chapel and start chanting, I come out of there and I feel 100 percent better. The problem virtually disappears. Answers come to me too, answers and dreams. Answers by just opening the book and you open it to the right page. This might sound goofy but it works. God's guiding you. The guardian angel."

Looking at icons generates reflection and tranquility. "They're like looking at a sweet grandmother's face or somebody you love very much or something. I guess that's kind of the feeling of peace, serenity, looking at icons. They're so inviting. The way they're painted, they take you, they come out to you to greet you."

Chanting has a different effect. "Even in the church it's almost trance-like. You're worshiping God, you start forgetting everything that's around you. Like in the church, I notice sometimes I sort of sway or keep time to music, I barely notice what's going on up front, really. I'm barely watching the priest or anybody in the church. I fixate on icons or stuff in the church, or on God in other words. There's a Holy Trinity over the altar painted on the ceiling. So I kind of fixate on that and my mind goes into almost like a trance. You could almost drop dead next to me and I'd probably jump from you falling on the floor or something. It's relaxing I guess. When you go in there you got problems, you had an argument with somebody or something, well it's gone when you walk out of there. You've relaxed. The problem maybe ain't gone but the frustration part maybe somehow has subsided."

Nearly all the music that he listens to now, said Gary, is church music. "That's part of my way of praying. Anger's a terrible thing, that's when you can't pray because if you're upset there's no use to it. When everything's smooth, which is most of the time, I get up and put a tape on, an hour or more. I listen to Byzantine chant either in English or Russian or Ukrainian or old Slavonic or whatever. And at the same time my mind's praying and I'm working--preparing my food for the day and whatever."

How does chanting and music relate to your art, your icons, the house, the way you live? I asked Gary.

"I think the easiest answer for that is I couldn't live without it. It's a difficult question to answer--it's a part of me and I can't live, there's no way I could live without that. Some people have their coffee in the morning, I gotta have my prayers and chanting and. . . . Is that a good enough answer? It's hard to pick it apart. It's just me, that's what I do. In reality, I don't see my life being any different than anyone else's life. I do what I do because I'm me, and that's it. Although I realize 'cause you're here, it's different, but to me it's not, it's my life." A few moments later he added, "I drank, I've done marijuana, I've done a lot of things in my life, but nothing is as rewarding as the silence and praying or singing and praising God."

Conclusion

In answer to the question of how chanting, aesthetics and mood affect are related, we see that in Gary Robertson's life they are integral to his attempts at identity construction, stress reduction and meaning making. He has had to cope with a childhood filled with anxiety, emotional abuse, disappointment and anger. Only recently at age 58-60 has he been able to describe disturbing scenes from his earliest years, in written comments reminding himself that he is not to blame, he was victim rather than cause. No wonder that in writing and in oral discourse he identifies with the Ukrainian Orthodox Church and clerics in the Soviet Union during the time of his youth: "We were a persecuted people." His mother rejected him, "the little bastard," as she denounced her ethnic heritage and the religion and lifestyle of her Polish mother and Ukrainian father. His breach birth scarred her beautiful body. She refused to breastfeed him. Gary disappointed her by being a boy rather than the girl that she had anticipated and for whom she had already bought clothing. He has filled his scrapbooks with poignant photos of himself and his grandmother, a few images of his mother accompanied by comments about her vanity, promiscuity and vindictiveness as well as many photos of boys or youths his own age but not girls. Next to a photo of Peter, Jerry and himself at age 17 or 18, Gary has written that he enjoyed going to Peter's home to spend time together working on the farm, that Peter married but died at age 38 of cancer; "God bless you Peter for being a good listener when I had so many problems of being forced to live with my mom. May your memory be eternal." After breaking away from his mother to live with her parents at age 16, Gary made "an extreme effort to absorb the culture" of his Polish-Ukrainian grandparents, learning music, prayers and holiday customs, joining Sokol at age 19-21 (a Polish folk music and dance organization) and in 1972, three years after his grandmother died, visiting the area of Western Ukraine where his grandparents were born nearly 75 years earlier.

By building his own house out of two pioneer log cabins, furnishing it with the antiquities of the neighborhood," creating a chapel inside and "living the way people used to live" as an elderly aunt remarked, Gary Robertson has constructed an environment, a lifestyle and his identity. The identity is a multifaceted one: builder, icon painter, lay monk, aesthete and cantor, among others. It has its contradictions. By virtue of having a Scottish immigrant father, Gary is "ethnic." But the ethnicity that he cultivates is one generation removed on his mother's side. As cantor he was no Ukrainian *djak*; his chanting was largely in English and Latin, reflecting his Canadian assimilation and years in Catholic parochial school. In building a chapel replete with dome, tetrapod and icons he brought the physical manifestations of his grandparents' religion into his own home, a "home church," while at the same time he sought acceptance in the local Ukrainian church and participation in the chanting with its "foretaste of a heavenly reality" (Drillock 1997: 183).

"Music not only describes but also elicits an emotional response in the listener," writes Sean Kelly (1993:83). "To listen attentively to music is not merely to know but also to feel the spirit of the piece. The experience of worship, for example, is very different if the choir is singing and the organ playing than if the priest is simply leading spoken prayer." This point is crucial to understanding what Gary Robertson sought as parishioner, created as cantor, lost, regained but lost again in the local church, forcing him back to the home church.

"The whole idea of it," said Gary regarding the Divine Liturgy in church, "the priest is up front leading the people continually on the road to salvation, with the responses and everything, and with the movement back and forth. I was trying to get as many people as I could singing. . . . And this constant rolling reply, just like a ball rolling, once he starts chanting--'Blessed be the Kingdom of the Father, the Son and the Holy Spirit'--and this should just roll right to the end in an hour and a half, two hours later. It's spiritually uplifting." As cantor, "I guess you forget about the people, you forget about the priest, you forget about everything. You're on this way, your procession to Heaven, that's what it is." The organ playing, the choir singing, the parishioners singing as one voice: "I would like to see them get back to that. I remember that as a kid, it sends chills up my spine. They would lift the roof right off the church, you would hear it outside."

Gary William Robertson, who bears the name of a Scottish immigrant, now dons the black cassock of a Ukrainian Orthodox priest. A year and a half ago, about the time he quit the local church in conflict with the priest over whether to chant or speak the liturgy, he began to let his hair and beard grow long, contributing to the image of a holy man. He listens to both Byzantine chants and New Age music while painting icons. Three years ago he instituted a strict dietary regime in order to improve his health; a year ago he had a local carpenter build a casket for him. For all the abuse heaped upon him by his mother, he visits her once a month in a home for the aged in Winnipeg. He also proudly displays her paintings in his house including a large oil painting of what Gary's sister would have looked like, if he had had a sister, who has Gary's features and resembles him closely.

I end this essay, as I began it in the epigram, with remarks by Piotr Ilyich Tchaikovsky (Orlova 1990:85). "So, I am a mass of contradictions; despite the considerable maturity of my years I have not come to rest anywhere, I have not calmed my anxious soul either with religion or with philosophy. Indeed, I would go out of my mind were it not for music. That is truly heaven's greatest gift to mankind as it blunders about in the darkness. Music alone brings light, and calm, and reconciliation." I think Gary Robertson--son of a Scotsman, who dresses as Orthodox clergy, constructor of his own identity through art and music, a folk builder, icon painter and cantor, a collector of antiquities who lives the way people used to live (except for tape deck, CD player and television) and a person uplifted spiritually while emotionally becalmed by music--would agree with the famous composer.

62

NOTES

* Gary Robertson regrets that because of disrupted schooling his writings suffer poor spelling and ungrammatical constructions. I have corrected spelling errors in passages quoted here for the sake of readability; photocopies of the original accounts are archived at the Canadian Museum of Civilization, along with indexes, transcriptions and audiotapes and videotapes. For unpublished, archived writings about Robertson and other icon painters, see Jones 1994c, 1995a, 1996b and 1998; for published works, see Jones 1996a, 1997a and Forthcoming.

REFERENCES

Baldwin, Karen. 1992. Aesthetic Agency in the Folk Medical Practices and Remembrances of North Carolinians. In *Herbal and Magical Medicine: Traditional Healing Today*, ed, J. Kirkland, H. F. Mathews, C. W. Sullivan III and K. Baldwin, pp. 180-195. Durham, NC: Duke Univ. Press.

Barasch, Moshe. 1992. *Icon: Studies in the History of an Idea*. New York: New York University Press.

Barida, Michael N. 1977. Iconography and Its Meaning. In *The Iconography of St. Nicholas' Church*, ed. The Ikon-Study Group, pp. 15-18. Toronto: St. Nicholas Ukrainian Catholic Parish.

Benson, Herbert. 1975. *The Relaxation Response*. New York: Avon Books.

Benson, Herbert. 1984. *Beyond the Relaxation Response*. New York: Berkley Books.

Bilash, Radomir B. 1994. Peter Lipinski, Prairie Church Artist. *SSAC Bulletin* 1:88:3-14.

Bouhuys Antoinette L., Gerda M. Bloem and Tom G. G. Groothuis. 1995. Induction of Depressed and Elated Mood by Music Influences the Perception of Facial Emotional Expressions in Healthy Subjects. *Journal of Affective Disorders* 33(4):215-226.

Buckwalter, K. C., J. Hartsock and J. Gaffney. 1985. *Music Therapy. In Nursing Interventions: Treatments for Nursing Diagnoses*, ed. G. M. Bulecheck and J. C. McCloskey, pp. 58-74. Philadelphia: Saunders.

Bronner, Simon J. 1985. *Chain Carvers: Old Men Crafting Meaning*. Lexington: The University Press of Kentucky.

Cook, J. D. 1981. The Therapeutic Use of Music: A Literature Review. *Nursing Forum* 20:252-266.

Cosentino, Donald J., ed. 1995. *The Sacred Arts of Vodou*. Los Angeles: UCLA Fowler Museum of Cultural History.

Danielson, Larry. 1986. Religious Folklore. In *Folk Groups and Folklore*

Genres: An Introduction, ed. E. Oring, pp. 45-69. Logan: Utah State University Press.

Davies, Douglas. 1994. Christianity. In *Picturing God*, ed. Jean Holm, pp. 41-69. London, New York: Pinter Publishers.

Drillock, David. 1997. Liturgical song in the worship of the Church. *St. Vladimir's Theological Quarterly* 41 (no. 2/3):183-218.

Ezzone, Susan, Carol Baker, Robin Rosselet and Eileen Terepka. 1998. Music as an Adjunct to Antiemetic Therapy. *Oncology Nursing Forum* 25(9):1551-1556.

Geertz, Clifford. 1966. Religion as a Cultural System In *Anthropological Approaches to the Study of Religion*, ed. Michael Banton, pp. 1-46. Edinburgh: Tavistock. Rpr: In *Reader in Comparative Religion*, ed. W. A.Lessa and E. Z. Vogt, pp. 204-216. 2nd ed., New York: Harper & Row.

_____ 1973. Religion as a Cultural System. In *The Interpretation of Cultures*, pp. 87-125. New York: Basic Books.

Georges, Robert A. and Michael O. Jones. 1980. *People Studying People: The Human Element in Fieldwork*. Berkeley: University of California Press.

_____ 1995. *Folkloristics: An Introduction*. Bloomington: Indiana University Press.

Goa, David J. 1989. Three Urban Parishes: A Study of Sacred Space. *Material History Bulletin* 29 (Spring):13-24.

Good, Marion. 1996. Effects of Relaxation and Music on Postoperative Pain: A Review. *Journal of Advanced Nursing* 24(5):905-14.

Hesser, Barbara. 1995. The Power of Sound and Music in Therapy and Healing. In *Listening, Playing, Creating: Essays on the Power of Sound*, ed. Carolyn Bereznak Kenny, pp. 43-50. Albany: SUNY Press.

Hordynsky, S. 1988. Icon. In *Encyclopedia of Ukraine*, ed. Volodymyr Kubijovyc, vol. II, pp. 294-297. Toronto: University of Toronto Press.

Hotz, Robert Lee. 1998. Study Suggests Music May Someday Help Repair Brain. *Los Angeles Times* 9 Nov., A1, A21.

Isajiw, Wsevolod W. 1991. Ethnic Art and the Ukrainian-Canadian Experience. In *Art and Ethnicity: The Ukrainian Tradition in Canada*, ed. Robert B. Klymasz, pp. 29- 37. Hull: Canadian Museum of Civilization.

Jones, Michael Owen. 1975. *The Hand Made Object and Its Maker*. Berkeley and Los Angeles: University of California Press.

_____ 1987. *Exploring Folk Art: Twenty Years of Thought on Craft, Work, and Aesthetics*. Ann Arbor: UMI Research Press. Logan: Utah State University Press, 2nd edition, 1993.

_____. 1989. *Craftsman of the Cumberlands: Tradition and Creativity*. Lexington: The University Press of Kentucky.

64

_____. 1991. A Folklorist's Viewpoint on Ukrainian-Canadian Art. In *Art and Ethnicity: The Ukrainian Tradition in Canada*, ed. Robert B. Klymasz, pp.47-57. Hull: Canadian Museum of Civilization.

_____. 1993. Why Take a Behavioral Approach to Folk Objects? In *History from Things: Essays on Material Culture*, ed. Steven Lubar and W. David Kingery, pp. 182-196. Washington, D. C.: Smithsonian Institution Press.

_____. 1994a. Applying Folklore Studies: An Introduction. In *Putting Folklore to Use*, ed. M. O. Jones, pp. 1-41. Lexington: Univ. Press of Kentucky.

_____. 1994b. How Do You Get Inside the Art of Outsiders? In *The Artist Outsider: Creativity and the Boundaries of Culture*, ed. Michael D. Hall and Eugene Metcalf, Jr., pp. 312-330. Washington, D. C.: Smithsonian Institution Press.

_____. 1994c. Ukrainian Byzantine Icon Painters and Paintings in Canada: A Preliminary Report on Researching a Tradition. Unpublished report, Canadian Museum of Civilization.

_____. 1995a. Folk and Academic Traditions among Byzantine Icon Painters in Western Canada. Unpublished report, Canadian Museum of Civilization.

_____. 1995b. The 1995 Archer Taylor Memorial Lecture: Why Make (Folk) Art? *Western Folklore* 54:253-276.

_____. 1996a. Icon Painters in Western Canada and the Conundrums of Classification: Why Creates Folk Art, When, and Why? In *The Icon in Canada*, ed. Robert B. Klymasz, pp. 7-33. Hull: Canadian Museum of Civilization.

_____. 1996b. Orthodox Religion and an Aesthetic, Symbolic Approach to Community. Unpublished Report, Canadian Museum of Civilization, 105 pp.

_____. 1996c. *Studying Organizational Symbolism: What, How, Why?* Newbury Park, CA: Sage.

_____. 1997a. Gary Robertson: Tradition, Ethnicity and the Aesthetics of Everyday Life. www.americanfolk.com.

_____. 1997b. How Can We Apply Event Analysis to "Material Behavior," and Why Should We? *Western Folklore* 56:199-214.

_____. 1998. The Aesthetic-Emotional Aspect of Orthodoxy: Interview Transcripts, Proposed Video and Possible Health Implications. Unpublished Report, Canadian Museum of Civilization.

_____. Forthcoming. The Aesthetics of Everyday Life, or What Do Ukrainian Icons and Orange County Bathrooms Have in Common? In *Self-Taught Art in America*, ed. Charles Russell.

Keleher, Serge. 1989. Ukrainian Church Iconography in Canada: Models and Their Spiritual Significance. In *The Ukrainian Religious Experience:*

Tradition and the Canadian Cultural Context, ed. David J. Goa, pp. 47-55. Edmonton: University of Alberta Canadian Institute of Ukrainian Studies.

Kelly, Sean F. 1993. The Use of Music as a Hypnotic Suggestion. *American Journal of Clinical Hypnosis* 36(2):83-90.

Kenny, Carolyn Bereznak, ed. 1995. *Listening, Playing, Creating: Essays on the Power of Sound*. Albany: SUNY Press.

Klymasz, Robert B. 1978. The Science in Folklore: The Case of Motif D1275-- "Magic Song." In *Folklore in the Modern World*, ed. Richard M. Dorson, pp. 273-280. The Hague: Mouton.

Lawless, Elaine. 1983. Brothers and Sisters: Pentecostals as a Religious Folk Group. *Western Folklore* 42:85-104.

Lofaro, Tony. 1995. Strength in Song: Singer Weaves Music into Therapy. *The Ottawa Citizen* 11 Nov:C3.

Matthew, Gervase. 1963. *Byzantine Aesthetics*. London: John Murray.

McDannell, Colleen. 1995. *Material Christianity: Religion and Popular Culture in America*. New Haven: Yale Univ. Press.

McCraty, R., B. Barrios-Choplin, M. Atkinson and D. Tomasino.1998. The Effects of Different Types of Music on Mood, Tension, and Mental Clarity. *Alternative Therapies in Health and Medicine* 4:75-84.

Milspaw, Yvonne J. 1986. Protestant Home Shrines: Icon and Image. *New York Folklore*12:119-136.

Morgan, David. 1998. *Visual Piety: A History and Theory of Popular Religious Images*. Berkeley: University of California Press.

Murphy, Declan C. 1988. Cicero and the Icon Painters: The Transformation of Byzantine Image Theory in Medieval Muscovey. In *The Byzantine Legacy in Eastern Europe*, ed. Lowell Clucas, pp. 149-164. New York: East European Monographs, Boulder; Distributed by Columbia University Press.

Orlova, Alexandra. 1990. *Tchaikovsky: A Self-Portrait*. Trans. R. M.Davison, Oxford: Oxford University Press.

O'Sullivan, R. J. 1991. A Musical Road to Recovery: Music in Intensive Care. *Intensive Care Nursing* 7:160-163.

Primiano, Leonard Norman. 1995. Vernacular Religion and the Search for Method in Religious Folklife. *Western Folklore* 54:37-56.

Quenot, Michel. 1991. *The Ikon: Window on the Kingdom*. Trans. A Carthusian Monk. Crestwood, N.Y.: St. Vladimir's Seminary Press.

Schlieper, Heiko C. 1986. Icons and Art: An Icon Painter's View. In *Seasons of Celebration: Ritual in Eastern Christian Culture*, ed. David J. Goa, pp. 45-48. Edmonton: Provincial Museum of Alberta.

Redmond, Layne. 1997. *When the Drummers Were Women: A Spiritual History of Rhythm.* New York: Three Rivers Press.

Roseman, Marina. 1988. The Pragmatics of Aesthetics: The Performance of Healing among Senoi Temiar. *Social Science and Medicine* 27(8):811-818.

Schwartz, Fred J. 1993. Music in Medicine. In *Current Research in Arts Medicine*, ed. Fadi J. Bejjani, pp. 375-378. Princeton, NJ: MedArt International.

Sherrard, Philip. 1990. *The Sacred in Life and Art.* Ipswich, U. K.: Golgonooza Press.

Soloukin, Vladimir. 1971. *Searching for Icons in Russia.* Trans. P. S.Falla. New York: Harcourt Brace Jovanovich; a Helen and Kurt Wolff Book.

Stepovyk, Dmytro V. 1991. The Ukrainian Icon in Canada. In *Art and Ethnicity: The Ukrainian Tradition in Canada*, ed. Robert B. Klymasz, pp.39-45. Hull: Canadian Museum of Civilization.

Vedantam, Shankar. 1995. Research Sings Praises of Musical Therapy. *The Ottawa Citizen* 21 Oct.:B8.

Vladyshevskaia, Tatiana. 1991. On the Links Between Music and Icon Painting in Medieval Rus. In *Christianity and the Arts in Russia*, ed. William C.Brumfield and Milos M. Velimirovic, pp. 14-29. New York: Cambridge University Press.

Vryonis, Speros, Jr. 1988. Preface. In *The Byzantine Legacy in Eastern Europe*, ed. Lowell Clucas, pp. v-xiv. New York: East European Monographs, Boulder; Distributed by Columbia University Press.

Yoder, Don. 1965/66. Official Religion versus Folk Religion. *Pennsylvania Folklife*15(2):36-52.

_____. 1974. Toward a Definition of Folk Religion. *Western Folklore* 32:2-15.

_____. 1996. Studying Organizational Symbolism: What, How, Why?

POUR LA SUITE DE LA « BEAUTÉ »
LE PARCOURS DE CLAUDE GOSSELIN
CHANTRE DE QUÉBEC DEPUIS 1943

par
Anne-Marie Poulin

« Je continue parce que c'est beau et je vais arrêter quand les gens ne me demanderont plus. J'adore ça! [1] ». C'est en ces termes que Monsieur Claude Gosselin, 67 ans, résume sa passion pour le chant en général et le chant sacré en particulier de même que sa volonté de continuer. D'où l'intitulé qui paraphrase le titre du film-culte de Pierre Perreault *Pour la suite du monde* (1962), titre d'ailleurs inspiré par Grand-Louis Harvey, agriculteur et chantre de l'île aux Coudres. Bien que le milieu et le mode de vie de l'insulaire diffèrent sensiblement de ceux de Claude Gosselin, résolument urbain et professionnel et qu'ils représentent des époques différentes, on retrouve chez l'un comme chez l'autre, un sens inné de la tradition et de la continuité de même qu'un respect analogue pour la beauté du chant liturgique.

Sur le plan historique les deux hommes s'inscrivent en outre, dans cette longue lignée de chantres[2] attestée depuis le Régime français dont le rôle a été largement reconnu et assuré jusqu'à l'*aggiornamento* de l'Église catholique romaine dans les années 1960. D'ailleurs, sous Mgr François-Xavier de Montmorency Laval, premier évêque de Québec (de 1674 à 1687), le maître-chantre figure parmi les cinq dignités majeures octroyées par la tradition ecclésiale (les quatre autres étant le doyen, l'archidiacre, le théologal et le pénitencier [sic]).

Quant aux chantres formant le chœur du Chapitre[3] de la Basilique, leur nomination quoique d'ordre mineur se situe au même niveau que celle des vicaires. Ce qui indique l'importance du chant sacré comme partie intégrante du culte et, de là, de la personne du chantre. C'est ce qui explique aussi les privilèges greffés à sa fonction tant dans les hauts lieux de l'Église que dans l'humble paroisse urbaine ou rurale. Pierre-Georges Roy rappelle d'autre part, que ces « personnages [...] qui touchent de près ou de loin au service de l'église [...] sont autant de dignitaires auxquels il n'est pas toujours permis de toucher impunément ». En font foi, les

---

[1] Entrevue réalisée le 11 novembre 1998.

[2] En ce début de parcours, le terme chantre s'applique uniquement à une personne qui chante dans un service religieux.

[3] Le Chapitre qui est composé de chanoines sert de conseil à l'évêque .

archives judiciaires de l'époque qui « pourraient faire, d'après Roy, le sujet de plus d'un poème héroï-comique[4] ».

Honneurs et privilèges

La nomination du Grand-Chantre du Chapitre de la basilique de Québec donne droit par exemple, d'introniser les chanoines qui sont *de facto* ses pairs. Quand en 1693 ces derniers s'abrogent du privilège à l'insu de leur supérieur, le Conseil souverain est saisi du problème qu'il règle en faveur de l'évêché et du Grand-Chantre[5]. De la même manière, des ordonnances régissent les devoirs des Fabriques[6] envers leurs chantres et les honneurs dûs à leur rang. Les *Statuts publiés* à la suite du troisième synode tenu à Québec en 1698 définissent clairement la voie à suivre en ce sens[7] :

> « Nous avons reconnu dans les Visites que nous avons faites des Paroisses de la Campagne, le besoin qu'elles avaient de Chantres pour aider aux Curés à chanter l'Office divin; et comme il est très difficle d'en trouver de bons, à cause qu'on ne peut leur accorder d'émoluments, nous avons cru à propos de régler que, puisqu'il est du devoir des Marguilliers d'en procurer aux Curés qui ne peuvent eux seuls chanter la grande Messe, ni les autres Offices divins dans les lieux où ils ne pourront point leur donner d'émoluments à cause de la pauvreté de la Paroisse, et où ils ne pourront leur fournir des surplis, *les dits Chantres, quoique non revêtus de surplis jouiront des prérogatives d'avoir le Pain-bénit, et l'Eau-bénite devant les Marguilliers, qui se doivent faire un plaisir de leur accorder les dites prérogatives* puisque c'est à eux à s'acquitter des obligations de l'Église, et à lui faire honneur. Cependant, *il ne sera pas permis indifféremment à toutes sortes de personnes de se mettre dans les Bancs du Chœur, pour chanter et jouir des avantages accordés aux dits Chantres*[8] mais seulement à ceux qui auront l'approbation du Curé, et l'agrément des Marguilliers.»

De même en 1709, le règlement VII du Conseil Supérieur concernant les honneurs décernés aux Seigneurs dans les églises ordonne que ce n'est « *Qu'après l'œuvre et le chœur, [que] le Seigneur aura le premier l'eau bénite par aspersion [...]* ». Étonnement, de telles compensations semblent suffire aux chantres, pourtant considérés indispensables au culte tout en y étant soumis et dont la fonction demeure tributaire du bon vouloir du curé, des marguilliers ou encore de la situation financière de la Fabrique!

---

4 Pierre-Georges Roy, « Les chantres et bedeaux sous le Régime français » *Le Bulletin des recherches historiques* vol. 6, n° 1, janv. 1940, p. 121.

5 Jacques Lacoursière, *Chronologie détaillée de la Nouvelle-France*, Québec, 1995, inédit.

6 Groupe de clercs ou laïcs qui veillent à l'administration des biens d'une église.

7 H. Têtu, C.O.Gagnon, *Mandements des évêques de Québec*, Québec, A. Côté et Cie., 1887. T.1, p. 372, art. 20.

8 Les italiques ne figurent pas dans le texte original.

Aussi, être chantre dans une paroisse n'est pas un emploi à temps plein. Pas plus d'ailleurs dans les hautes sphères de l'Église où le cumul des fonctions est généralisé. Le chanoine[9] tout comme l'agriculteur, le médecin, le bedeau et le fonctionnaire peut de la sorte être chantre. Au niveau paroissial, la fonction de maître-chantre relève généralement d'un laïc et suivant le contexte social de l'époque favorise la gent masculine. Il en est de même pour les membres du chœur. Toutefois, n'est pas chantre qui veut:

> Que l'on admette à faire partie de la maîtrise de l'église que des hommes d'une piété et d'une honnêteté reconnues et qui par leur tenue modeste et religieuse pendant les offices liturgiques se montrent dignes du rôle sait qu'ils remplissent. (Pie X, *Motu Proprio*, 1903, n° 14).

Compte tenu des nombreuses célébrations religieuses, deux, parfois trois hommes, se partagent la tâche et les honneurs dus à leur rang. Parmi ces bénéfices figurent l'usage gratuit d'un banc d'église pour leur famille et l'accès aux stalles dans le chœur ou au banc de chantres généralement situé au jubé. Cette structure généralement sculptée et de taille imposante est toujours surélevée par rapport aux bancs des fidèles et des servants de messe.

Un des grands privilèges du chantre en titre est de pouvoir « se produire » dans une paroisse voisine. Toutefois, là où plusieurs bonnes voix sont reconnues la situation prend parfois une tournure inattendue comme le rapporte le journal *L'Événement* de Québec du 7 septembre 1898[10] :

> « Une bataille dans une église. Deux chantres se donnent des coups de poing.»
> L'Église de St-David de Lauberivière [en aval de Québec] vient d'être le théatre d'une scène disgracieuse, pour ne pas dire scandaleuse. Il y eu dimanche quinze jours, deux chantres se sont donnés des taloches au chœur de l'orgue et voici pourquoi cette bataille a eu lieu en présence de toute la paroisse. Les paroissiens de St-David sont allés, il y a quelque temps, en pèlerinage au sanctuaire de la Bonne Ste-Anne. L'un des deux chantres en question s'est installé auprès de l'orgue et a entonné tous les morceaux de l'office divin, malgré les insistances de l'autre chantre qui voulait avoir l'honneur d'entonner à son tour dans une église étrangère.
> Il y a dimanche quinze jours, le chantre qui n'avait pas entonné à Ste-Anne, s'est mis au lutrin à St-David et n'a pas voulu que son compagnon chante à son tour. Ce dernier froissé dans son amour propre lança un coup de poing à son voisin et celui-ci

---

9 Charles-Amador Martin (1647-1711), chanoine (1684) et fils du célèbre Abraham Martin dit l'Écossais qui a laissé son [pré]nom aux plaines d'Abraham est un musicien accompli, un compositeur et est reconnu comme un « habile chantre ». Comme musicien, il compose le chant de la Messe et de l'Office de la Sainte-Famille, une dévotion introduite par Mgr de Laval à son arrivée dans la jeune colonie. Premier curé de la nouvelle paroisse Notre-Dame-de-Foy près de Québec (1698), ce second prêtre canadien est actuellement commémoré dans la toponymie de Sainte-Foy . (*Carrefour*, Ville de Sainte-Foy, 20ᵉ année, n° 14, nov. 1998, p. 6.

10 *L'Ancêtre*, Société de généalogie de Québec, vol. 25, n° 1-2, oct.-nov. 1998, p. 57

riposta aussitôt. Il s'ensuivit un échange de coups de poing ou une bataille en règle dans l'église.

       Ce grand scandale produisit presque une panique. L'organiste, Mlle Lemelin, tomba sans connaissance. Des amis parvinrent cependant à mettre fin au combat et à rétablir la paix dans le lieu saint. On nous a dit que l'un des combattants devait faire amende honorable dimanche dernier, mais nous n'avons pu vérifier le fait.

Le costume constitue une autre distinction du chantre traditionnel. Suivant les moyens financiers de la paroisse les chantres réunis en chœur dans la nef revêtent le surplis blanc à longues et larges manches sur une soutane noire. Lorsque le chantre (avec ou sans assistant) donne la réplique au célébrant à partir du premier banc d'église ou du jubé, le vêtement liturgique n'est pas exigé.

Devoirs du chantre paroissial

       Tout au long du XIXe siècle et de la première moitié du XXe siècle, le chantre est tenu de participer aux messes quotidiennes et dominicales, aux fêtes solennelles et calendaires comme Noël, Pâques et la Fête-Dieu, aux offices religieux tels les vêpres, le Salut du Saint-Sacrement, les Quarante-Heures, les mois de Marie et du Sacré-Cœur. Il doit en outre « se conformer exactement aux règles que l'Église a tracées pour la musique sacrée[11] » dans le *Calendrier pour les chantres* publié par le Comité interdiocésain de la Musique sacrée de la Province de Québec[12]. Sur demande, le chantre doit préparer et être disponible pour les mariages, les services funèbres ou autres événements paroissiaux comme l'intronisation d'un nouveau curé, la visite de dignitaires, les bénédictions diverses (école, nouvelles cloches, croix de chemin, semences, érablière, etc.). Enfin, la majorité des chantres sont tenus de former un chœur avec les gens désignés par le curé.

       Quant au chantre « à la voix de stentor », il peut remplir d'autres tâches sociales comme diriger les chants de « procession » de la fête « nationale » de la Saint-Jean-Baptiste ou encore être crieur public ou encanteur pour la paroisse. La « criée du dimanche matin » qui se faisait sur le parvis de l'église, consiste à faire état de la situation générale de la paroisse, annoncer les corvées et les décisions municipales, faire part d'objets perdus ou retrouvés, etc. Le Jour des Morts, le 2 novembre, le chantre transforme la criée habituelle d'information en une « criée pour les âmes » qui est une vente aux enchères à partir d'objets d'artisanat, de

---

[11]   *Discipline diocésaine....* 3e édition. Québec, L'Action catholique, 1937, p. 94, n° 2.

[12]   Actuellement, le Comité de liturgie diocésaine par décret de l'évêque propose les chants et thèmes appropriés aux divers Temps liturgiques. Les chorales paroissiales et chantres s'en tiennent à ces propositions pour éviter les contresens liturgiques.

produits de la cuisine ou de la ferme dont les profits servent à faire chanter des messes « aux chers disparus » de la paroisse[13].

Embauche et rémunération

Parce que la nomination et le renvoi du chantre traditionnel sont du ressort du curé, on peut croire que la situation est acceptée d'emblée. Or, le cas Chartier présenté ici démontre le contraire : voulant se protéger, un chantre de l'Acadie du Haut-Richelieu « rédigea une formule d'engagement qu'il fit contresigner par le curé, renversant ainsi l'usage habituel […][14] » :

> « Je soussigné m'engage à chanter les offices paroissiaux de la paroisse de l'Acadie et à enseigné [sic] le plein chant aux jeunes gens qui voudront l'apprendre aux conditions suivantes, savoir:
>
> « mon salaire sera de cent piastres par année, avec droit au casuel déterminé par l'évêque
>
> « J'exige un avis de trois mois avant le terme de mon engagement quand mes services ne seront plus requis, et je m'engage à donner le même avis, trois mois avant la fin de mon année de chant si je désire cesser d'être maître-chantre.
>
> « fait et passé à l'Acadie le premier juin mil huit cent quatre vingt dix neuf et signé par moi et Monsieur le curé. »
>
> Oscar Chartier [1899]
> J. L. Gaudet, ptre curé.

Indépendamment des conditions d'embauche, le poste de maître-chantre n'a jamais été « très payant à moins que le titulaire ne bénéficie du casuel[15] des messes [fixé par le diocèse]. Le chant des dimanches et fêtes d'obligation ne comporte pas de rémunération. Il n'y a que les grand'messes chantées durant la semaine qui rapportent quelque argent[16] ». Pour compenser, la Fabrique verse un salaire selon ses moyens ou l'interprétation qu'elle se fait du service à l'église. De telle sorte que les émoluments varient considérablement d'un endroit à l'autre, voire d'une époque à l'autre. Jean-Baptiste Neveu par exemple, chantre à l'Assomption entre 1780 et 1797, reçoit comme émoluments, 30 minots de blé, 100 livres de lard et 50

---

13 Yvon Desautels, « La coutume de nos ancêtres. La Criée », *Vidéo-Presse*, vol.9 n° 3, novembre 1979, p. 12.
14 Pierre Brault, *Histoire de l'Acadie du Haut-Richelieu*, St-Jean-sur-le-Richelieu, Éditions Mille Roches, 1982, p. 81.
15 Revenu incertain et variable d'un office.
16 Ernest Mercier, Notre-Dame-du-Rosaire, étape de l'amitié, s.l., s.éd., 1983, p. 170.

francs, sans préjudice du casuel[17] ». Un siècle plus tard, en 1884, Louis-Martin de Saint-Romuald de Farnham, reçoit « 72 dollars payables par paiement égaux de 6 dollars, à chaque fin de mois. Toutefois, on ne lui accorde aucun droit aux casuels des grand-messes, mariages, services et sépultures [18] ».

Dans certains cas, la Fabrique ne verse aucun salaire jugeant que le casuel devait suffire. C'est ainsi qu'entre 1853 et 1901, MM. Sévère Dugas et Simon Richard ont chanté « à bon marché » dans leur paroisse pendant plus de quarante-huit ans[19]. Là où il y a plus d'un chantre en titre comme dans le cas Dugas/Richard et que les deux participent au service quotidien, le modeste casuel est partagé. De plus, dans l'éventualité où un chantre s'absente, il défraie lui-même le coût d'un remplaçant, et ce, même après 25 ou 30 ans de loyaux services! Vers 1955, M. Laurent Gosselin, père de Claude, reçoit 30 $ pour chanter 30 messes par semaine, une somme intéressante pour l'époque et qu'il n'a pas à partager avec le second chantre.

Force est de reconnaître que dans l'esprit de l'église et des fidèles, et ce, pendant près de trois siècles, « un véritable chantre qui a le sens de la fonction ne mesure pas son rendement et son empressement aux sous dont on le paie[20] ». En effet, malgré les conditions offertes ou imposées le chantre persiste et chante! De plus, là où il est apprécié, sans concurrent ou tout simplement indélogeable, il demeure souvent en poste de longues années!

La fidélité du chantre

Un des aspects non négligeables du chantre est sa fidélité à la tâche. À ce chapitre, les exemples foisonnent. Retenons entre autres le cas particulier de l'octogénaire Adolphe Biron de Pointe-du-Lac près de Trois-Rivières. *Le Petit Journal* du 16 mai 1948 indique en gros titre : « À 80 ans, il chante la messe de son 70e anniversaire comme chantre dans la même église ». Rien dans l'article n'indique que son mandat était terminé! Ou à la veille de l'être!

Johnny Tremblay de Grande-Baie est chantre pendant 67 ans. « Ça finit le 2 avril 1934. Le curé m'a dit : "Vous ne reviendrez plus"[21] ». Édouard Lincourt

17   Christian Roy, *Histoire de l'Assomption*, L'Assomption, Édité par la Commission des fêtes du 250e, 1967, p. 496.
18   Lorenzo Proteau, *Pépère et mémère*, Boucherville, Les Publications Proteau, 1992, p. 344.
19   A.-C. Dugas, *Histoire de la paroisse de Saint-Ligouri, Comté de Montcalm, P.Q.*, s.l., s.éd., 1902, p.105.
20   Guy Fortin, s.s.s. « Le beau métier de chantre », *Index des chorales de la région métropolitaine de Québec*, (1955) s.éd., n.p.
21   V.T., [Victor Tremblay] ptre, « Mémoires d'un vieillard», *Saguenayensia*, vol. 3, n° 1, janvier-février 1961, p. 18.

de la paroisse de Saint-Théodore-d'Acton, instruit dans le plain-chant par le curé de la paroisse, devient chantre en 1873 à 14 ans. Ayant rempli fidèlement son rôle pendant 66 ans, il s'arrête en 1939 à l'âge de 80 ans. On dit même que lors d'une intervention chirurgicale [et sous anesthésie] il chantait un Alléluia [22]! ». Grand-Louis Harvey de l'île aux Coudres reste en poste quatre décennies jusqu'à l'âge de 75 ans. Avec l'avènement de la nouvelle liturgie en 1968-1969, il abandonne. « [...] j'ai dit, Bonsoir la visite! J'su descendu du jubé [...] pi j'ai pas remonté [...]». À Québec, Laurent Gosselin, père de Claude œuvre 35 ans, à l'église de Jacques-Cartier jusqu'à l'âge de 58 ans alors que son fils, maître de chapelle à l'église Saint-Cœur-de-Marie demeure en fonction pendant 42 ans (1955-1997).

Le Québec et ses « chantres à voix »

Depuis le Régime français, le chantre d'église au Québec est maintes fois associé à une voix forte et sonore[23]. Au XIXᵉ siècle notamment, la fonction incombe le plus souvent au « chanteur à voix » ayant le style « opéra » et dont la prestance lui permet en plus de faire office de crieur public. Plusieurs écrivains en témoignent et les monographies paroissiales leur rendent moult hommages sous forme d'articles, d'anecdotes, de courtes biographies, de photographies et de nomenclatures. À telle enseigne que la « gloire » d'une paroisse semble reposer, en sus des dimensions de l'église ou de la prestance de certains curés, sur la force vocale de ses chantres ou de la chorale. C'est ainsi que Benjamin Sulte, dans son histoire de Trois-Rivières, ne tarit pas d'éloges sur cinq maîtres-chantres dont la « renommée » s'étend depuis la Nouvelle-France jusqu'en 1887[24].

Sulte évoque d'abord Leclerc, chantre / agriculteur dont les hymnes et chansons vers 1710 pouvaient être entendus sur une distance de deux milles « au moins »; ensuite Charles Malavoine, médecin qui prend la relève en 1730; suivi de Jean-Baptiste Badeaux en 1754, « qui avait une voix sympathique et vibrante [...] dans l'esprit du plain-chant [...] »; « son fils, Joseph Badeaux, [qui suit] sa trace au tournant du XVIIᵉ siècle avec une voix qui eut rempli une vaste cathédrale et qui « brisait les vitres » de l'église paroissiale. [L'auteur ajoute qu'] après avoir abandonné le chœur pour raison d'âge, il ne se gênait pas de reprendre de son banc les chantres qui entonnaient de travers ou qui faussaient »; et à partir de 1830, « le docteur Georges-Edouard Badeaux [fils de Joseph] raviva le lustre de[s] maîtres-chantres ». Sulte dira de ce dernier qu'il a côtoyé « qu'il était de ces hommes qui ne savent pas qu'ils sont artistes et qui, cependant, s'emparent de nous par

22   En collaboration, *La petite histoire de la paroisse de Saint-Théodore-d'Acton*, s.l., s.éd., 1942, p. 53-54
23   Sur ce point, le Québec accuse une certaine avance sur l'Europe. Selon R. Mancini musicologue, ce n'est qu'à partir de 1831 (en France) que « la magie de la vocalise » cède à « la puissance de la voix et surtout des notes aiguës ». *Universalis*, 1995, p. 367.
24   Benjamin Sulte, *Trois-Rivières d'autrefois*, Montréal, Ed. Edouard Garand, vol.19, 1932, p. 74-77.

la force même de leur vertu et de leur talent ». Transporté par la qualité de la voix du chantre Badeaux, Sulte ira jusqu'à affirmer qu'il « a fait autant pour le sentiment religieux que tous les prédicateurs qui ont prêché, de 1830 à 1870, dans l'église paroissiale de Trois-Rivières ».

Enfin, plus près de notre époque, Ovide Tremblay à Jacquau à Marc chantre-bègue des Éboulements dans Charlevoix, attire les louanges suivantes : « Celui qui a une fois entendu le célèbre chantre [...] a cru, peut-être avec raison entendre mieux que Caruso[25] ».

L'engouement pour ce type de chantre et les tensions entourant son rôle se poursuivent jusqu'à la veille de Vatican II. Encore en 1955, on rappelle que la véritable mission du chantre d'église est de relever l'éclat de la liturgie plutôt que de chercher à « éblouir ou à mousser sa popularité vocale [26] ». Ce qui démontre que le solo est peut-être préféré au chant grégorien qui est essentiellement collectif et nivèle les voix. Cependant le timbre de la voix n'est qu'un problème parmi d'autres.

Résonnances et dissonances

En effet, la qualité sonore n'est pas toujours garante d'une voix juste. À cet égard, Marius Barbeau rappelle une anecdote impliquant son ancien curé, J.-T Alfred Chaperon de Québec. « Sa grande voix, dit-il, qui ne manquait pas de timbre ne l'empêchait pas de chanter archi-faux. Il faisait détonner les chantres, et l'organiste lui-même se mêlait dans ses anches et dans ses flûtes [27] ».

Quant au chantre laïque peu ou pas formé en latin ou en grégorien, ce sont des difficultés d'un autre ordre qui surgissent. Louis Harvey qui commence à pratiquer le plain-chant à l'âge de 18 ans admet que sans instruction préalable « c'était de l'ouvrage pour moé [...]. J'avais peur de manquer [...] C'était bien terrible [...] Ça m'a pris un gros mois pour comprendre [où] était la note de sol. Un gros mois[28] ». D'autres apprennent la musique au son et mémorisent les paroles. Ce qui donnent parfois des cantiques improvisés ou des messes chantées sans modifier une mesure, une note de leurs gammes pendant de longues années[29]. Il arrive aussi que les réponses en latin provoquent de curieux écarts d'interprétation. Par exemple, ce « Méo r'cule pas, Méo r'cule pas, Maxime non

25   Léonce Boivin, *Dans nos montagnes (Charlevoix), Les Éboulements*, s.n., 1945, p. 111.
26   Fortin, Guy.s.s.s. *op.cit.*
27   *Revue trimestrielle canadienne*: 1943:381. v.a. Lawrence Nowry, *Man of Mana. Marius Barbeau. A Biography.* Toronto, NC Press Limited, (c1995). 448 p. ill.
28   Gaston Blackburn, ptre. «Enquêtes folkloriques à l'Ile aux Coudres(sic), *Saguenayensia*:, mars-avril 1979, p. 30
29   Pierre-Paul Turgeon, *La vie à Ste-Claire pendant 150 ans*, s.l., s.éd., 1975, p. 87.

plus racule pas » en lieu et place du *Mea culpa, mea culpa, Mea maxima culpa*[30]. (Trad. Par ma faute, par ma faute, par ma très grande faute.) À la décharge du chantre formé sur le terrain, la valeur morale et chrétienne de celui-ci a toujours préséance sur la qualité de la voix [31].

Les grands virages

Loin d'être uniques dans les annales paroissiales ces récits occultent cependant des tensions autrement plus importantes qui apparaissent au XIXe siècle entre la liturgie et la musique lui étant destinée. Dans un dossier sur la musique liturgique, ses enjeux et les problèmes rencontrés au Québec[32], Jean-Claude Breton fait voir que trois courants de pensés s'affrontent à l'époque : les tenants de la tradition des XVIIe et XVIIIe siècles [privilégiant l'art vocal], ceux voulant développer une musique plus contemporaine [voix et instruments] et enfin, les partisans du chant grégorien et l'œuvre de Palestrina, perçue comme un pivot du chant polyphonique. Le conflit, dit-il, a frappé le compositeur de la musique de l'hymne national canadien, Calixa Lavallée (1842-1891) ... [qui] avait mis sur pied une chorale mixte extrêmement compétente [dans une église] à Montréal[33]. Citant Paul Cadrin, professeur de musicologie théorique à l'Université Laval, Breton note que de nouvelles normes en musique imposées par l'église rendaient le travail de Lavallée impraticable. « Incapable de trouver un compromis, Calixa Lavallée a émigré aux États-Unis. Il est mort en exil, sans jamais s'être remis de cette blessure morale. »

Au début du XXe siècle, poursuit Breton, le *Motu Proprio* de Pie X met définitivement un terme aux diverses tendances, signalant du coup le triomphe du traditionnalisme. Dès lors, sont bannis de l'église le style opéra, l'utilisation des voix féminines dans les chœurs et l'emploi d'autres instruments que l'orgue après plus d'un siècle de ces coutumes. Les répercussions de l'édit ont touché le Québec près de 30 ans plus tard. Descendant d'une longue lignée de musiciens d'église, Paul Cadrin se souvient : « L'impact du *Motu Proprio* a bouleversé la vie de mon grand-père quand, au milieu des années 30, le curé a exigé qu'il se départisse de l'orchestre et de la chorale de voix mixtes qu'il entraînait depuis des années. Le

---

30 *Ibid.*

31 Fortin, Guy s.s.s. *op.cit.*

32 Jean-Claude Breton, « Dossier. Si on chantait... » *Présence Magazine* , vol. 4, n° 6, mai 1995, p. 15-25.

33 Lavallée œuvre à l'église Saint-Jacques et non à Saint-Charles comme l'indiquent Breton dans son texte (voir DBC:XII:578-580 et Eugène Lapierrre, *Calixa Lavallée. 1842-1891. Musicien national du Canada*. Montréal/Paris, Fides, Les Publications de la Société historique de Montréal, 1966, 291 p.

grand-père a quitté à regret sa bien-aimée tâche de maître de chapelle et il est mort sans avoir pu y œuvrer de nouveau[34] »

L'impact du *Motu Proprio* résonne à nouveau en 1955 quand le pape Pie XII « prône le chant grégorien et la polyphonie comme des modèles exclusifs et universels ». Toutefois, moins de dix ans plus tard, Vatican II modifie radicalement la donne. Désormais l'Église oscille, selon le théologien Roger Mager, entre « la réaffirmation de la primauté du latin mais ouverture aux langues vivantes; la réaffirmation de la primauté du grégorien mais ouverture au chant populaire ». (*Congrégation des rites*, 1967). C'est dans ce contexte éclaté que le chantre Claude Gosselin formé dans la tradition classique se retrouve au mitan de la trentaine.

Il connaît alors une Église qui troque sa langue et sa musique originales - le latin, le grégorien - au profit des langues vernaculaires et de la création de textes modernes se voulant « plus accessibles ». Il est témoin du chant choral cédant sa place au chant d'assemblée dirigé par un « animateur » le plus souvent sans formation musicale. Le but étant de favoriser une participation plus « active » de la communauté à la célébration de la messe. C'est ainsi que dans la foulée des changements conciliaires, le rôle-clé tenu jusque-là par le chantre est marginalisé sinon éliminé, ses interventions suspectes et sa crédibilité par rapport aux efforts de renouvellement mis à rude épreuve. Au vent de renouveau s'ajoute également la forte désaffection religieuse de la société québécoise, qui a pour effet de sonner le glas en quelque sorte au chantre et à son répertoire traditionnel. De fait, à l'instar des rites, signes et symboles comme les processions, vêpres, Fête-Dieu, Rogations, la statuaire, l'encens, les médailles et le missel, le chantre semble voué à la disparition. À moins de profiter comme Claude Gosselin, d'un contexte et de conditions exceptionnels - pour un certain temps!

En quête d'une musique sacrée

Depuis la bourrasque vaticane, il y a trente ans, musiciens, pasteurs, compositeurs et diffuseurs de la musique liturgique essaient de (re)créer une qualité musicale propre à inspirer les fidèles tout en leur assurant une participation active. Suivant l'interprétation des textes conciliaires parfois contradictoires, la nouvelle musique est censée refléter la « noble simplicité »[35], soit la même qualité attribuée jusque-là au grégorien et à la polyphonie pourtant « construits » sur plusieurs siècles! C'est dire tout le défi du compositeur actuel!

Il appert non sans surprise que « la mise en place, au plan des textes et de la musique, des chants, notamment ceux de l'assemblée, s'est avérée ardue. Déjà

---

[34] Breton, *op.cit.*

[35] *Sacrosanctum Concilium*, 1963, art. 34

[...] en 1965, un des pères de la réforme, le jésuite Joseph-André Jungmann estimait que cette tâche dépasserait les forces d'une seule génération ». D'où l'intérêt du premier bilan effectué sur ce problème complexe en 1993.

Un premier bilan

La problématique du changement des trente dernières années dans le domaine de la musique sacrée (voix et intruments) fait alors l'objet d'un symposium international organisé par l'école de musique de l'Université Laval en collaboration avec la revue (française) *Musique sacrée-l'Organiste* et tenu les 20 et 21 mai 1993. « Sous le titre, *Chant et musique liturgiques en pays francophones,* les participants, venus de toutes les régions de l'Est du Canada, de même que de la France, s'y sont penchés sur un large éventail de questions, autant théologiques que pratiques, liées à la pratique de la musique dans le cadre de la liturgie ». La publication des Actes visait un seul objectif, « nourrir la réflexion et l'action de tous ceux que préoccupe la qualité de la liturgie[...][36]».

L'importance du symposium impose que l'on s'y attarde pour fins d'éclaircissement. D'une part, pour mieux cerner le contexte dans lequel le chantre d'église a évolué au Québec au cours du présent siècle, pour connaître les réalisations et les principaux artisans du mouvement actuel et pour apprécier ensuite l'expérience particulière de Claude Gosselin, témoin-clé *in situ* des périodes pré et postconciliaires. Monsieur l'abbé Paul Boily, directeur de l'Office national de liturgie et directeur de la revue *Liturgie, foi et culture* [au Québec] résume fort bien la situation du mouvement liturgique depuis 1903 au Canada francophone de même que les perspectives d'avenir par rapport aux enjeux théologiques et culturels et par rapport à ses besoins les plus urgents. Le texte qui suit reprend d'importants extraits de sa conférence d'ouverture au symposium[37].

I. SITUATION
Le mouvement liturgico-musical au Canada. [1903-1993]

Au Canada, le mouvement liturgico-musical issu du *Motu Proprio* [1903] de saint Pie X a trouvé un écho large et fidèle dans les écoles de chant grégorien d'abord. Des centres comme l'Abbaye de Saint-Benoît-du-Lac, l'École de musique de l'Université Laval, la Faculté de musique de l'Université de Montréal, l'Université Saint-Paul d'Ottawa ainsi que plusieurs écoles diocésaines de musique sacrée ont donné au chant grégorien, à la polyphonie sacrée, à la musique d'orgue et à la musique d'ensemble

---

36   Paul Cadrin (ss la dir.de) *Chant et musique liturgiques en pays francophones....* Québec, Université Laval, 1994, 171 p.
37   Boily, P. « La musique litrugique en francophonie. Situation et perspectives au Canada », *Chant et musique liturgiques en pays francophones....* (ss la dir. de Paul Cadrin) Québec, Université Laval, 1994, p. 3-13.

instrumentale une place de choix. Ils ont permis aux musiciens d'église de recevoir une solide formation, généralement poursuivie jusqu'à nos jours dans certains milieux, avec les adaptations nécessaires requises par l'évolution de la science paléographique ou celles de la pastorale d'aujourd'hui. Qu'on nous permette de nommer ici dom Georges Mercure, O.S.B., de Saint-Benoît-du-Lac, Mgr Elzéar Fortier et Marius Cayoutte de l'Université Laval, et l'abbé Clément Morin, P.S.S., de l'Université de Montréal. Mentionnons parmi les écoles de formation, celle des Petits chanteurs du Mont-Royal, celle de la Maîtrise du chapitre de Québec et celle des Petits chanteurs de Trois-Rivières. Il faut aussi souligner la récente initiative du Cégep de Drummondville qui a mis sur pied un cours « Musique et liturgie » proposé à plusieurs diocèses et dont les initiateurs sont M. Gilles Fortin et M. l'abbé Claude Thompson.

Après les années soixante, l'Action musicale liturgique (AML) fondée par un laïc, M. Claude Tessier, qui s'était d'abord occupée de la diffusion du chant grégorien chez le peuple chrétien, amorça le virage entraîné par la réforme liturgique de Vatican II. Le premier *Bulletin de la Commission nationale de liturgie* lançait en 1965 les cours d'été que l'AML organisa jusque vers les années 1980: des Européens comme Rimaud, Gelineau, Veuthey, Reboud, Akepsimas, Moreau, aussi bien que des Canadiens, comme Farley, Gignac, Paradis, Tessier, Chouinard, Fontaine, donnèrent des sessions intensives de musique sacrée et de liturgie dans le sens de ce que demandait Vatican II. L'AML travailla aussi durant l'année dans plusieurs diocèses - Rimouski, Chicoutimi, Saint-Hyacinthe, Sainte-Anne-de-la-Pocatière, Sherbrooke - et y assura une transition pas toujours facile, mais assez heureuse.

Quelques années plus tard, en 1969, Armand Chouinard, eudiste, fondait à Québec le centre ALPEC (Animation et liturgie par l'expression et la communication), qui fit surtout appel à des créateurs québécois et se préoccupa de la liturgie pour les communautés de jeunes. Dans le recueil publié par Alpec, on trouve des noms comme Pierick Houdy, Claudette Melançon, Jean-Louis Racine, Patrice Vallée, Armand Chouinard. Alpec assura des sessions brèves, mais intensives, non seulement au Québec, mais aussi dans les provinces Maritimes et les province de l'Ouest. Alpec-Les Prairies a pris le relais et poursuit avec dynamisme un travail d'animation sur le terrain.[...]

Entre-temps, le diocèse de Montréal, appuyé par une équipe interdiocésaine, publiait en 1966 son *Livret des fidèles* qui cherchait à donner à l'ensemble des assemblées liturgiques un livre de chant de base tenant compte de tout ce qui s'était écrit de valable jusqu'alors, tant en Europe qu'ici. Malheureusement, le livre de la chorale qui aurait dû lui succéder n'a pas pu être réalisé, surtout à cause de l'opposition des éditeurs. On a dû recourir à des blocs de fiches et aux partitions originales des compositeurs d'ici. Néanmoins, le *Livret des fidèles* a joué un rôle important chez nous dans le cadre de la mise en place d'un chant d'Église dans l'esprit de Vatican II. En témoignent les approbations que la Commission épiscopale de liturgie pour le Canada et l'Assemblée des évêques du Québec lui ont accordées dès le départ.

À la différence du *Livret des fidèles*, le *Recueil ALPEC* est d'abord conçu comme un livre de chorale. D'autres livrets de participation publiant des chants méritent d'être mentionnés. Le plus répandu, même en France maintenant, est sans doute le *Prions en Église*, conçu par *Novalis*. Après avoir publié les refrains de la collection *Chantons en Église* du Centre catholique d'Ottawa dans les années soixante, le *Prions en Église* s'est fait l'écho du *Livret des fidèles*, puis, plus tard, des publications d'Alpec, de la revue *Vie liturgique de Québec* et d'autres recueils. Pour leur part, les Bénédictines du Précieux-

Sang de Mont-Laurier éditent, dans le livret mensuel *Liturgie de gloire,* les adaptations en français du *Graduel romain* par dom Georges Mercure, O.S. B. Celui-ci a aussi publié en 1966 une étude et des tons de récitation pour les mélodies du sanctuaire, qui se veulent une fidèle traduction en français des tons latins correspondants, encore utilisés à l'Abbaye de Saint-Benoît-du Lac.

Il convient ici de souligner que le *Bulletin national de liturgie* a publié les tons officiels des préfaces, des prières eucharistiques et du « Notre-Père » en français, ainsi qu'un ordinaire de messe recommandé pour le Canada *La Messe de l'Assemblée.* La Commission épiscopale de liturgie patronne aussi, depuis 1991, la publication de la série *Psaumes et acclamations* pour l'ensemble de l'année liturgique, commande faite à un certain nombre de compositeurs de chez nous par l'Office national de liturgie et diffusée avec la collaboration de Novalis. Ce projet permet une contribution de nos musiciens professionnels à l'enrichissement d'un « Répertoire de chants rituels pour l'Église du Canada ».

Il serait trop long d'énumérer ici toutes les publications faites chez nous depuis 1965. Déjà le premier *Bulletin de la Commission nationale de Liturgie* a dressé la liste de 16 ordinaires de messe, et on n'a pas cessé d'en publier depuis. Je voudrais tout de même mentionner quelques maisons d'édition qui cherchent à faire connaître des œuvres pour la liturgie.
- Les Éditions LAUDEM, rattachées à l'Association du même nom regroupant depuis 1992 les organistes liturgiques du Canada, ont publié diverses compositions liturgiques de Gilles Leclerc, Claude Thompson et Jean Le Buis.
- Le diocèse de Montréal a publié des chants de Jacques Faubert et de Pierre Grandmaison à l'occasion de grands événements comme le 150e anniversaire du diocèse de Montréal et le 350e anniversaire de la fondation de Montréal, entre autres.
- D'autres courants, comme les Éditions RM du Cap-de-la-Madeleine, ont fait paraître dans les années soixante-dix des chants populaires d'André Dumont et autres.
- Les éditions Pontbriand font paraître les recueils de chants de Robert Lebel, dont quelques titres sont repris dans les fiches françaises, tandis que les Éditions du Cénacle publient les chants de s. Madeleine Dubé, O.P.

Cette énumération […] démontre une volonté ferme de la part des divers milieux musicaux d'Église de répondre aux vœux de Vatican II, les uns s'efforçant de conserver une tradition musicale de grande valeur tout en s'adaptant aux besoins nouveaux de notre temps, les autres cherchant dans la culture ambiante l'expression de la quête spirituelle de l'homme d'aujourd'hui.

II. PERSPECTIVES
Enjeux théologiques
Comme je l'ai déjà souligné […] la pastorale de la musique pour la liturgie comporte des enjeux théologiques. Le chant et la musique liturgiques sont porteurs de la foi de l'Église. Le père Jean-Louis Angué, directeur du Centre national de Pastorale liturgique et secrétaire de la Commission épiscopale de liturgie (France), écrivait avec pertinence : « Pour beaucoup de chrétiens, évêques, prêtres ou laïcs, la musique n'est qu'un […] décor supplémentaire, un ornement, qui n'entretient pas de lien structurel avec la foi elle-même. Or la musique et le chant font partie intégrante de la confession

de la foi, de la *lex orandi*, non seulement en étant à la base d'attitudes spirituelles essentielles, comme la louange ou le rassemblement des fidèles [...] en un seul corps, mais encore en jouant un rôle d'anamnèse, de mémoire, en nous faisant ruminer ou conserver le contenu de la foi. [...] L'enjeu de la musique n'est donc pas seulement d'ordre esthétique, il est à proprement parler théologique [...] même si c'est par mode de convenance et de façon non nécessaire » (« Une charte pour la musique d'Église », *La Maison de Dieu*, n° 186, p. 92-93).

Pourtant, sous prétexte que la liturgie devait correspondre au « vécu », un grand nombre de chants faisant souvent appel à une émotivité superficielle et instantanée ont pénétré nos liturgies, quand on ne va pas jusqu'à utiliser tels quels les textes et musiques de chansons populaires qui n'ont rien à voir avec le mystère célébré, quand ce ne sont pas des ballades absolument incongrues dans une célébration liturgique.

Devant cette tendance à la facilité, nous devons engager nos fidèles et nos musiciens d'Église à croire aux valeurs propres à la liturgie. La liturgie a son langage. Tout en tenant compte des réalités présentes, on ne peut faire abstraction du principe fondamental de la liturgie, rappelé à l'article 24 de la Constitution conciliaire, à savoir que les Saintes Écritures sont la source principale d'où jaillissent les chants liturgiques. Dieu met dans notre bouche la réponse des psaumes, dont la valeur humaine, théologique et christologique est plus que jamais actuelle: « Des profondeurs, je crie vers toi Seigneur! » chante notre monde actuel confronté au défi de la mort planétaire. Et les hymnes, cantiques, séquences, proses qui constituent le patrimoine chrétien actuel ont jailli d'une méditation assidue, d'un goût savoureux et vivant de la Sainte Écriture. Qu'on pense au *Veni Creator Spiritus*, au *Stabat Mater*, au *Crux fidelis*, au *Victimae paschali laudes*...

Il y a aussi des textes de base de la liturgie qu'on ne saurait diluer dans des traductions « ramollies » ou dans des formes étrangères à leur esprit aussi bien qu'à leur lettre. C'est le cas des chants dits de l'ordinaire de la messe, dont la traduction et l'adaptation musicale posent encore des problèmes importants. Je pense ici en particulier au *Pater* et au *Sanctus*, textes majeurs de la liturgie, s'il en est. Les experts en musique et en traduction liturgiques doivent continuer à travailler pour trouver des solutions valables musicalement. C'est en retournant à la rigueur du texte biblico-liturgique qu'on pourra trouver des solutions acceptables. *Mutatis mutandis*, il faut en dire autant du *Kyrie* et du *Gloria in excelsis*, qu'on a trop souvent accommodés en des supplications pénitentielles insipides ou en des adaptations qui en changent l'orientation et la nature.

Par exemple, le Gloria est d'abord une hymne christologique : la doxologie trinitaire ajouté par la suite, *Cum sancto Spiritu*, ne commande pas une structure trinitaire. C'est normalement une composition continue, et non à refrain, comme tendent à faire bon nombre de compositeurs qui se veulent populaires en ramenant tout à la forme rondeau.

Enjeux culturels

Si nous croyons que la liturgie a ses valeurs propres, il n'en reste pas moins vrai que le monde de notre temps et l'évolution de la culture posent des problèmes redoutables à la musique liturgique. Des questions vitales se posent aux musiciens d'Église. Notre civilisation a le goût du spectaculaire, elle promeut la consommation à outrance, le prêt-à-porter, l'individualisme qui fait dire à plusieurs que la religion et la foi sont des questions purement privées. Comment concilier ces tendances avec la liturgie qui se veut d'abord prière d'Église, anamnèse de gestes immémoriaux, union des cœurs dans une même voix ?

Par ailleurs, le trésor de notre musique liturgique nous apprend aussi que, selon les temps et les époques, selon l'évolution du langage musical, la musique liturgique s'est adaptée aux diverses cultures. Certes, le chant grégorien demeure le modèle inégalé où le texte est si bien servi par la musique. Mais des génies aussi divers que Pérotin, Machaut, Palestrina, Monteverdi, Bach, Mozart, Schubert, Stravinsky, Poulenc, Bernstein et combien d'autres, ont cherché à dire, dans la langue de leur époque, la gloire de Dieu et la condition humaine. Pourquoi le musicien d'aujourd'hui ne pourrait-il pas arriver à trouver l'expression musicale contemporaine juste?

Que sera ce langage musical? Sera-t-il modal comme dans le chant grégorien et beaucoup d'œuvres modernes? Tonal comme dans la grammaire classique de l'âge de la tonalité? Tributaire d'une tonalité élargie par l'influence du chromatisme et l'usage plus généralisé des dissonances? Un langage encore plus à l'avant-garde, comme en ouvrent la piste, à titre d'exemples chez nous : le *Te Deum* de Roger Matton, les *Vêpres de la Vierge* de Gilles Tremblay? Et que sera son rythme? La musique sacrée de demain sera-t-elle confinée dans la carrure rythmique habituelle? Épousera-t-elle la liberté rythmique du chant grégorien, du folklore et de beaucoup d'œuvres modernes, s'aventurera-t-elle dans les rythmes heurtés des musiques contemporaines?

Et si l'orgue garde sa place privilégiée au sein de la liturgie, comme le rappelle la *Constitution sur la Sainte-Liturgie* au n° 120, l'évolution de notre musique occidentale n'a-t-elle pas admis l'orchestre à la tribune de l'orgue depuis Monteverdi et Bach, en passant par Haydn et Mozart jusqu'à nous? Avec l'évolution actuelle de la musique contemporaine où les instruments de percussion jouent un si grand rôle, qui pourra nous dire où devrait s'arrêter le choix de tels instruments pour convenir, comme le dit la Constitution, à un « usage sacré »? Dans un contexte de fête populaire, la *Messe québécoise* de Pierick Houdy n'utilise-t-elle pas les cuillers? Et Gilles Tremblay, dans les *Vêpres de la Vierge,* ne fait-il pas appel au tam-tam?

Autant de questions qui se posent aujourd'hui aux musiciens liturgistes dans le cadre de ce que l'on appelle l'« inculturation » et qui ne concerne pas seulement les pays africains ou asiatiques, mais aussi les nôtres, comme les essais plus ou moins heureux des trentes dernières années nous l'ont appris.

L'Église et sa liturgie jouent ici [...] un rôle culturel irremplaçable, à la fois en conservant le trésor de la musique sacrée et en ouvrant large les portes de la création aux compositeurs d'aujourd'hui. Il faudrait en particulier souligner que la liturgie est à peu près le seul lieu de notre civilisation qui fasse place à la cantillation dans sa pureté primitive et dont est fort loin le récitatif d'opéra. Que penser alors de la tendance générale à faire disparaître la cantillation des textes sacrés au profit de la seule parole dite, même dans des textes importants comme la *Préface* ou la *Prière eucharistique*?

Besoins particulièrement urgents

[...] il faut appeler les divers agents et services qui travaillent en musique liturgique à une plus grande concertation. Ce travail d'équipe se doit d'exister tant au cœur de nos paroisses que dans les divers paliers de l'Église. Si l'assemblée célébrante est appelée à créer l'unanimité par le chant, comment cela pourra-t-il se faire si les organismes destinés à la promouvoir dispersent leurs efforts dans tous les sens?

Ici, au Canada, nous pensons en particulier à la publication d'un livre de chant pour l'ensemble de notre Église francophone qui viendrait prendre le relais du *Livret des fidèles* de 1966 dont les lacunes sont évidentes. Le secteur anglais de l'Office national de liturgie au Canada propose un modèle à cet égard. Déjà en 1972, il publiait le *Catholic Book of Worship*, comprenant le livret de chorale, le livre des fidèles et le livre de l'organiste. Réédité en 1980, le *Catholic Book of Worship* II, est un succès d'édition. Beaucoup de travail a été déjà accompli à divers paliers, notamment au Conseil national de musique pour la liturgie (CNML) et dans beacoup de diocèses.

Dans cette remise à neuf, qui ne se voudra pas un frein à la création, au contraire, il faudra davantage tenir compte de la distinction des genres et des formes. D'une part, le *Graduel romain* est bâti presque entièrement sur la psalmodie et les antiennes. D'autre part, la tendance, en paroisse surtout, a été de renverser la vapeur au profit du cantique ou de l'hymne à refrain. Au point que Claude Duchesneau parle, dans un article récent, de « généralisation inflationniste de la structure refrain-couplet» (*La Maison-Dieu*, n° 192). Il faudra se rappeler la grande distinction des genres - cantillation, psalmodie, hymnodie - et leurs multiples formes: dialogues, acclamations, cantillation de lectures, cantillation de prières, psalmodie responsoriale, alternée ou d'accompagnement, litanies, chants processionnaux, hymne strophique ou à refrain, motet, répons, etc. Il y a là une variété qui est essentielle à une liturgie chantée vivante, où chorale et animateur, assemblée, organiste et autres instrumentistes vont trouver stimulation et inspiration.

Il y a eu chez nous de nombreux créateurs, d'inspiration variée et de compétences diverses. Des efforts sérieux ont été faits pour publier des œuvres valables. Par exemple, en ce qui concerne le psaume responsorial de la messe et l'acclamation à l'Évangile, l'Office national de liturgie a voulu faire sa part en faisant appel, depuis 1990, à la collaboration d'une douzaine de compositeurs canadiens pour mener à bien la tâche de créer des mélodies pour les dimanches et fêtes des trois années liturgiques. Et ce n'est là qu'un début.

[Observations][38]

... [Ces observations] traduisent les convictions que portent actuellement la Commission épiscopale de liturgie et l'Office national de liturgie.

[1re observation : le religieux non critiqué]

La première a trait à ce que le père Tillard appelle « le retour du religieux applaudi de façon non critique ». Retour où le merveilleux et surtout, l'émotion deviennent la valeur dominante et régulatrice, risquant de compromettre le contenu formel de la foi. Il y a chez nous tout un répertoire de chants utilisés en liturgie qui sont de cet ordre. Il est étonnant de constater le peu de vigilance de la part des personnes responsables des célébrations, qui souvent se montrent si pointilleuses envers certains textes liturgiques, si serviles à l'égard d'autres formules proposées à titre de suggestion alors qu'il y aurait place à une saine créativité, et, au contraire, si laxistes envers certains chants qui, par le texte ou par la musique - ou par les deux -, sont étrangers à la foi commune de l'Église et au mystère célébré et qui n'ont pas leur place dans une célébration liturgique.

[2e observation : la liturgie « confisquée »]

[...] La liturgie est trop souvent confisquée par des personnes qui imposent aux assemblées leurs goûts, se comportant en « propriétaires » et oubliant ainsi ce que la

---

[38] Le titre et sous-titres entre crochets sont de l'auteure de cet article.

Constitution sur la liturgie a fortement rappelé : l'assemblée est le sujet intégral de l'action liturgique. Elle a droit à la prière officielle de l'Église et à des formes d'expression qui soient à la hauteur du mystère célébré. Dans son document, *L'Esprit chante en nos cœurs*, la Commission épiscopale de liturgie le soulignait avec clarté: « Organistes, animateurs, choristes et compositeurs accomplissent dans l'Église une tâche indispensable pour donner vigueur et élan à la prière communautaire.[...] Il s'agit d'un travail qui exige compétence, application et recherche constante de qualité [...] ». [3ᵉ observation : refus d'un modèle unique].
Cependant [...] ces exigences de qualité ne trouveront pas de réponses adéquates dans l'uniformisation ou le retour à un modèle unique. La réforme liturgique de Vatican II commande désormais un mouvement permanent de mise à jour. L'adaptation de la liturgie aux diverses cultures indique que la pluriformité est le chemin obligé pour vivre la véritable catholicité. Il en va de l'être même de l'Église et de son avenir au cœur de ce monde et de ce temps. Jean XXIII en avait bien saisi l'urgence : « L'Église n'est pas un musée archéologique. Elle est l'antique fontaine du village qui donne l'eau aux générations contemporaines, comme elle la donnait à celles d'hier ».
Pour nous, musiciens et liturgistes, c'est là un immense chantier dans lequel, je le souhaite, tous trouveront la joie de servir [...].

Si l'analyse du père Boily met en lumière une situation globale, elle éclaire peu cependant celle de l'« ouvrier » de chantier. Celui qui a dû se (re) positionner face à la « brise vaticane » où la volonté de changement a souvent été synonyme de *tabula rasa*. Le survol du parcours personnel de Claude Gosselin propose d'apporter un certain éclairage sur ces interrogations. Tout en reconnaissant que l'exemple unique ne saura seul traduire la réalité complexe de l'ensemble des chantres francophones de l'Église catholique du Québec (l'histoire du chantre au Québec reste à faire) il permet néanmoins de poser un regard plus intime sur le phénomène d'adaptation à une situation incontournable et, plus important, de dévoiler de precieux indices sur le sens d'une démarche personnelle. Un sens qu'il est légitime de croire qu'il peut être partagé par des pairs.

Aux origines du parcours de Claude Gosselin, chantre

Monsieur Claude Gosselin est né le 16 janvier 1932 dans la paroisse Jacques-Cartier de la Basse-Ville de Québec. Très tôt, l'avant-dernier fils d'une famille de neuf enfants se montre fort doué pour le chant. Il dit tenir ce talent de son père Laurent, baryton, qui pendant 35 ans chante cinq messes tous les matins après sa nuit de travail! Aussi à onze ans, le jeune Gosselin est inscrit à la Maîtrise (chorale) du Chapitre de la basilique de Québec où, de 1943 à 1945, il reçoit une solide formation en chant liturgique sous la gouverne « stricte » de l'abbé de Smet. M. Gosselin avoue sans ambages que ces années de formation ont été et demeurent les plus marquantes et « les plus heureuses de sa vie ». Ce sont elles d'ailleurs qui continuent à l'inspirer. Fidèle à sa formation, M. Gosselin paraphrase même Pie X dont le *Motu Proprio* a grandement influé sur la liturgie au début du XXᵉ siècle, en rappelant que pour lui « chanter équivaut à prier sur de la beauté ». À l'évidence, M. Gosselin qui est issu de l'école musicale classique y demeure fidèle!

L'*Alma Mater*

La Maîtrise fréquentée par M. Gosselin est fondée en 1915 avec le soutien du cardinal Bégin. Première du genre en Amérique du Nord et toujours active, l'institution a formé plus de 2000 jeunes dont 1500 finissants. Son premier directeur, l'abbé Placide Gagnon, préside quatre ans aux destinées de la jeune chorale alors connue sous le nom de la Maîtrise Notre-Dame. En 1919, l'abbé Joseph de Smet d'Ostende en Belgique prend la relève et assure la direction (d'une main de fer, dit-on) pendant 34 ans, jusqu'à sa mort en 1953. « Cet important mandat qui remonte aux débuts de la Maîtrise en a fait, en quelque sorte, le patron de l'institution[39] ». D'ailleurs après son décès, la Maîtrise effectue jusque vers les années 1970 des visites annuelles sur sa tombe.

Sous la gouverne de l'abbé de Smet la Maîtrise franchit une étape importante. En 1947, elle est reconnue par la Fédération internationale des manécanteries de Paris ce qui lui permet de porter le nom « Petits chanteurs à la Croix de Bois » de Québec. Par manécanteries on entend « chanteurs du matin » ce qui est en effet « le but premier » [d'une] Mané […] et sa raison d'être [40] ».

De 1954 à 1978, l'abbé Georges Marchand dirige la Maîtrise à son tour. C'est durant son mandat que le volet instrumental est introduit au curriculum et que le nombre de maîtrises semble avoir atteint son apogée[41]. Toutefois, son départ après 24 ans marque la fin d'une époque. « Une époque qui correspond à toute une philosophie de l'enseignement, celle d'avant-hier […] où les professeurs sont des éducateurs qui consacrent leur vie à la cause pédagogique [où la] vocation professorale coïncide souvent avec une vocation religieuse […][42] ». En effet, depuis la sécularisation de la société québécoise, la réorganisation scolaire et les difficultés financières évoquées par l'archevêché à la fin des années 1970, la « Mané » relève de la Commission scolaire catholique de Québec, est laïcisée, admet les jeunes filles (1981) - bien qu'au début, la pratique du chant se fait séparément des garçons - et cesse de chanter quotidiennement à la cathédrale. Elle continue cependant d'y assurer le chant à la messe dominicale une fois par mois. Suivant sa

---

[39] Hélène de Billy, *Education Québec*, vol.11, n° 5, mars 1981, p. 34.

[40] *Ibid.*

[41] En 1953-1954, la Fédération canadienne des petits chanteurs, affiliée aux Petits chanteurs à la croix de bois de Paris, compte 113 chorales dont 107 au Québec. Les six autres sont situées dans l'est ontarien.

[42] H. de Billy, *op.cit.*

nouvelle orientation séculaire, l'institution répond désormais au nom « La Maîtrise de Québec ».

La Maîtrise de Québec en 1945-1946 sous la direction de l'abbé Joseph de Smet. Jusqu'au printemps 1947, le costume solennel des jeunes chantres est une réplique exacte du costume de chanoine. On aperçoit Claude Gosselin dans la deuxième rangée, deuxième à partir de la gauche.

La Maîtrise : lieu de formation, d'appartenance et de distinction

À l'époque de monsieur Gosselin (1943-1945) la Maîtrise est réservée exclusivement aux garçons « de bonnes familles » âgés de huit à treize ans suivant la mue de leur voix. Outre la scolarité régulière, les apprentis consacrent une heure et demie par jour à la technique du chant et à la vocalise, à l'apprentissage du répertoire religieux classique (le grégorien et la polyphonie), à l'histoire de la musique sacrée en lien avec leur répertoire et à la discipline exigeante du chant choral. La Maîtrise prépare également des concerts grand public où se cotoient les chants sacré, classique et folklorique. Dès la deuxième année de formation, les garçons assurent une présence quotidienne (sauf le samedi) à la messe de 8 h à la basilique-cathédrale et à la grand-messe dominicale. C'est ainsi que le jeune Claude prend le tramway six jours par semaine en direction de la Haute-Ville pour remplir ses obligations de chantre. Outre l'enseignement spécialisé, les étudiants de la Maîtrise se distinguent par deux habits de circonstances : l'uniforme scolaire et l'habit solennel pour la grand-messe et autres occasions spéciales. L'habit scolaire de couleur bleue est composé d'un pantalon court, d'une veste-chandail et de bas aux genoux avec une chemise blanche à col ouvert. Sur le chandail figure l'emblème de la Maîtrise.

Jusqu'en 1947, le costume solennel consiste en une réplique exacte de l'habit de chanoine, soit le soutane noire et le surplis blanc superposé d'un rochet (mantelet) cramoisi[43]. Par suite de l'affiliation de la Maîtrise de Québec aux Manécanteries de Paris en novembre 1947, le costume sacerdotal fait place à un vêtement plus sobre composé d'une aube blanche et de la petite croix de bois, symbole des manécanteries. Présent à cette époque charnière, Claude Gosselin porte d'abord l'habit de chanoine et comme jeune adulte prêtant main-forte à la chorale, revêt l'aube blanche.

L'aggrégation du Petit Chanteur à la Maîtrise est d'ailleurs souligné par une cérémonie de prise de l'aube [44] :

> Pour les offices religieux et la deuxième partie de leurs concerts, les Petits Chanteurs revêtent l'aube blanche, l'amict et le cordon bleu, et portent la petite croix de bois qui leur a donné son nom. L'aube n'est pas un simple costume d'apparât mais a une signification particulière. Après quelques mois d'apprentissage, le nouveau-venu est, par son travail, sa conduite et sa piété, admis à revêtir l'aube. La cérémonie a lieu au soir du 2e lundi du mois de décembre de chaque année.
>
> Accompagné de son parrain, un Petit Chanteur plus âgé, le candidat entre dans la basilique-cathédrale par l'allée centrale portant son uniforme bleu marine et en chantant le psaume *Laudate Pueri Dominum*. Il se dirige vers le sanctuaire où Monseigneur de la basilique l'attend pour bénir son aube blanche. Durant les prières liturgiques propres à cette cérémonie, il revêt son aube et rejoint ensuite ses compagnons près du trône de l'évêque. La cérémonie se termine par un salut du saint sacrement.
>
> Désormais vous serez admis à présenter à l'autel, l'encens, l'eau, le vin du sacrifice de la messe. Vous aurez l'honneur d'aider le prêtre dans la célébration du saint sacrifice et des offices liturgiques, et vous approcherez ainsi tout près du Dieu qui réjouit votre jeunesse. Mais ce n'est pas assez pour vous de consacrer à Dieu vos cœurs et vos mains; vous voulez encore lui consacrer vos voix, et les faire servir à chanter la beauté de son nom et à proclamer la grandeur de sa gloire. Vos lèvres exprimeront désormais la prière publique et officielle de l'Église. Et vos chants, qui n'auront pas d'autre but que la gloire de Dieu, vous aideront et aideront les autres à mieux s'unir à l'action du prêtre et à mieux prier.

La voix est mûre

À quatorze ans, la voix de l'adolescent Gosselin mue pour se fixer définitivement comme ténor. Bien qu'ayant quitté officiellement la Maîtrise, il continue néanmoins à lui prêter son concours lors des messes dominicales, des concerts et à l'occasion de certaines tournées. De fait, en 1949, une photo de la Maîtrise parue en page couverture du *Sélection du Reader's Digest* confirme sa participation[45].

---

[43] À l'occasion du 75e anniversaire de la fondation de la Maîtrise à Noël 1990, le costume d'apparat traditionnel est reconstitué et porté pour la circonstance.

[44] *Les Petits Chanteurs à la Croix de Bois de Québec*, s.l., s.éd., s.d., n.p. [1950 ?]

[45] *Sélection du Reader's Digest*, vol.4, n° 22. Montréal, 1949, 177 p. (ill.)

La même année, Claude Gosselin franchit l'âge adulte en formant avec trois « anciens » de la Maîtrise, l'ensemble Les Collégiens-Troubadours[46]. Munis de leur bagage musical et d'une formation classique du Petit Séminaire de Québec, les quatre amis partent à la conquête du grand public.

En route   (1949-1966)

L'ensemble Les Collégiens-Troubadours est actif pendant dix-sept ans soit de 1949 à 1966 et connaît un grande popularité au Québec grâce à la radio et à la télévision naissante. Outre les concerts, émissions de variétés, commerciaux, le quatuor réalise trois séries de 39 films d'un quart d'heure pour le compte de Radio-Canada ayant pour thème *La Route*. Baluchons au dos, les « collégiens » sillonent - en temps réel - villes et villages du Québec alors que le répertoire de folklore et des « belles chansons françaises » de Trenet, Brassens, Ferré, etc., qu'ils interprétent est préenrégistré à Montréal.

À titre individuel, Claude Gosselin se perfectionne en étudiant l'art lyrique au Conservatoire de musique de Québec où ses principaux professeurs furent Dina Maria Naricci et Raoul Jobin. Dès l'âge de 24 ans, il participe au concours prestigieux du Prix d'Europe et effectue à 27 ans, une tournée de 40 concerts avec Les Jeunesses musicales du Canada alors sous la direction de Raoul Jobin. Deux ans plus tard, il tient le premier rôle dans l'opéra *L'Enfant prodigue* de Debussy avec Napoléon Brisson et un second rôle, celui d'Arlequin dans *Le Magicien* de Jean Vallerand.

Comme soliste, il participe à de nombreuses productions d'opéra avec le Théâtre lyrique de la Nouvelle-France et l'Opéra de Québec où il tient des rôles importants dans les opéras, *Madame Butterfly*, *Manon*, *La Traviata*, les *Contes d'Hoffmann* et aussi dans des opérettes, la *Chauve-Souris* et *La Veuve Joyeuse* dans laquelle il tient les rôles de Camille de Coutançon et de Destillac dans deux productions différentes[47].

Nouvelles voies 1967-1997

Après la dissolution des Collégiens-Troubadours (1966), M. Gosselin devient réalisateur des émissions musicales de Radio-Canada à Québec. Cet emploi d'une durée de 25 ans, soit de 1967 à 1992, lui permet de cotoyer les grands de la chanson, à réaliser des disques pour eux et à faire connaître de nouveaux talents du Québec dans le domaine. Son statut d'employé en régime libre lui permet en outre de poursuivre ses intérêts et de se produire en public.

---

[46]   Le nom du groupe est conçu par Paul Legendre de Radio-Canada.
[47]   Document de presse. Archives privées de Claude Gosselin.

Notamment de continuer à faire du chant choral, à participer à des concours et festivals pour chorales (Toronto, Ottawa, Vancouver) et éventuellement de retourner à l'institution qui l'avait formé cette fois-ci comme directeur.

M. Gosselin parle de cette brève période, de 1983 à 1985, avec beaucoup d'enthousiasme appréciant surtout que ses étudiants continuent à le reconnaître en le saluant lors de rencontres et concerts. Un des meilleurs souvenirs de son court séjour à la maîtrise est le voyage en Europe avec une vingtaine de jeunes chanteurs pour la rencontre internationale des *Pueri Cantores*. Il était alors accompagné de l'abbé Claude Thompson, président de la section canadienne des Petits Chanteurs à la Croix de Bois et ardent défenseur de la formation des jeunes par le chant.

Semper fidelis

En dépit de ses nombreuses activités, M. Gosselin ne quitte jamais le chant sacré demeurant membre des chorales de l'église Saint-Jean-Baptiste dans la Haute-Ville et de la paroisse de la Nativité de Beauport. En 1955, sa fidélité à la musique liturgique et son talent évident lui valent d'être nommé maître de chapelle à l'église Saint-Cœur-de-Marie à Québec. Sous sa direction, la chorale atteint un très haut niveau de qualité musicale. D'ailleurs pendant plus de 40 ans, la messe en grégorien[48] fera la renommée du chœur et de la paroisse. Une paroisse décrite par Claude Gosselin comme « sensible au beau »

Comme Maître de chapelle, M. Gosselin profite d'une rare liberté pour continuer à chanter selon la tradition classique, pendant et après Vatican II. Les Eudistes dont relève la paroisse « ont eu selon lui le bon jugement de nous laisser faire[49] ». De fait, « Il fallait bien, disaient-ils, avoir au moins un endroit où la musique liturgique traditionnelle soit maintenue ». Avec d'heureuses conséquences pour la fabrique, la chorale et les mélomanes pendant quatre décennies.

Il y a bien eu selon Claude Gosselin, des ajustements et l'ajout de quelques « chansonnettes religieuses » en français après le Concile mais « c'est le grégorien que les gens voulaient entendre ». Non pas que lui-même ait été rébarbatif aux

---

[48] Luc Noppen, Lucie K.Morriset (dir.) *Lieux de culte situés sur le territoire de la Ville de Québec. Fiches analytiques*. Ville de Québec. Service de l'urbanisme, Division du design urbain et du patrimoine. T. 1. fiche 13 août 1994, p. 102

[49] Cette attitude correspond assez bien à l'esprit des origines de la paroisse « créée en 1918 pour satisfaire la clientèle exigeante du secteur de la Grande-Allée, lasse du clergé diocésain ».(Noppen/Morriset.*Ibid*. p. 97) En bout de piste, le diocèse a eu raison de la paroisse un peu trop unique à ses yeux.

nouvelles créations. À preuve, sa participation à l'enregistrement de l'œuvre magistrale de Pierick Houdy, *La Messe québécoise* en 1979[50].

Aussi, après avoir survécu en quelque sorte à la désaffection religieuse des années 1960-1970, aux efforts plus ou moins réussis de renouveau dans la musique liturgique et à la réduction de la densité démographique de la paroisse, la fabrique cède sous le poids du discours implacable de la rationalisation qui a rejoint le diocèse. Claude Gosselin dirige la chorale lors de la messe de fermeture de la paroisse le 21 décembre 1997.

À nouveau « troubadour »

Actuellement, la renommée de la chorale Saint-Cœur-de-Marie se poursuit dans l'Ensemble vocal Claude Gosselin. Formé de huit à douze « anciens et anciennes », l'Ensemble sillonne la région donnant des concerts classiques mais aussi et surtout répondant aux nombreuses demandes pour chanter le grégorien à des services religieux. Devenus en quelque sorte des « chantres-troubadours », ils desservent plusieurs paroisses de la banlieue de Québec.

En dépit de certains revers, M. Gosselin avoue avoir eu une vie heureuse et privilégiée. Heureuse parce qu'il a pu intégrer le chant à toutes les étapes de sa vie. Privilégiée d'avoir eu comme modèles son père et l'abbé de Smet, d'avoir reçu et pu profiter d'une formation de qualité qui continue à lui servir et, enfin, de pouvoir jouir d'une bonne santé lui permettant encore de chanter.

En guise de conclusion

Le parcours de Claude Gosselin chantre est à la fois exceptionnel, marginal et essentiellement esthétique. Qu'il ait traversé l'époque charnière de Vatican II sans trop de heurts et avec le même répertoire est en soi remarquable. Par ailleurs, sa fidélité au grégorien et à la polyphonie de la Renaissance fait qu'il s'est toujours démarqué de la majorité de ses contemporains pré et postconciliaires. Chez les premiers, l'écart apparaît au niveau de la maîtrise de la technique vocale. Auprès du spécialiste actuel du renouveau, la distinction est davantage manifeste par rapport au répertoire. Préférant « laisser les savants s'arranger entre eux », Claude Gosselin s'appuie sur ce vaste réservoir de chants liturgiques romains qui remonte au IVe siècle. « Une valeur sûre » dit-il où l'adéquation entre texte (latin) et musique (grégorien/ polyphonie) demeure inégalée jusqu'à nos jours. D'où d'ailleurs sa grande qualité esthétique qui semble résister au temps.

Comment expliquer autrement le renouveau d'intérêt pour ce genre classique sinon par la beauté et l'enchantement qu'il continue à inspirer.

---

50 Le disque obtient le Premier prix du Conseil canadien de la musique.

Rappelons à cet effet les « critiques unanimement louangeuses » du « son brillant, pas éclatant » des Tallis Scholars, chorale qui depuis 25 ans « suscite l'engouement par la qualité de son plain-chant et de la polyphonie [51] »; le *Top-10* du temps des fêtes 1994 des *Meilleures œuvres du chant grégorien* qui fracasse des records de vente avec ses 260 000 exemplaires)[52] ; ou encore la remontée populaire du chant grégorien qui rejoint « paradoxalement [...] des jeunes gens n'ayant jamais connu ce type de chant dans leurs liturgies[53]». Enfin, la demande régionale pour l'Ensemble vocal Claude Gosselin semble à son tour, confirmer l'intérêt actuel.

Cette tendance participerait à un retour au religieux amorcé dans les années 1980 où la recherche de l'au-delà et du sensible s'alimente à des sources primitives. Dans le cas présent, le chant rituel de l'Église catholique romaine qui s'enracine à partir du IVe siècle tient lieu de support. En outre, « Comme toutes les religions s'accordent à attribuer la naissance du monde au son (Jean I, 1: « Au commencement était le verbe »...) », et à sacraliser le chant (voire parfois le chantre), le chant liturgique romain évoque les origines de la parole[54] et de là ses premières cantillations. Dans cette perspective le cheminement de Claude Gosselin rejoint la poésie universelle. De fait, comme porteur d'un art sacré millénaire destiné à rehausser l'éclat du culte et à rapprocher l'homme de son Dieu, le chantre d'église semble investi d'une mission esthétique. Dès lors, le sens premier s'unit au second consacrant le « poète » du culte comme un véritable chantre de la beauté!

BIBLIOGRAPHIE

BOILY, Paul, « La musique liturgique en francophonie. Situation et perspectives au Canada », *Chant et musique liturgiques en pays francophones*. Actes du symposium international organisé par l'École de musique de l'Université Laval en collaboration avec la revue *Musique sacrée-l'Organiste* et tenu les 20 et 21 mai 1993. Québec, Université Laval, École de musique, Faculté des Arts, 1994, p. 3-13.

---

[51] Clément Trudel, « Hymne à la voix » *Le Devoir*, les samedi 5 et dimanche 6 décembre 1998, p. B12.

[52] Endisqué par le Chœur des moines bénédictins de l'abbaye Santo Domingo de Silos à 200 km au nord de Madrid en Espagne.

[53] Anne-Marie Lapalme, « Le chant liturgique en français: formes anciennes et création contemporaine », *Chant et musique liturgiques en pays francophones* (ss la dir. de P. Cadrin). Québec, Université Laval, 1994, p. 60.

[54] Roland Mancini, « Chant » *Universalis 5*, Paris, 1995, p. 366.

BRETON, Jean-Claude. « Dossier. Si on chantait.... » *Présence Magazine*, vol.4 n° 26, mai 1995, p. 15-25.

CADRIN, Paul (ss la dir. de). *Chant et musique liturgiques en pays francophones*. Actes du symposium international organisé par l'École de musique de l'Université Laval en collaboration avec la revue *Musique sacrée-l'Organiste* et tenu les 20 et 21 mai 1993. Québec, Université Laval, École de musique, Faculté des Arts, 1994, 171 p.

COMITÉ INTERDIOCÉSAIN DE MUSIQUE SACRÉE DE LA PROVINCE DE QUÉBEC. *Code de Musique sacrée* et *Liste de pièces recommandées pour le culte divin (Messes, motets, cantiques, morceaux d'orgues*. Québec, Les Presses universitaires Laval, 1952, 86 p.

FELLERER, Karl Gustav. *The History of Catholic Church Music.* Translated by Francis A Brunner.C.Ss.R. Baltimore, Helicon Press, 1961, 235 p.

NEMMER, Erwin Esser. *Twenty Centuries of Catholic Church Music.* Connecticut, Greenwood Press, 1978, 213 p.

NOPPEN, Luc, Lucie K. MORRISSET. (ss la dir. de). *Lieux de culte situés sur le territoire de la Ville de Québec. Fiches analytiques.* 2 tomes. Ville de Québec, Service de l'urbanisme, Division du design urbain et du patrimoine, 1994, 606 p.

PERREAULT, Pierre. *Pour la suite du monde. Récit.* Photographie de Michel Brault. [Montréal], L'Hexagone, 1992, 304 p.

Sélection du Reader's Digest, vol.4, n° 22. Montréal, 1949, 177 p. (ill.).

TÊTU H.,Gagnon, C.O., *Mandements des évêques de Québec. T.1 1659-1740,* Québec, A. Côté et Cie.,1887, p. 372, art. 20.

THOMPSON, Claude. *Document sur la musique sacrée.* s.l., s.éd. (1986), 15 p.

TRUDEL, Clément, « Hymne à la voix », *Le Devoir*, le samedi 5 et dimanche 6 décembre 1998, p. B.12.

SOURCE SONORE

Entrevue avec M. Claude Gosselin, le 11 novembre 1998, 85 min.

PERSONNES RESSOURCES

Mme Cécile Binet, directrice de la Maîtrise de Québec
Mme Guay, archiviste-bénévole de la Maîtrise de Québec
M. Pierre Lafontaine, Archives de l'Archidiocèse de Québec (AAQ)

SOURCES ARCHIVISTIQUES

Les Archives de l'Archidiocèse de Québec
- monographies / documents divers sur la paroisse Saint-Cœur-de-Marie
- programmes-souvenirs /dernier concert d'église (sous la direction de Claude Gosselin)
- règlement des maîtrises
- programmes de concerts sacrés de la Maîtrise du Chapitre de Québec (chorale d'enfants)
- texte sur le rite de l'oblation des enfants dans une maîtrise
- Index des chorales de la région métropolitaine de Québec (1955)
- dépliants de recrutement des jeunes garçons de la 3e année pour la Maîtrise du Chapitre de Québec (1963, 1982, 1983, etc.)
- articles de la presse régionale sur la Maîtrise - 1981, 1994, 1997

La Maîtrise de Québec
- dépliant publicitaire (1999)
- dessin de la reconstitution du costume sacerdotal traditionnel / fête du 80e anniv. (1995)
- photos de la Maîtrise en costume sacerdotal, en aube blanche, en uniforme scolaire

Archives privées, Claude Gosselin
- découpures de presse, photos, programmes de concerts, cassettes d'émissions radiophoniques.

AU-DELÀ DE LA TRADITION...

Rôle et fonction d'un chantre dans la survie d'une église: l'exemple de Iwan Semenovich Kozachok à l'église Sainte-Marie-la-Protectrice de Montréal

par
Claudette Berthiaume-Zavada

Introduction

Au-delà de la tradition, au-delà de l'icône, au-delà de la prière, le chant transcende la matière. Parce qu'il est impalpable, il est immatériel; parce qu'il est immatériel, il est spirituel.

Dans le rite orthodoxe, la parole divine, la prière, prennent place dans une continuité musicale non interrompue du premier mot prononcé au dernier, continuité qui circule entre le prêtre officiant, le chantre, le lecteur, le chœur et les fidèles. Cette symbiose caractérise le rite orthodoxe, si bien que sans le chant, le rituel orthodoxe serait inexistant. Le « musical » est ici indissociable du « religieux » et vice-versa.

Un texte n'est pas simplement dit ou récité : il est chanté, c'est-à-dire plus ou moins chanté. En effet, le rituel est tissé d'un ensemble nuancé et diversifié d'ondulations rythmiques et mélodiques, qui prennent forme à l'intérieur d'un ambitus plus ou moins grand de complexités rythmiques et d'ornementations plus ou moins élaborées. Entre la psalmodie et les grands chœurs polyphoniques complexes à 8 et 12 voix, diverses formes prennent place, lesquelles sont relatives à la spécificité fonctionnelle et rituelle des pièces musicales et à ceux qui les exécutent. Ces formes diverses constituent l'art de la cantillation.

Cet article, élaboré à la suite d'une enquête de terrain à Montréal, vise à rendre compte de deux aspects reliés à la tradition cantoriale au Canada, qui ont particulièrement retenu notre attention : l'un concernant l'importance capitale et l'apport particulier d'un chantre dans le maintien de la tradition religieuse; l'autre focalisant sur une forme particulière et spécifique de la cantillation dans le rite orthodoxe, c'est-à-dire la lecture de l'épître, qui se situe, aux points de vue formel et stylistique, à la ligne de démarcation entre la récitation parlée et la récitation chantée[1].

Considérations générales sur les pratiques musicales religieuses chrétiennes byzantines, orientales et orthodoxes à Montréal

Montréal compte plus de quarante églises chrétiennes de rites byzantin, orthodoxe et oriental. Ces paroisses groupent plus de deux cent mille citoyens montréalais de diverses ethnies. Grecs, Libanais, Égyptiens, Syriens, Arméniens,

Russes, Serbes, Roumains, Bulgares et Ukrainiens sont réunis par des rites et traditions nous faisant remonter aux temps les plus anciens de la chrétienté que la mémoire collective a pu conserver au fil des millénaires.

C'est autour de ces pratiques religieuses que les liens ancestraux avec le lieu d'origine subsistent et sont constamment consolidés dans la régularité du calendrier liturgique.Par contre, les contraintes de la vie urbaine et contemporaine de même que celles imposées par le milieu d'implantation se manifestent à différents niveaux. Un regard sur le panorama cosmopolite montréalais nous permet d'observer, juxtaposés dans un axe synchronique, la diversité et les transformations des pratiques musicales associées à une tradition commune, chrétienne et orientale, diversifiée selon les ethnies et à l'intérieur de ces ethnies, selon les strates migratoires. Cette situation privilégiée fournit des indices évidents sur les rapports entre les modalités d'expression musicale et le contexte social dans lequel elles prennent place.

Les musiques religieuses, intimement liées aux pratiques religieuses régies par un rituel, une tradition et un canon immuables se transforment (lorsqu'il y a mutation) moins rapidement que les autres formes d'expression musicale identitaire en milieu d'implantation culturelle où des contraintes d'adaptation imposent à la tradition des transformations parfois radicales. Dans les pratiques religieuses et, conséquemment les pratiques musicales religieuses traditionnelles, le processus s'opère dans un temps plus long. D'où l'intérêt particulier de l'étude des musiques sacrées telles que pratiquées dans les églises de rite byzantin, orthodoxe et oriental où la tradition a encore bien peu subi de mutations dans la performance du rituel, malgré certaines stratégies d'adaptation, dans certains cas, conditionnées par le mode de vie moderne et le contexte culturel ambiant.

Les espaces sonores qui englobent les composantes musicales d'une cérémonie religieuse de rite orthodoxe/byzantin/oriental peuvent se définir comme suit :

- le chant[2] intégré à la liturgie et indispensable au déroulement du rituel, impliquant les prêtres officiants, diacres, lecteurs, chantres ou psalmistes soit en solo soit en petit groupe de trois ou quatre;
- le chant exécuté par le chœur qui participe également au déroulement de la liturgie (messes et compositions spécifiques) et insère des chants religieux (cantiques/hymnes) appropriés aux différentes fêtes et célébrations du calendrier liturgique. Les fonctions musicales du chœur peuvent être assumées par une chorale (dans le cas des messes spéciales et cantiques) ou par la participation spontanée de l'assistance (pour les cantiques et hymnes). Il arrive souvent que l'assistance se joigne spontanément à la chorale pour l'exécution d'hymnes et de cantiques plus connus.

Bien que la séquence du déroulement liturgique soit identique dans les différentes églises, c'est au niveau de la performance et de l'interprétation que l'on retrouve plus ou moins de distanciation par rapport aux versions écrites originales et à la tradition orale. C'est à ces deux niveaux distincts, ci-haut mentionnés, que la différenciation des pratiques musicales peut s'observer. En général, les diversités culturelles et transformations conditionnées par le milieu sont plus apparentes dans le répertoire et la performance du chœur alors que la musique liturgique proprement dite et intégrée au « canon » demeure plus immuable et garante de l'authenticité de la tradition. Toutefois, lorsqu'on observe des transformations à ce niveau, les paramètres suivants sont l'objet de variantes plus apparentes : l'ornementation / la précision d'exécution et la justesse des micro-intervalles dans les différents modes / l'exécution du *ison* (bourdon continu accompagnant les incantations et les psaumes) / l'aspect « théâtral » et la gestuelle du prêtre associés au chant / la manière dont le chant « circule » entre les participants et qui révèle un consensus et une complicité collective. En ce sens, l'église copte de la Vierge-Marie, les églises grecques Koimisis tis Theotokou et Evangelismos tis Theotokou, nous relient directement aux éléments d'une tradition religieuse qui remonte aux IIIe et IVe siècles.

Quant à la participation spontanée de l'assistance, elle est généralement étroitement liée à la provenance des participants. La participation est plus dynamique dans les paroisses qui regroupent une immigration plus récente connaissant la langue et le répertoire et dont la moyenne d'âge est plus élevée. Il en est de même de la participation aux rituels traditionnels. Chaque paroisse est constituée de composantes sociales uniques et les différents modes d'expression musicale en sont conséquents. Dans certaines églises, l'influence du milieu d'implantation est inexistante et dès le portail franchi, toutes les composantes visuelles, musicales et de comportements nous transportent au lieu d'origine de la tradition. C'est le cas de la petite église grecque orthodoxe Koimisis tis Theotokou où nous avons assisté au rituel du *Psychosabaton* (Samedi des esprits / âmes / défunts). Les cantiques y sont chantés par l'assistance alors que la liturgie est chantée par un « psalmiste » accompagné par deux chantres qui exécutent l'*ison*.

D'autres paroisses tentent de s'adapter au contexte social et culturel ambiant tout en maintenant la tradition. L'église copte de la Vierge-Marie à Brossard représente un exemple intéressant. Trois styles musicaux et tout à fait contrastants y sont juxtaposés pendant la même cérémonie :
- un petit chœur d'hommes, dirigé par le soliste (chantre principal) exécute le chant liturgique traditionnel et les psaumes en langue copte; il s'agit de monodie, très ornementée et comprenant des micro-intervalles;
- l'assistance chante des cantiques en langue arabe, sur des modes parfois occidentalisés, sans complexité ornementale et intervallique, toujours à l'unisson;

- un chœur d'enfants chante en anglais et occasionnellement en français et en arabe des cantiques connus tels *Ave Maria, Il est né le divin enfant,* etc.

Notons que dans certaines églises, l'un des signes les plus visibles de transformation et de modernisation est la réduction et même le remplacement du « musical » par le « parlé » et la simple récitation. Il en résulte évidemment un office religieux raccourci et plus adapté aux contraintes temporelles de la vie moderne et urbaine.

Dans cette perspective comparative, l'église orthodoxe ukrainienne Sainte-Marie-la-Protectrice, sur laquelle nous nous attardons dans cet article, présente un intérêt particulier : c'est la plus récente des églises orthodoxes ukrainiennes à Montréal et elle constitue un lien direct avec la tradition musicale liturgique kyivaine grâce au chantre et directeur de la chorale qui a assuré la continuité de cette tradition musicale religieuse depuis la fondation de la paroisse en 1952 jusqu'en 1997, année où ce dernier dut abandonner l'exercice de ses fonctions à cause de la maladie.

L'église ukrainienne orthodoxe Sainte-Marie-la-Protectrice, un cas particulier

La paroisse fut fondée le 23 avril 1952 par un groupe de réfugiés ukrainiens de foi orthodoxe, venus au Canada après la Seconde Guerre mondiale. Le R. P. Petro Archanhel's'kyj a d'abord célébré la Divine Liturgie dans une salle louée en attendant la construction d'une église qui fut commencée en 1959 et consacrée le 10 octobre 1961 par l'archevêque Mykhail de l' Église grecque-orthodoxe ukrainienne du Canada. L'iconostase fut terminé en 1972.

Deux facteurs donnent à l'église Sainte-Marie-la-Protectrice un statut particulier dans le maintien de la tradition musicale religieuse ukrainienne :

- d'une part, les paroissiens arrivaient directement d'Ukraine; il s'agit donc d'une première génération. Mais cette situation n'est pas nécessairement significative par rapport à la tradition puisque les pratiques religieuses du pays d'origine faisaient l'objet, à l'époque du régime communiste soviétique non seulement de restrictions mais d'interdiction totale sous peine d'emprisonnement. À cet égard, il est intéressant de noter ici que les églises ukrainiennes au Canada déjà existantes depuis la première strate migratoire ukrainienne de la fin du XIXe siècle, ont joué un rôle important dans le maintien de la tradition religieuse, et ce, malgré les transformations subies dans le processus de transmission en contexte d'éloignement et d'absence de communication avec le pays d'origine. Le maintien de la tradition musicale religieuse et de son authenticité était d'autant plus précieux à l'époque où celle-ci prenait place au Canada qu'elle faisait l'objet d'interdiction en Ukraine même. Parlant des nouveaux arrivants d'Ukraine du début des années cinquante, dont un grand nombre avaient été dépourvus de la pratique religieuse pendant plusieurs décennies, une informatrice s'exprimait ainsi : « […] ils ne nous enseignaient pas, <u>nous </u>leur enseignions […] »[3].

- dans ce contexte, avec ce nouvel influx de réfugiés, l'arrivée du musicien Iwan Kozachok eut un impact considérable dans le milieu musical ukrainien montréalais puisqu'il s'amenait avec un bassin de connaissances musicales acquises en haut lieu de la tradition musicale religieuse, c'est-à-dire le monastère de Potchaïv. Dès la fondation de la paroisse, Iwan Kozachok assuma la direction de la vie musicale religieuse de la paroisse par diverses fonctions dont la création et la direction d'une chorale, le rôle de *diak* (chantre), de lecteur et récitant des textes sacrés. C'est précisemment grâce à sa polyvalence et par l'exercice de ses fonctions multiples qu'il eut un rôle prépondérant dans la survie de la paroisse à un moment crucial de son histoire.

Dans l'attente d'un prêtre...

De 1976 à 1978, par suite du manque de prêtres au Canada, la paroisse s'est retrouvée sans prêtre. Pendant toute cette période qui dura plus de deux ans, Iwan Kozachok devint le chantre multiple et omniprésent : chaque dimanche, les fidèles de la paroisse se réunissaient autour de ce dernier, qui maintenait à lui seul le déroulement des parties de la liturgie pouvant prendre place sans le prêtre officiant. I. Kozachok dirigeait le chœur qui chantait les hymnes, assumait le rôle de *diak* par la lecture des «Heures » (3e et 6e) avant la liturgie et récitait l'épître. Il exécutait aussi les récitations du diacre. Durant cette période d'incertitude, I. Kozachok a effectivement assuré à lui seul la survie et la continuité de la tradition religieuse par la tradition musicale. C'est ainsi que de semaine en semaine, le chantre a nourri l'espoir des paroissiens. Grâce à sa ténacité, à ses compétences et à sa connaissance approfondie des différentes formes du chant liturgique, il a non seulement gardé l'assiduité, la fidélité et la loyauté des paroissiens à leur église jusqu'à la venue du R. P. Zacharie Revko mais il a maintenu la tradition vivante et entretenu ainsi la mémoire collective de la pratique religieuse par la pratique musicale.

Iwan Semenovich Kozachok

Iwan Semenovich Kozachok est né en Ukraine et a étudié la musique dans la ville de Kremianets en Volhynie (alors en territoire polonais). Dès l'âge de 12 ans, il étudiait et chantait la musique liturgique au monastère de Potchaïv. Lors d'une visite de l'évêque au monastère, ce dernier fut très impressionné par sa lecture de l'épître et incita fortement le jeune chantre à poursuivre ses études musicales religieuses. On y célébrait alors la liturgie en ancien slavon.

Après la fin de la Deuxième Guerre mondiale, Iwan Kozachok fuit les bolcheviques et émigra à Salzbourg, en Autriche. De 1947 à 1949, il y organisa un chœur ukrainien. C'est en 1949 qu'il vint au Canada. Il occupa d'abord le poste de chef de chœur à l'église ukrainienne orthodoxe Saint-Georges à Lachine (Québec). Il y assuma les fonctions de *diak*, de lecteur de l'épître et de directeur du chœur pendant trois ans. En 1952, Kozachok a accepté le poste de chef de chœur à l'église ukrainienne orthodoxe Sainte-Marie-la-Protectrice à Montréal (Québec); il occupa ce poste jusqu'à récemment soit pendant 45 ans.

À Montréal, il fut également fondateur et directeur du chœur Moloda Ukraïna, du chœur d'hommes de la Fédération ukrainienne nationale et du chœur de femmes auprès de l'organisation Prosvita à Montréal. Il fut aussi le directeur du chœur du Millénaire de la chrétienté en Ukraine réunissant les chœurs des trois églises orthodoxes ukrainiennes de Montréal soit la cathédrale Sainte-Sophie, l'église Saint-Georges de Lachine et l'église Sainte-Marie-la-Protectrice.

Kozachok réalisa également de nombreux arrangements et composa un «Notre Père» (*Otche nash*, non publié).

C'est grâce au talent, à la compétence, aux connaissances, à la formation antérieure de son directeur Iwan Semenovich Kozachok que le chœur de l'église Sainte-Marie-la-Protectrice a maintenu la tradition musicale liturgique. Motivé par son esprit religieux et une dévotion à son patrimoine, ce musicien dévoué et vigilant a su communiquer l'esprit du chant religieux aux membres de sa chorale. Musicien érudit religieux, il a su transmettre son savoir et il pouvait assumer selon les besoins les rôles respectifs de directeur de chœur, de *diak*, de lecteur. Dans cet esprit, il donna des cours de « direction chorale » à Pointe-Saint-Charles afin d'assurer une relève, il format les choristes de Sainte-Marie-la-Protectrice, leur enseigna la lecture musicale et transmit à certains d'entre eux l'art de la récitation de l'épître selon le style kyivain. Kozachok établit ainsi un lien direct entre la tradition liturgique de Kyiv et le nouveau milieu d'implantation. « [...] Kozachok nous a enseigné la manière qu'il connaissait [...] il n'en connaissait pas d'autre [...] » (une choriste)[3].

Spécificité de la tradition musicale à l'église Sainte-Marie-la-Protectice

La continuité assurée par le même directeur et chantre pendant une période de 45 ans a largement contribué à l'ancrage d'un esprit et d'un style qui caractérise la performance musicale qui prend place à cette petite église. L'homogénéité des voix, de l'interprétation et du « vécu » musical, confère au chœur une couleur vocale particulière et un fondu qui donne l'impression souvent d'un seul instrument vocal à la texture harmonique plutôt que d'un ensemble de plusieurs voix superposées. La souplesse de la respiration et le naturel dans l'expression musicale transmettent aisément la dévotion et véhiculent la prière et les textes sacrés dans une symbiose musicale qui enveloppe les fidèles dans un espace sonore sacré tout au long du rituel.

Un autre aspect contribue aussi à cette qualité musicale particulière : la plupart des participants partagent aussi leurs activités musicales avec la musique traditionnelle ukrainienne d'essence vocale et polyphonique. Leur participation à la musique religieuse orthodoxe ukrainienne s'inscrit donc dans un ensemble culturel naturel et spontané et non comme une activité artificielle et hors-contexte.

Le souci de préserver la tradition et son authenticité a prévalu jusqu'à présent et n'a pas cédé, comme dans certaines autres paroisses, devant les contraintes de la vie moderne et urbaine. À titre d'exemple, Sainte-Marie-la-Protectrice est une des rares églises au Canada où non seulement le chantre (*diak*) mais le chœur participe à la « Vigile » (*Sviata Vsenitchna*), cérémonie qui prend place le soir de la veille des principales fêtes[4].

Notons que l'un des premiers signes visibles de l'éloignement de la tradition et de l'authenticité du rituel orthodoxe est la réduction des parties chantées et le remplacement de la cantillation par la simple récitation. Les causes de cette transformation peuvent être variées et conditionnées soit par l'absence de musiciens qualifiés et aptes à remplir ces fonctions, soit par des facteurs de réduction du temps de célébration du rituel dans un processus d'adaptation imposé par les conditions de vie moderne. La simple lecture d'une prière prend beaucoup moins de temps que sa récitation chantée. Il en est de même pour les textes sacrés de l'épître et de l'évangile dont la récitation cantillée en « montée systématique » a été abandonnée dans plusieurs églises mais qui prévaut encore sous cette forme à Sainte-Marie-la-Protectice.

La voix de l'Apôtre...

Parmi les formes de cantillation qui prennent place dans le rituel liturgique orthodoxe, un des plus énigmatiques et difficile à cerner est la lecture de textes sacrés, entre autres celle de l'épître, en « montée systématique ».

L'on s'entend en général pour définir la cantillation comme une forme mélodique religieuse, plus proche de la déclamation que du chant proprement dit, entremêlée parfois de vocalises; synonyme de récitatif liturgique, le terme s'applique aux diverses formes de récitatifs adoptés pour la lecture des textes sacrés. La cantillation occupe une place importante dans le déroulement de la liturgie chrétienne et est confiée à divers exécutants tels le prêtre officiant, les diacres, sous-diacres, chantre et lecteur. En général, la cantillation occupe une situation intermédiaire entre la récitation horizontale (recto-tono) et la psalmodie qui comporte dans certains cas une ornementation élaborée (Honegger, 1976; Brenet, 1926).

La cantillation prend place à l'intérieur d'un ambitus intervallique plus ou moins large et à l'intérieur de cette marge consiste en ondulations rythmiques et mélodiques plus ou moins amples et variées selon le statut de la pièce dans la liturgie, le texte auquel elle est rattachée et l'interprète. Ce qui importe ici, ce n'est pas la stylisation mélodique comme telle mais la bonne audition des paroles, l'impression qu'elles produisent sur l'auditeur. N'oublions pas qu'à une époque où les fidèles n'avaient pas les moyens de lire, le but de la cantillation était de transmettre un enseignement oral à l'assemblée. Conséquemment, le texte doit être transmis sans équivoque et passer par l'oreille et non par les yeux sur le livre. Il s'agit d'assurer dans l'assistance un état de réceptivité, d'hyper-attention à propos duquel on pourrait presque parler de magie. L'aspect musical sert ici à amplifier l'éloquence dans l'énonciation du texte.

Dans cette optique, la lecture solennelle de l'épître, confiée au « lecteur » s'inscrit sous la rubrique de la cantillation. Le caractère solennel de la proclamation de la parole sacrée est ici véhiculé par la « montée systématique »

Description générale d'une lecture de l'épître « en montée systématique »

La lecture traditionnelle et solennelle de l'épître dans le rite orthodoxe se caractérise par la « montée systématique » qui consiste en une élévation graduelle de la voix en cours de récitation. L'espace sonore de la récitation cantillée se situe en général à l'intérieur d'un ambitus approximatif de quarte plus ou moins précise avec comme point de départ, généralement le son le plus grave du registre naturel du lecteur. Effectuée par un léger glissando à peine perceptible, cette élévation graduelle de la voix ponctue la fin de chaque phrase et est parfois préparée en filigrane à l'intérieur du registre de fréquences propre à chaque verset. Effectivement, il ne s'agit pas ici d'une hauteur définie soutenue en « recto-tono » mais plutôt d'une région de hauteur ou d'une bande de fréquences modulatoires à l'intérieur de laquelle se place la voix pour la récitation de chaque verset. La dernière note de la phrase, haussée à un palier supérieur est prolongée et après une respiration, sert de nouveau point de départ au verset suivant. La distanciation minimale et micro-intervallique entre les différents paliers représente l'aspect le plus intriguant et le plus spécifique de cette forme de cantillation. (Voir les tableaux).

Du son grave et caverneux de départ, associé au flou de la mouvance ascendante intervallique, se dégage une sensation d'immatérialité : ce n'est pas la voix du lecteur que nous entendons, c'est la voix de l'Apôtre. Ce processus musical non seulement donne du relief à la parole de l'Apôtre mais par la « montée systématique » vers un sommet franchement affirmé, amplifie le caractère solennel de la lecture du texte sacré.

Un exemple spécifique

L' exemple illustré ci-dessous est extrait de la récitation des deux épîtres lors de la célébration de la messe de la fête de Sainte-Marie-la-Protectrice, patronne de la paroisse du même nom, le 18 octobre 1998. Il y avait pour cette occasion spéciale deux lecteurs soit un pour chaque épître. Bien que chaque lecteur possède sa méthode personnelle (tradition orale) d'interprétation et d'énonciation du texte cantillé, nous pouvons quand même dégager certaines caractéristiques générales. À cet effet, nous présentons ici une analyse de la première lecture. Notons que la transcription graphique présentée ici ne vise pas une reproduction exacte du phénomène sonore mais représente plutôt une esquisse des composantes principales au niveau de l'organisation sonore, élaborée à la suite d'une analyse spectrale du phénomène[5].

Le premier tableau est une esquisse de la « montée systématique » réalisée lors de la récitation de la première épître. On peut y observer onze phrases réparties sur onze paliers qui peuvent se définir plutôt comme des régions de hauteur ou des bandes fréquentielles approximatives à l'intérieur desquelles prend place la récitation des textes. La dernière montée, suivie d'une quarte descendante constitue la terminaison cadentielle de la récitation de l'épître (voir Tableau I).

(Tableau I)

Première lecture cantillée : esquisse de la montée systématique

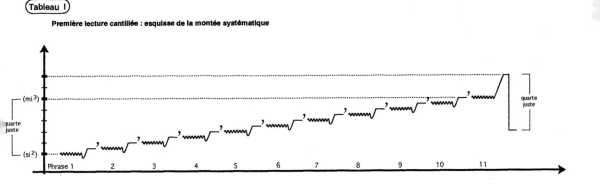

Le second tableau offre une description détaillée de l'énonciation d'une phrase. Notons que chaque phrase se termine par une note prolongée qui suit une élévation de la voix en glissando (voir Tableau II).

102

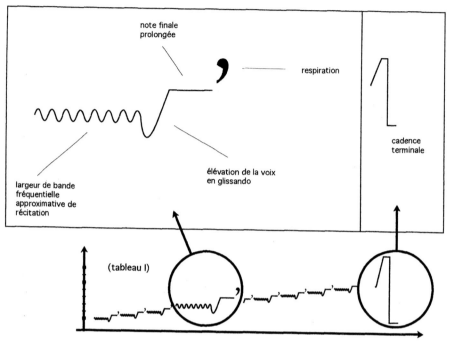

Tableau II

Description détaillée d'une phrase

note finale
prolongée

respiration

cadence
terminale

élévation de la voix
en glissando

largeur de bande
fréquentielle
approximative de
récitation

(tableau I)

Le troisième tableau présente une mise en parallèle des fréquences de l'échelle tempérée et des fréquences identifiées lors d'une analyse spectrale des fréquences et des relations intervalliques telles que perçues dans la récitation de la première épître. Pour faciliter la comparaison, nous utilisons le système préconisé par Ellis pour mesurer l'écart intervallique entre les demi-tons. Selon ce système, chaque demi-ton est égal à 100 « cents ». Le demi-ton, dans notre système musical est le plus petit intervalle entre deux notes (hauteurs). Or, dans la lecture de la première épître, il y a entre le premier palier et le dernier, un intervalle de quarte juste; dans notre système avec échelle tempérée, la quarte juste englobe **six degrés équidistants** soit cinq demi-tons; dans la lecture de la première épître, la même quarte juste est divisée en **onze paliers** (degrés), dont les écarts intervalliques **non équidistants** sont beaucoup plus petits que le demi-ton de l'échelle tempérée.

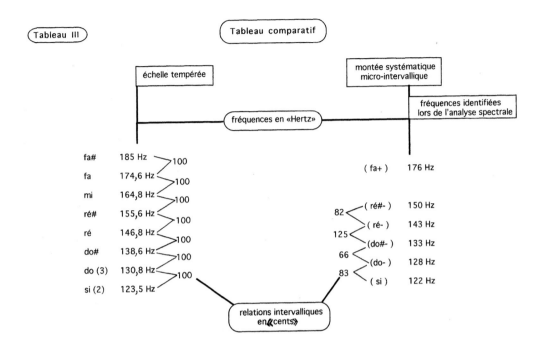

Notons que la lecture de la deuxième épître était répartie en huit paliers, toujours dans un ambitus de quarte, ce qui occasionne aussi des écarts intervalliques plus petits que dans l'échelle tempérée. Cette deuxième lecture révélait aussi des fins de phrases ponctuées par une note longue soutenue en tremolo et un glissando ascendant vers le palier supérieur. À la différence de la première lecture, la note terminale de chaque phrase était précédée d'une broderie inférieure sur un intervalle de tierce mineure.

Sans prétendre à aucune généralité et dans un but purement descriptif, les caractéristiques que nous voulons mettre en relief par ces illustrations graphiques des composantes musicales de la « montée systématique » analysées ici sont les suivantes:

• l'ambitus de quarte /quinte à l'intérieur duquel s'effectue la « montée systématique »;

- l'approximation de la largeur de bande fréquentielle à l'intérieur de laquelle prennent place les différents paliers de la « montée systématique »;
- les micro-intervalles non tempérés et non équidistants qui relient les différents paliers;
- l'élévation de la voix en glissando;
- les notes prolongées qui ponctuent chaque phrase;
- les différentes manières d'ornementer et de ponctuer les fins de phrases;
- une cadence finale marque l'arrivée au sommet de la montée;
- les différentes manières de présenter la cadence finale à la fin de la récitation cantillée.

Vivacité et fragilité de la tradition

La récitation solennelle et traditionnelle de l'épître qui prend place à l'église Sainte-Marie-la-Protectrice de Montréal illustre bien la vivacité et l'immuabilité d'une tradition qui a transcendé les siècles, voire le millénaire, par le processus de la transmission orale, et ce, malgré les oppressions politiques, les déplacements des populations et les pressions d'acculturation subies en milieu d'implantation.

Toutefois, le contexte de vie moderne et urbaine représente une menace grandissante au maintien de l'authenticité des pratiques musicales liées à une fonction qui, socialement et religieusement perd graduellement sa raison d'être originale et son sens profond. En ce sens, la situation actuelle de l'église Sainte-Marie-la-Protectrice est précaire et révèle bien la fragilité de la tradition, tributaire d'éléments contextuels sociaux, économiques et culturels en mutation perpétuelle.

Depuis la fondation de la paroisse Sainte-Marie-la-Protectrice, la menace de survie de la paroisse se manifesta sous différentes formes. Les deux premières décennies connurent l'édification de la paroisse, de l'église et de tous ses éléments : architecture, iconostase, chœur. Pendant la troisième décennie l'absence prolongée de prêtre a mis en doute l'existence même de la paroisse. Depuis plus récemment, alors que tous les éléments sont en place pour le bon fonctionnement de ce lieu de culte, on assiste à une réduction flagrante du nombre de paroissiens et de fidèles que assistent aux offices religieux : le statut économique plus élevé des nouvelles générations et leurs activités professionnelles favorisent le déplacement des nouvelles familles vers les banlieux plus éloignées de Montréal, ce qui occasionne forcément un mode de vie où la hiérarchie des priorités est conditionnée par ces nouvelles situations et un sens des valeurs différent.

Cette situation contraignante ne peut qu'avoir des conséquences directes sur les pratiques musicales : par exemple, la diminution du nombre de choristes, la réduction de la variété du répertoire, la rareté des adeptes plus spécialisés , voire de ceux qui peuvent chanter dans la langue vernaculaire, les transformations au niveau de la prononciation ou encore l'éloignement de l'authenticité stylistique. Aussi, la « relève », bien intentionnée et si compétente soit-elle dans le maintien de la tradition, n'a plus à qui transmettre ses compétences et sa connaissance de la tradition. Ce qui demeure de ce premier lien direct avec la grande tradition de Pochaïv par le chantre Kozachok, bien que profondémment ancré chez ceux qui maintiennent encore la tradition, est d'une grande fragilité et risque de n'avoir pour lieu d'existence que les quelques enregistrements qui subsitent (voir discographie), d'autant plus précieux vu cette situation.

Le sort de la tradition musicale liturgique est en effet intimement lié à la pratique dans son contexte propre et implicitement dépendante des conditions culturelles, historiques et sociales à l'intérieur desquelles elle prend place. Mais dans ce contexte, le rôle de ceux qui se sont voués, et continuent encore de le faire aujourd'hui, à la tradition cantoriale sous toutes ses formes est crucial. Le maintien de la tradition et de son authenticité dépend en grande partie de ces connaisseurs qui se font à tour de rôle la voix de l'Apôtre, la voix de Dieu à travers les écritures , le prolongement de la voix du prêtre ou encore la voix qui engendre celles des choristes. Ces fonctions confèrent au chantre un statut particulier dans le déroulement de la liturgie et dans la société dans laquelle prend place cette liturgie.

NOTES

1. Cet article a été élaboré à la suite d'une enquête de terrain réalisée à Montréal pendant les deux dernières années et financée par le Musée canadien des civilisations.
2. Notons la présence à Montréal d'un chœur byzantin formé uniquement d'hommes, c'est-à-dire de prêtres et de psaltistes provenant de neuf églises orthodoxes grecques de Montréal, qui se sont donné pour mission de préserver la tradition musicale byzantine dans sa forme la plus pure.
3. Extrait d'une entrevue à Montréal, octobre 1998.
4. Nous renvoyons le lecteur au document vidéographique inédit *Vigile et Messe pour la fête de Sainte-Marie-la-Protectrice* (Musée canadien des civilisations et Laboratoire de recherche sur les musiques du monde, LRMM, Faculté de musique, Université de Montéal) et au disque *Sviata Vsenitchna* (La Sainte Vigile), voir discographie ci-contre.
5. Nous remercions M. Myke Roy du secteur électroacoustique de la Faculté de musique de l'Université de Montréal pour sa disponibilité et ses observations lors de l'étude des composantes vocales et de l'analyse spectrale de ce phénomène.

BIBLIOGRAPHIE

BOULTON, Laura

1969   « A Glimpse into Byzantine and Orthodox Music », *The Music Hunter, The Autobiography of a Career,* Doubleday & Company, Inc. New York, chap. 31, p. 480-488

BERTHIAUME-ZAVADA, Claudette

1989   « Stratégies musicales de préservation et d'adaptation chez les Ukrainiens montréalais », *Revue de musique folklorique canadienne,* 17:40-46

1994   « La vie musicale ukrainienne à Montréal : caractéristiques et spécificités », *La vie des Ukrainiens du Québec* , sous la direction d'Alexandre Biega, Éditions Basiliens, Toronto, p. 181-204

1994   *Le chant ukrainien, une puissance qui défie les pouvoirs,* Thèse de Doctorat, Faculté de musique, Université de Montréal

BRENET, Michel

1926   *Dictionnaire pratique et historique de la musique,* Paris

CORBIN, Solange

1961   « La cantillation des rituels chrétiens », *Revue de Musicologie,* Société française de Musicologie, vol. XLVII, juillet 1961

HONEGGER, Marc

1976   *Dictionnaire de la musique,* « Science de la musique, techniques, formes, instruments », direction Marc Honneger, éd. Bordas

KUTASH, Ihor G.

1994   « Les origines et les caractéristiques de la HROMADA orthodoxe ukrainienne Sainte-Sophie de Montréal, Québec », *La vie des Ukrainiens du Québec,* sous la direction d'Alexandre Biega, Éditions Basiliens, Toronto, p. 121-137.

MOROSAN, Vladimir

1991   « Liturgical Singing or Sacred Music? Understanding the Aesthetic of the New Russian Choral School », in *Christianity and the Arts in Russia* , Cambridge University Press, Cambridge, p. 124-131

1991   *One Thousand Years of Russian Church Music, Monuments of Russian sacred Music,* series I , Volume I, Musica Russica, Washington, DC

PICARDA, GUY
1993 « The Evolution of Church Music in Belorussia »,
*Christianity and the Eastern Slavs, California Slavic Studies
XVI*, University of California Press, vol.1, p. 328-357

STESKO, FEDIR
1935 *The Influence of Czech Musicians in Ukrainian Music (The
History of Galician-Ukrainian Religious Music)*, traduction
en anglais : Kristina Alda, non publié

WELLESZ, Egon
1959 *A History of Byzantine Music and Hymnography*, Oxford

WERNER, Eric
1959 *The Sacred Bridge, The Interdependence of Liturgy and
Music in Synagogue and Church during the first Millenium*,
New York, Columbia University Press

WYNNYCKY, Nadia
1994 « L'Église grecque catholique ukrainienne de Montréal », *La
vie des Ukrainiens du Québec*, sous la direction d'Alexandre
Biega, Éditions Basiliens, Toronto, p. 109-121.

ZMIJENKO SENYSHYN, Halina
1992 *Documentation chronologique de l'histoire
organisationnelle et de la vie paroissiale des Ukrainiens de
la Province de Québec au Canada*, The Basilian Press
Ukrainian Inc., Etobicoke (Ontario).

DISCOGRAPHIE

Sviata Vsenitchna (*La sainte Vigile*), Chœur orthodoxe ukrainien de l'église
Sainte-Marie-la-Protectrice, Montréal. Directeur : Iwan S. Kozachok; prêtre
officiant : R. P. Hryhorij Fil'; lecteur : Iwan Hawrylovych Perederij; solistes :
Mme Vira Buresh, Mme Pawlina Korsavenko.
   Ce disque comprend sept chants extraits de la divine liturgie de la Vigile,
rarement chantée par le chœur dans les églises d'aujourd'hui.

Velykyj Pist (**Le Grand Carême**), Chœur orthodoxe ukrainien de l'église Sainte-
Marie-la Protectrice, Montréal. Directeur : Iwan S. Kozachok; solistes : Vera
Bures, Nadine Zwetkow, Claudia Melnyk Yevshan Communications Inc., 1984.
   Ce disque comprend des extraits de liturgie kyivaine, des compositions de
Bortniansky et de Turchaninov.

VIDÉOGRAPHIE

«Vigile et Messe pour la fête de Sainte-Marie-la-Protectrice», Chœur orthodoxe ukrainien de l'église Sainte-Marie-la-Protectrice, Montréal. Directrice, Claudia Melnyk; enregistrement vidéo, Yuri Zawada, Laboratoire de Recherche sur les Musiques du Monde, Université de Montréal, 1998.

Enregistrement vidéo inédit de la Vigile et de la Messe pour la fête de Sainte-Marie-la-Protectrice, réalisé à l'église du même nom, le 18 octobre 1998 par Yuri Zawada. Document d'archive dont la cassette originale « DV » a été déposée au Laboratoire de Recherche sur les Musiques du Monde de l'Université de Montréal (LRMM) qui a fourni l'équipement; une copie a été déposée aux archives de la paroisse et une copie a été déposée au Musée canadien des civilisations qui a financé le projet.

CANTORS AND GODPARENTS IN UKRAINIAN FOLKLORE

by
Bohdan Medwidsky

Ukrainian traditional society is commonly depicted as being dominated by peasants supporting themselves by their agricultural pursuits. Though well-grounded in history, this stereotypical portrayal sidesteps the importance of non-peasants as significant members of that society. For example, Ukraine's period of Kyivan Rus' included a coterie of princes, boyars and assorted retinues who ruled over the population and, among other things, employed professional entertainers for diversion and amusement purposes. Initially, many of these performers were foreigners invited to amuse the nobility at their courts; but with the passing of time local *skomorokhy* evolved, many of whom put on shows not only in the princes' courts or in urban areas but also travelled to the countryside to amuse the peasants in their villages.[1] Even though these entertainers became well known to the village folk, their migratory nature always made them outsiders in as far as the more sedentary local population was concerned.

Somewhat later on, in the 16th and 17th centuries, another group of minstrels, the *kobzari* and *lirnyky,* followed in the footsteps of the *skomorokhy.* Making their living from singing and playing on a *bandura* or *lira*, they also were not part of the peasant class but rather reflected their ideas and thoughts about this class from the outside. Analyzing the position of the Ukrainian *kobzari* and *lirnyky*, Natalia Kononenko says:

> By stressing the contradictions relating to Ukrainian minstrelsy as an occupation, I want to indicate that this is a "liminal profession." Liminal means something on the margin, something unusual - something not in the middle of the structure of society, but something on the periphery. To be a peasant in traditional Ukraine meant to live an ordinary life in the center of the social structure. To be occupied as a *kobzar* or *lirnyk* meant to live on the periphery. That is in a "liminal position." People and professions on the periphery are characterized by contradictions and opposing views or relations, they view the structure of society from a position beyond it.[2]

---

[1]Filiaret Kolessa, *Ukrains'ka usna slovesnist'* [1938] (reprint, Edmonton: Canadian Institute of Ukrainian Studies, University of Alberta, 1983), pp. 6-7. Russel Zguta traces the origin of these entertainers in his *Russian Minstrels: A History of the Skomorokhi* (see pp. xiii, 3-8)

[2] Natalia Kononenko, "Suspil'nyi status ukrains'kykh kobzariv i lirnykiv," *Ukrains'ka literatura: Materialy I konhresu Mizhnarodnoi asotsiatsii ukrainistiv* (Kyiv, 27 serpnia - 3 veresnia 1990 r.) (Kyiv, 1995), p. 296 (trans. B.M.).

Others, too, functioned as minimal figures on the periphery of Ukraine's peasant class: for example, reeves, priests, cantors, blacksmiths, folk midwives, folk healers, salt traders or in some cases persons who took on even more peripheral transitional functions in society such as baptismal sponsors or godparents, breast-feeding mothers, best men at weddings, seasonal carolers or mummers, etc., can all be listed as liminal figures. A study of their functions, official and otherwise, would encompass many pages. In this short essay I wish to deal with only two such figures in Ukrainian society: the cantor/reader, etc. (*diak* [plural form, *diaky*]) and the godparent (*kum* [masc.sing.form], *kuma* [fem.sing.form], *kumy* [plural form, either / both male or female; note also that in Ukrainian the relationship between godparents and biological/natural parents is not differentiated terminologically: both refer to each other as *kum*). Although peripheral and understudied in the existing scholarly literature, both of these functions have been and still are very important for Ukrainian agricultural and current urban societies.

Historically, Ukrainian cantors played a vital role in the church service, in literacy and the education of peasants, as intermediaries between the illiterate and literate parts of society, and even in the development of national consciousness of the local populace. This vital activity of cantors is evidenced by their overrepresentation (in comparison to their number) in the 19th century Ukrainian national movement in Galicia.[3] The category of baptismal sponsorship (as represented by godparents) gained importance in all spheres of society with the

---

[3] John-Paul Himka, *Galician Villages and the Ukrainian National Movement in the Nineteenth Century* (Edmonton: Canadian Institute of Ukrainian Studies, University of Alberta, 1988), p. 105. Metropolitan Andrii Sheptytsky wrote an appeal addressed to cantors suggesting that these church officials were expected to be role models in their parishes. In his special letter (dated December 1939) to the cantors, the Metropolitan wrote:

> Considering you as helpers or assistants of the clergy, I turn to you in this letter of mine to encourage your work on the introduction of congregational singing. It is most beautiful when you conduct a choir in four voices, but it is even better and more important that under leadership all the people were singing because this way all those present in church are absorbed in prayer. It is correct to say that who sings - prays twice. Because he himself prays and he helps the people to pray. The general singing of the whole church without comparison helps people to pray more than the singing of one or even several people. Singing is one of the very important pastoral instruments in the formation and education of a Christian soul. Therefore, you church cantors consider this as a most important message of God. Your duty is to provide the development of Christianity in human souls by a devout and godly singing and by organizing of a community-wide singing. I can assure you that he who among you will fulfill this sacred duty for God's glory and for the love of your fellow men and women, he will not be left without the reward that Jesus Christ has assigned to his apostles. Peace be to you! - A.M. (*Pys'ma-poslannia Mytropolyta Andreia* [Yorkton: Logos?, 1961], p. 6).

promulgation of Christianity as Ukraine's official, state religion in 988 A.D. Henceforth, baptism and all its attributes was part and parcel of the social life of every person who adhered to the Christian faith, whether they lived in villages or urban centres. Still, the liminal nature of both the *diaky* and the *kumy* placed these functionaries in an ambivalent situation. On the one hand some might have preferred to have less to do with these liminal types; yet on the other hand, they were crucial in the performance of the church rites linked to a person's life cycle. The cantor would be expected to assist at the church baptism, the church wedding and at the funeral. The godparents would be expected to sponsor the newly born at the baptismal celebration (an enterprise that would also involve some cost). Wedding gifts would also be expected later during the life cycle, although a godparent might or might not outlive his or her godchild.

From the standpoint of Eastern Christianity it is important to note that both cantors and godparents were/are involved in some fashion with the ritual or sacrament of baptism. Both were expected to be churched (i.e., baptized, given church instructions and members in good standing). While the connection between churching and cantorship was somewhat fluid and subject to many changes since early Christianity, sponsors/godparents, on the other hand, were screened in accordance with a hard set of regulations. The recent *Code of Canons of the Eastern Churches,* for instance, specifies the following requirements for godparents:

> Can. 685 - §1. For a person to fulfill validly the role of a sponsor it is necessary that he or she:
>
> 1° be initiated with the three sacraments of baptism, chrismation with holy myron and the Eucharist;
>
> 2° belong to the Catholic Church, with due regard for §3;
>
> 3° have the intention of carrying out the responsibility of sponsor;
>
> 4° be designated by the person to be baptized or the parents or guardians, or, if there are not any, by the minister;
>
> 5° not be a father, mother or spouse of the person to be baptized;
>
> 6° not be bound by excommunication, even a minor one, suspension, deposition or deprived of the right of acting in the function of a sponsor.
>
> §2. To assume licitly the role of sponsor, in addition to what is required, the sponsor should be of the age required by particular law and lead a life in harmony with the faith and the role to be undertaken.
>
> §3. For a just cause, it is permitted to admit the Christian faithful of another Eastern non-Catholic Church to the function of a sponsor, but always at the same time with a Catholic sponsor.[4]

---

[4] *Code of Canons of the Eastern Churches* (Canon Law Society of America, 1992), p. 343.

Other baptismal obligations for parents, pastor and sponsors are provided in Canon 686:

> Can. 686 - §1. Parents are held to the obligation that the infant be baptized as soon as possible according to legitimate custom.
> §2. The pastor is to see that the parents of the infant to be baptized and those who are given the function of sponsor, be instructed as to the meaning of this sacrament and the obligations connected with it and that they are prepared for an appropriate celebration of the sacrament.[5]

While godparents/sponsors were committed to the responsibilities listed above, cantors, who were congregation leaders, had to have an intimate knowledge of liturgical services and offices to fulfill their responsibilities. The following passage describes how this evolved.

> ...during the times of the early Church, sacred singing was given by the entire congregation. This congregational singing was taken over from the synagogue in as much as the first hymns of the Church were mainly taken from the Psalms and the original congregation was composed of Christians from Judaism. But because not all members of the congregation knew how to read or had the books, it was established that for the purpose of avoiding cacophony only one person would sing a hymn and the rest would join by singing the refrain of the hymn or by repeating the last words where there was no refrain. The singing on the part of the congregation of a part of a hymn had developed into a kind of a choir as we understand it today. The celebrant would begin the singing and the entire congregation would follow. But because not all celebrants were in a position to lead the rendering of a hymn, the function and office of cantor gradually came into being.[6]

Although the literature dealing with the history of the development of cantorship in the early Church tends to stress various aspects of this ecclesiastical office, certain general tendencies or outlines can be discerned. Some sources suggest that the authorities of the early church saw the need for an official cantor to prevent heresy from making its way into a congregation. "One of the reasons for which the office of cantor was established in the worship of the Church was the concern that heretical teachings could be furtively introduced into sacred hymns and thus be spread among the faithful."[7] With an official cantor leading the congregation, this possibility would be neutralized. Furthermore, some rules and regulations were established by the Church authorities for the duties and moral behaviour of cantors. "There are decisions of even Ecumenical Councils that regulate the office and personal life of cantors as bearers of the grace by the 'laying

---

[5] Ibid., pp. 343/345.
[6] Rev.Nicon D.Patrinacos, *A Dictionary of Greek Orthodoxy* (Minneapolis: Light & Life Publishing, 1984 [fourth Printing 1997], p. 69.
[7] Ibid.

on of hands'."[8] Other sources suggest that minor Church officials were inducted into their positions by being "given a special blessing and dedication" and that this was not an "ordination."[9] Some sources referring to the leadership of Christian congregations mention a distinction made between cantors and readers or lectors. Thus, an Arabic version of the *Canons of the Apostles* mentions women performing the duties of the lectorate. According to this same Arabic version "one and the same person very often performed the offices both of cantor and lector, as quite natural in the smaller churches."[10] These developments have led to a situation where for the Orthodox Church "today's cantor (Psaltes) must be a Reader because besides singing, reading Psalms and other hymns, he has the authority to read or sing the Apostolic passage of the day."[11]

The importance of cantors as congregational leaders is also noted in Ukrainian publications, as exemplified by the following excerpt:

> One cannot do without cantors; without them our beautiful chant is disappearing and our rite is diminishing in our church.
>
> A good cantor in the parish is the right hand of the priest, he is the connection between the priest and the parishioners; he is the assistant and is even often a counselor to the priest mainly in local matters.
>
> A good cantor can also provide a lot of good for our people working in village institutions like the reading halls, in commercial cooperatives such as the dairy industry, credit unions, etc. as well as teaching the illiterate, conducting the local choir, directing amateur plays, concerts and even acting as a community secretary, etc. Such peripheral activities could also provide additional income for the cantor.[12]

From the above it is clear that both *diaky* and *kumy* needed similar credentials: both had to be accepted and regarded as members of the Church and perhaps not only as members but also as role models. Unfortunately, an exemplary lifestyle was not always possible. There is a significant amount of Ukrainian folklore about cantors and sponsors in which one can, on the one hand, note positive depictions of these two offices in keeping with Christian expectations, and on the other hand, a contrasting situation, where the folk description is very much opposite to the Christian ideal.

[8] Ibid.
[9] Kucharek, *The Sacramental Mysteries: A Byzantine Approach*, p. 301 (including footnote 31 on the same page).
[10] Johannes Quasten, *Music & Worship in Pagan & Christian Antiquity*. Translated by Boniface Ramsey, O.P. (Washington, D.C.: National Association of Pastoral Musicians, 1983), p. 81.
[11] Patrinacos, p. 316.
[12] Sviashch. Ihn. K. "Diakivs'ki spravy," *Nyva* (L'viv), XXX, no. 8-9 (1928), p. 318.

In order to come to a more detailed analysis of the folk depiction one should, first of all, examine the characterizations available in non-ecclesiastical sources about cantors and sponsors. Very apt summaries have been provided in *Ukrains'ka mala entsyklopediia* edited by Ievhen Onats'kyi (1894-1979). One entry reads as follows in translation:

> A CANTOR [*diak*] is a church singer and reader; the term is derived from the abbreviation of the word deacon [*diakon*]. Cantors taught in schools during the kozak period in Ukraine and later. They were also called *USTAVNYKY* (see below). Almost all of them were sons of priests, had some education and later some of them also entered the priesthood. For their teaching they were paid with grain and other products of that nature. Besides this it was the students' duty to give them special gifts and offerings. The breviary and Psalter served as school texts from which the children learned the alphabet and perfected/improved their reading abilities...They taught the *ustav* style of writing (from which the word *ustavnyky* is derived) and calligraphy according to the old manner. We know from the biography of T. Shevchenko about the rough schooling he had to endure under the drunk cantor Bohors'kyi, from whom he learned grammar, the breviary and the Psalter, but from whose beating he had "to escape into the world to find people who would give him a sound moral upbringing..."[13]

The cantor has become a favourite figure in Ukrainian satirical folksongs and comedies where he plays the role of a Don Juan caricature. Professor M. Sumtsov indicated in his time that the ironic songs about the courting/lovemaking of the cantor based, without doubt, on local every day life situations, could also have been borrowed from western European literature where the courting or lovemaking of clergymen was widely used in novelas, facetiae and songs of *mienensaenger*.[14]

---

[13] From the autobiography of Shevchenko one may conclude that he was taught by several cantors and none of them treated their pupils very well. The same autobiography mentions that "When he was going on eight years of age, having lost his father and mother, he found refuge with a church sexton [in the Russian original - *d'iachok*] in a school as his pupil-*drudge*. After a most difficult two-year ordeal he learned grammar, the breviary, and finally, the psalm book. The sexton, realizing that his pupil-*drudge* had ability, used to send him in his stead to read prayers for the souls of serfs who had passed away, for which he paid him every tenth kopeck in remuneration. But despite such flattering attention from his strict Spartan teacher, on one of the many days and nights when the Spartan teacher and his friend... were dead drunk, the pupil-*drudge*, baring the buttocks of his mentor and benefactor, without a twinge of conscience, gave him a good dose of the rod. Having avenged himself to the full and purloining a book with pictures, that very night he ran away to the little town of L... where he found himself a teacher of painting,." (Taras Shevchenko, "Autobiography," *Selections: Poetry, Prose* [Kiev: Dnipro Publishers, 1988], pp. 142-3).

[14] Prof. Ievhen Onats'kyi, "Diak,"*Ukrains'ka mala entsyklopediia: Knyzhka tretia: Litery D-Ie* (Buenos Aires: Nakladom Administratury UAPTserkvy v Argentini, 1958), p. 397.

In his entry about sponsors/godparents, Onats'kyi provides even more extensive depictions of these types, making good use of Ukrainian folk customs and beliefs. According to this entry, the godparents are the godfather and the godmother that hold the child at baptism, in relationship to the father and the mother of the child. The Ukrainian people distinguish three categories of godparents:

1. INVITED or SUMMONED GODPARENTS. They were usually selected from among one's relatives who are liked and respected and occasionally from among good acquaintances and friends. They usually selected people with good spiritual characteristics because they believed that these would transfer to the child. They also made certain that the godfather was rich, because a rich godfather was considered security for a child's future. Poor people especially tried to find rich people as godparents in order to get a nice present from them. It was considered bad taste to refuse this request because it was a sin 'to refuse the cross' [i.e., to serve as a sponsor].

People did not like to change invited godparents: if the children did not die then they would call the same godparents for subsequent newborns. But if the children died then one had to look for others [i.e., a new set of godparents for subsequent newborns].

2. ENCOUNTERED GODPARENTS. When children died or were not fortunate in general, then when a new child was born the first people encountered on the road were asked to become godparents. This custom can be observed among other people as well, for example in Germany.

3. BOUGHT GODPARENTS. When a baptized child was sick for a long time, this was ascribed to a bad selection of godparents. Then bought godparents were used. The child was passed across the threshold of a corridor or a window to those asked to become bought godparents. Upon accepting the child, the bought godparents gave some money for it, dressed it in a new shirt which they brought with them and from that time on they substituted for the godparents ...

After the baptism godparents become like members of the family and take on duties towards the child in case of the death of the parents. Especially, they must bring gifts. There is no question regarding the christening linen [chrisom] since it is given by the godparents because this is required by religious regulations. Besides that they would generally give bread or buns. In the Hutsul region they gave larger presents as well: a sheep, a horse, a shirt, a warm coat made of coarse material or they announced what they would donate in the future.

It is generally understood that after baptism the godparents become spiritually related among themselves (to one another). Therefore, the Roman Council of 721 already forbade godparents to enter into sexual relations. From this, it was understood that living together and adultery among godparents was considered an especially serious sin. The Ukrainian story about the "Godparents' Valley" near Boryshpil' states that the godparents who sinned there were transformed into ducks and the same valley became a lake ... However, [Ivan] Manzhura remarked that in the folk consciousness, the relationship between godparents and the understood sinning by committing adultery among them is differentiated: godparents, in relationship to the parents of the child whom they baptized, are considered such close relatives that adultery among them would really be a mortal sin; on the other hand, adultery between the godfather and the godmother, friends who held the child at the baptism, was compared to regular adultery, that is, also a sin, but a very common one in life. Folksongs that deal with sex among godparents really have these godparents-friends in mind: "The young kozak Nechai is drinking mead with his [female co-] godparent Khmel'nyts'ka…"

Ordinarily one pair of godparents was invited [to a baptism], but whoever wanted greater honor invited several pairs of godparents. If there was someone who wished that his child grow well, he would also call several pairs of godparents, because if there were more godparents, then even if one pair was unlucky, the second one might be luckier and the child would live well.[15]

These descriptions show how, in Ukrainian folklore, the image of cantors and godparents is ambivalent, i.e., both positive and negative. Cantors, for instance, were indispensable in the education of the village inhabitants, but at the same time they were often caricatured and satirized. In the case of the godparents, this contradiction appears as well, as outlined above: according to belief, their positive moral traits are passed on to the newly baptized child; yet, on the other hand, in the imagination of the Ukrainian folk community, godparents are also commonly involved in sexual transgressions.

In tracing the complexity and variety of the depictions of cantors and godparents in Ukrainian folklore, one should, however, avoid simplistic generalizations. It is not always possible to explain, for example, the amorality of a godfather, gypsy, or a blacksmith simply as a product of the class factor as Britsyna suggests.[16] The folkloric manifestations of cantors and godparents, as well as other examples of folklore, should be analyzed in all the multiplicity of their representation within the imagination and craftsmanship of the Ukrainian folk and considering all possible shades and colours. The differences between the idealized depictions of these figures in ecclesiastical literature and their folkloric manifestations can be seen as strictly dogmatic postulates on the one hand, and less officially sanctioned oral forms of entertainment on the other hand. This analysis proceeds from the point of view of the folk.

Let us first deal with the concept of baptismal sponsorship, which is widely represented in Ukrainian folklore, especially in religious legends, folk songs and even in historical legends. One folkloric example showing godparenthood in a positive light (at least from a Ukrainian/ancient Rus' standpoint) is the legend about the baptism of Princess Ol'ha in Byzantium around 955,[17] considered to be

---

[15] Ibid.: "Kumy,"*Knyzhka VI: Litery Kom.-L.* (Buenos-Aires: Nakladom Administratury UAPTserkvy v Argentini, 1960), p. 790.

[16] O.Iu.Britsyna, *Ukrains'ka narodna sotsial'no-pobutova kazka (spetsyfika ta funktsionuvannia)* (Kyiv: Naukova dumka,1989), p. 52.

[17] Sviashch. Iu. Fedoriv. *Istoriia tserkvy v Ukraini* (Toronto: Ukrains'ka Katolyts'ka Tserkva v Kanadi, 1967), pp. 30-1.

one of the oldest Ukrainian legends.[18] In order to avoid the emperor's pressure to marry him, she asks him to become her godfather. When he agrees but continues his advances, Ol'ha reminds Constantine that according to Christian teachings godparents cannot marry their godchildren. Thus, the rules pertaining to godparentship save Ol'ha from an unwanted liaison.

The depiction of godparenthood in the legend about Princess Ol'ha is rather straightforward. Other tales are more complicated. Some legends focus on antagonistic relationships between godparents and biological/natural parents (in Ukrainian neither is differentiated terminologically, i.e., both refer to each other as *kum*). That is to say, ideal Christian conduct is sometimes shown in opposition to wayward human behaviour. Such a situation occurs in the religious legend, "St. Nicholas as a Godparent." In this legend St. Nicholas's role as a virtuous godfather is contrasted with that of his godchild's biological father, who is not only a negative type but is also a poor and extremely greedy peasant. Here we see two men (*kumy*) related through the ceremony of baptism: one represents Christian ideals, and the other is opposed to these virtues. On the one hand, St. Nicholas personifies the qualities of spiritual mercy inasmuch as he endeavours to convert the sinner, to instruct the ignorant, to advise the doubtful, to comfort the sorrowful. On the other hand, we have a poor peasant, who, notwithstanding the fact that he keeps getting wealthier and wealthier seems to have no qualms about committing such sins as pride, covetousness (greed), envy, and anger, which are in direct contradiction to the Christian virtues of humility, generosity, contentment, and patience (meekness).

In this legend, St. Nicholas, seeing a poor and sad man on the road, and learning that the fellow was unable to find a godfather for his child, readily agrees to fulfil this function. The Saint also helps the poor peasant escape from his poverty and patiently satisfies all of the peasant's desires, which one by one become more and more excessive. Eventually, the peasant even becomes the emperor, but this too is not enough for him. The peasant-emperor then journeys to St. Nicholas's for dinner and desires the palace and the orchard that the latter has. The peasant turns to the saint, saying:

My dear *kum*, I will ask you about something..." - And St. Nicholas says: "About what?" - He says: "Give me this orchard and all of the palace." - And St. Nicholas says [...]: "No, only after death." – Then the emperor shouted at his army, saying: "Take this *kum*, that old man, and throw him into this slough (for all the good he had done for him!) - But Saint Nicholas had not finished saying this fully, when already his servants approached him (the emperor). And that emperor, immediately the emperor's clothing disappeared and he became that old [peasant] man, the *kum*. And the servants approached him and take this old man - they carry him outside the town, this old man, the emperor himself,

---

[18] Filiaret Kolessa, *Ukrains'ka usna slovesnist'*, p. 144.

and throw him outside the gates into this slough, and the bubbles rose above him. And the emperor begins to say: "*Kum, kum, kum, kum!*"- and St. Nicholas stands on the side near that slough and says: "You are going to keep croaking till Judgment Day in this slough where the frogs mock each other! Don't you remember I was a *kum* for you, and I helped you so much to escape your poverty, and you intended to throw me out of paradise, me a saint... And I ordered you thrown into a hellish bottomless pit for that, that you complained about God, that you were poor, and you escaped poverty and even became an emperor, and didn't pay any attention to anybody except yourself, that no one else is as powerful as yourself, because you are the emperor. And if God in the highest, would blow with his holy spirit on your army, then you and your power would be carried away up to the clouds. Don't you remember that I did not let you perish and you thought, that you would not allow me to live on this earth, to spend my life in this paradise...[19]

The opposition of good and evil in this legend offers a moral since the peasant-emperor later was made to pay for his sins and sent to hell. The folklorized depiction of St. Nicholas provides a role model according to which people should conduct their lives on the straight and narrow. In this portrayal, the churched sponsor (the peasant-emperor) reflects popular notions and exemplifies how folklore makes use of the liminal image of a *kum* to condemn human failings.[20] In the extensive text of this legend about St. Nicholas as godfather (the original is 8 pages long) we have an example of a structurally complex model of the sponsor relationship, demonstrating both the church and the folk interpretation of the *kum* category.

In the humorous folksong "*Iak do kumy ne khodyty*" [How Can One Help Not Visit a Godmother] the opposition of the Christian ideal in baptismal relations and human transgressions is absent. The satire is directed toward the amorality of extramarital sexual relations in a village context. The protagonists in this song are folklorized versions of a male *kum* and female *kuma*). The *kum* in this song represents a loose-living rogue who is attracted by the beauty of other men's wives and who pays them visits. He explains his deeds in a comical way:

How is one not to visit the *kuma*,
If the *kuma* approves,
If the *kuma* is young,
As beautiful as a star?...
How is one not to visit the *kuma*,

[19] Ibid., pp. 175-6.
[20] The etiological legend "Vidky vzialasia zhaba" [Where Did the Frog Come From] (*Lehendy ta perekazy* (Kyiv: Naukova dumka, 1985, p. 88) is a variant of the St. Nicholas text. In this much shorter text, instead of St. Nicholas, who plays the role of the ideal godfather, we have Jesus Christ, who delivers a poor man from his misery. Having become rich, the former poor wretch shuns his *kum*, Jesus Christ, and chases Him and St. Peter out of his house. When Jesus attempts to calm his *kum* down, the latter responds: "The devil is your *kum*, not I." Then Jesus sends him off to a hell-like place, transforming him into a frog.

> Even if it were far?
> And the *kuma* has sweet lips,
> It is easy to kiss them. [21]

In this song both the lecherous godfather-*kum* and his paramour, the godmother-*kuma*, are presented in a negative and satirical manner. But why is it that godparents/*kumy* have been selected to underline negative conduct? It seems that the disparaging folk depictions connected with these images operate on at least two levels. Firstly, the individuals in this song are undeniably friendly with one another (there are three of them - the godfather and the natural parents), and these kinds of close relations, in folkloric material, are easily depicted as sexual. Secondly, the relationship with its associated liminalities lends itself to the projection of human failings and weaknesses. Here the basic purpose of the satire is to ridicule the negative human traits symbolized by the folk song's description of extramarital behaviour. As in the legend about St. Nicholas, the religious precepts regarding sponsorship are also implied. In this case, however, we have the absence rather than the presence of virtuous behaviour.

Similar situations in which the dichotomy between worldly realities and religious ideals emerge are found in tales about cantors. For example, a negative portrayal of a sinning cantor is represented in the folktale "*Diak-muzyka*" [the Cantor-Musician]. In this text the hero is described as a sinner "because he frequented married women."[22] In the tale "*Diak-muzyka*" just as in the previous texts about the *kumy*, a liminal, folklorized image of the cantor is used. The liminality of this tale's hero is not limited to his cantorship, but is also suggested by the fact that he is a musician. Divine intervention plays an important part in this legend and this intercession brings about the salvation of the sinning cantor. According to this legend, the cantor is invited to play his fiddle for the forces of evil, who want to take possession of his soul. Close to midnight, the devils "stopped dancing and they gave the cantor a gun and they told him to shoot at the window. And when they placed the gun in his hands, they turned the barrel towards him and the stock towards the window."[23] The cantor is saved from death because he has a habit of making the sign of the cross. When he begins to do this, he sees the image of Jesus Christ, from whose wounds blood was flowing. As a result of this vision, the sinning cantor falls to the ground, losing consciousness. The next morning, when he regains his senses, "he looks, and he is sitting on a

---

[21] *Ukrains'ki narodni pisni: Rodynno-pobutova liryka.* Chastyna 1: Pisni pro kokhannia (Kyiv: "Dnipro," 1964), p. 289.

[22] "Diak-muzyka,"*Halyts'ko-rus'ki narodni liegendy*, I, zibrav Volodymyr Hnatiuk, *Etnografichnyi zbirnyk*, T.XII (L'viv 1902), p.204.

[23] Ibid.

mound in some reeds and near him is [the food] that he had eaten yesterday, urine and horse manure, and instead of money there were broken pieces of clay. From then on the cantor no longer went around to visit other people's married women."[24] In this instance, God not only teaches the cantor a lesson, but also saves his life. Again, we have a situation in which the positive church ideal of a cantor is contrasted with that of a sinning cantor. The sinner was subjected to Divine punishment because he did not act in accordance with church teaching. By disciplining the sinner, God cleansed his soul from evil and set him on the path of righteousness.

A similar contrasting of cantors as saints and sinners obtains in the humorous tale "Why Do Cantors Not Go to Heaven?" In this tale we have a cantor who wants to get to paradise. His friend, also a cantor, spends three years in purgatory and then is let into paradise. Thereafter, he visits the first cantor, who is still alive. The visitor tells his friend that during his three years in the afterworld, not one other cantor had made it to heaven. The first cantor, having heard this report, "left the cantor's profession and is working now on the land."[25] In this tale cantors are shown to be sinners who do not fulfil their cantorial obligations piously and who also lack Christian zeal. As a result of this poor work ethic, they end up in hell and not in paradise. As suggested earlier, the negative side of this coin also implies a positive antithesis, in this case the church concept of cantorship. That is, if "cantors do not go to heaven" it is because they are supposedly sinners and because they do not conform to the church concept of cantorship. It is important to note, however, that the protagonist in this tale obviously aspired to enter paradise. But learning that no other cantor had entered heaven during the time that his friend had been in purgatory, the protagonist decides to do some honest work (at least in accordance with Ukrainian mainstream agricultural society). He "quit the cantor's job and is working on the land." He leaves behind his liminal occupation and tills the soil in order to become worthy of a place in paradise. Thus, in this tale, traditional agricultural pursuits offer a true and preferred path to paradise along with the realization of church ideals. It may be interpreted that the stereotypes who find themselves in liminal positions cannot, at least from the viewpoint of a villager (the main bearer of folklore in Ukrainian traditional society), become figures who can achieve the church ideal; but on the other hand, the honest work of tillers of the soil provides the possibility of nearing, if not achieving, this ideal.

While the cantor in the previous tale serves as a negative folk figure, in the historical legend "Karmeliuk and the Cruel Lord" the cantor achieves a more

---

[24] Ibid., p. 205.

[25] "Chomu diaky ne idut' do neba," Halyts'ko-rus'ki narodni liegendy, II, *Etnografichnyi zbirnyk*, T. XIII (L'viv, 1902), p. 107.

positive personification. In this tale, the legendary 18th-century Ukrainian hero, Karmeliuk, fighting the oppressive lords, disguises himself as a cantor to teach the cruel lord a lesson and to stand up for justice:

Once upon a time there was a lord: gentle, most gentle, quiet, very quiet, benevolent, most benevolent. [He went around] always flattering people and with sighs, greeting others by bowing down, but people feared him more than merciless fire, more than the plague and the violent pestilence. Because if a poor wretch came late for work, then you may be certain, that the lord would send his steward and the latter would take away only a quarter of the person's possession. And if the poor wretch would be late a second time, then it's half [of the property], and if he was disobedient, [he would take] the whole household... But to beat or to scold - God forbid! And how much suffering did the people go through with him, how many bleeding tears were shed, how many unfortunate orphans were left behind when their mothers departed to the other world through hunger and illness! And once this lord left for church. He made his confession and returned home by coach, but in the forest, he hears something shouting in the back, and it's the church cantor who is running after him and shouting for him to wait. The lord stopped his horses, and the cantor said so and so, your eminence, the priest father forgot, what the sins were that you had confessed to him, so he sent me to catch up with you that you would repeat the confession, because he has to say a prayer for your sins. Well, the lord goes and repeats: - I confessed - he says, - so that God would forgive my grave sins, that somehow on Holy Friday I took [some] greasy meat into my mouth and somehow unwittingly I pinned my cat's tail down and I also told the coachman an abusive word...- Aha, - says the cantor, - and that's all, your eminence? - That's all, - says the lord. - Aha, - says the cantor, your eminence forgot one more little sin, that is your wealth, that you raised from the tears of orphans. And he immediately took off his cantor's clothing and the lord, when he sees that this is Karmeliuk, he really begins to raise a fuss, and Karmeliuk then, right away, takes a poplar tree and bends it down, for he was strong, he bent it down and then put a rope around the lord's neck quickly and says: - Well, rise, your eminence, there you will report the rest of your sins..." and he let the poplar tree move upwards.
And only the wind whistled.[26]

In this tale Karmeliuk assumes the guise of a cantor to teach the cruel lord a lesson. The liminality of cantorship provides a folkloric vehicle that condemns the conduct of the cruel lord but does little, if any, damage to the cantorial profession or to Karmeliuk's heroic reputation

One can note from these few examples that godparents and cantors enjoy a wide spectrum of representation in Ukrainian folklore. It includes both positive and negative depictions of these types, as well as intermediary samples with more

---

[26] *Lehendy ta perekazy*, p. 281.

neutral traits, their positive or negative features expressed less ostentatiously. Among the previously discussed folk portrayals, St. Nicholas, without doubt, represents the most positive depiction of a godfather, serving as an example of a proper sponsor and a generous saint in Ukrainian folklore. One can find Princess Ol'ha on the same level of godliness, even though somewhat distanced from the image of St. Nicholas. Devoid of religious sainthood (though conferred posthumously), Ol'ha is very much a folk heroine who uses her wit and wisdom to defend herself against the erotic desires of Emperor Constantine. The image of Karmeliuk as cantor has a more neutral position because the folk hero was not a real cantor. But such neutrality can be viewed in a positive light, because it comes about as the result of the combination of the concept of cantorship with the very positive image of the folk hero, Karmeliuk. In the legend "Why Do Cantors Not Go to Heaven," the cantor at first seems to have a positive image; however, this perceived trait dissipates because of the negative associations linked to this office and the hasty departure of the protagonist from his position. Other figures seem to have a more negative image. This is especially the case with the portrayal of the poor peasant in the legend "St. Nicholas as Godparent," as well as with the protagonists of the humorous folk song "How Can One Help Not Visit a Godmother." This is also the situation with the figure of the sinning cantor in the legend "The Cantor-Musician," even though the negative depiction of this image is somewhat mitigated by the fact that he maintained some redeeming features.

Thus, speaking about cantors and godparents we note two opposite poles in Ukrainian folklore which could conditionally be termed as the poles of sinners and saints, which, in fact, represent the notions of good and evil. At the same time, we have a whole gamut of possibilities which exist between those two basic extremes reflecting real life, where human nature hardly ever appears as a paragon of virtue but, more often, where it is enmeshed in a constant struggle between good and bad. In the sampling above, the folk concept of good appears to coincide with church precepts regarding godparents and cantors, and their opposites are the popular concepts that personify the weaknesses of human nature and which are ridiculed in folklore. Thus, we notice a dichotomy between those behaviours that are, on the one hand, sanctioned by the church, and, on the other, others that are not.

In spite of the differences between sponsorship and cantorship, there are many commonalities in their folkloric depiction. In view of their important community functions and elevated status in real life, it would seem that their distorted depiction in folklore is overly abundant. This incongruence can perhaps be explained by the liminality of both types. In ancient cultures strangers (i.e., liminal types) were subjected to rites of befriending and neutralization (including

extreme physical measures) for the well-being of the rest of the group.[27]
Nowadays ridicule or satire has an equivalent socializing and equalizing effect and
these means are frequently used in folk literature, as shown above. It is the satirical
element deployed with regard to godparents and cantors in the process of their
folklorization that has transformed some of these figures from saints to sinners.

---

[27] A. Van Gennep mentions that "Some peoples kill, strip, and mistreat a stranger without
ceremony, while others fear him, take great care of him, treat him as a powerful being, or take
magico-religious protective measures against him." This statement is expanded in his
explanation that the intention of these rites are to make the strangers "neutral or benevolent."
The Rites of Passage, translated by Monika B. Vizedom and Gabrielle L. Caffee (Chicago: The
University of Chicago Press, 1960), p. 26.

The musical culture of the Doukhobors is completely oral. A member of the choir or congregation begins each verse to establish the pitch and tempo, whereupon the entire group joins in, either to continue singing the principal inner melody begun by the soloist or to provide contrapunctal parts above and below. There is no conductor.

Kenneth Peacock, *Songs of the Doukhobors* (1970)

"GOD IS IN FRONT OF ME"
CANTORS OF THE OTTAWA JEWISH COMMUNITY, 1998

by
I. Sheldon Posen

V'khulam potkhim et pihem	And all open their mouth
Bik'dusha u-v'tahara	With holiness and purity
B'shira u-v'zimra	With song and melody
U'm'vorkhim u'm'shab'khim	And bless and praise
U'm'fo'arim u'ma'aritzim	And glorify and reverence
U'makdishim u'mamlikhim	And sanctify and exalt
Et shem ha'el...	The name of the Lord...

from *Ha-Sidur Ha-Shalem* (Daily Prayer Book) p. 341

"You have to be very careful and understand who you're standing in front of when you *daven*. I want to do the best job I can, because God is in front of me."
Cantor Daniel Benlolo

Introduction

This is a preliminary report on *khazanut*[1]—the Jewish cantorial art—as it is practised in the synagogues of Ottawa, Canada[2]. It is based on interviews I

---

[1] Please see my "Glossary of Hebrew and Yiddish Terms" at the end of this report. A brief guide to the Hebrew-Yiddish orthography used here follows.

a	"o" as in "mother"
ay	"i" as in "bite"
e	"e" as in "met"
ey	"a" as in "plate"
i	"ee" as in "peer"
kh	"ch" as in "Bach" (German)
o	"o" as in "vote"
u	"oo" as in "doom"

conducted at the end of 1998 with each of five professional *khazanim* (cantors) and one lay *khazan* (cantor) in the city. The interviews were designed to draw out the cantors' perceptions of what they do, of stability and change in their repertoires, and of their role in their congregations and in the Jewish community. I hope one day to continue this research—to compile data on the history and musicology of *khazanut* in Ottawa, to collect perceptions of synagogue song and *khazanut* from congregation members, and to document the music of prayer services in the city's synagogues.

Some Backgrond

The Ottawa Jewish community, which numbers about 13,000, is of medium size compared to others in Canada: larger than the one in Calgary or Halifax, significantly smaller than Montreal's or Toronto's. The community has a history as a relatively active, prosperous, and religiously committed one, and thanks in part to an influx of Jews from Montreal in the past ten years, it is growing. At the end of 1998, Ottawa had at least one synagogue belonging to each of the mainstream divisions of modern Judaism—Orthodox, Conservative, and Reform, plus one congregation belonging to each of two newer, "left-of-centre" movements, Reconstructionist and Chavura, that endorse (among other things) "egalitarian" participation in services by both males and females.

Only Orthodox and Conservative congregations in the city have a professional *khazan*. It is a coincidence that in 1998 many are new in their positions. **Agudath Israel** (Conservative) recently appointed Cantor Stephen Chaiet and granted emeritus status to his retired predecessor, Cantor David Aptowitzer, after 40 years of service at the *shul* [synagogue]. Congregation **Beth Shalom West** (Orthodox) selected Daniel Benlolo as their first, full-time cantor in 1995. The *khazan* at Congregation **Beth Shalom** (Orthodox), Ya'ir Subar, was just appointed last year. The *khazan* who now has held office the longest in Ottawa is Pinkhas Levinson at **Machzikei Hadas** (Orthodox). The cantors range in age from mid 40s to early 70s. Only Cantor Chaiet is Canadian-born; Cantor Aptowitzer is from Poland, cantors Subar and Levinson are from Israel, Cantor Benlolo was born in Morocco.

' used to ensure a glottal break between vowels, or a pronounced break between abutting consonants, thus *ba'al t'fila*, "BAH-al teh-FEE-lah."

[2] I am grateful to *khazanim* David Aptowitzer, Daniel Benlolo, Stephen Chaiet, Pinkhas Levinson, Ya'ir Subar, and to lay cantor Floralove Katz for their patience in explaining their cantorial art and for sharing their insights and opinions with me. The words are theirs, but the responsibility for their interpretation in this report is, of course, my own.

The Reform synagogue **Temple Israel** uses a number of lay, amateur cantors selected from among its members. One was interviewed for this study: Floralove Katz, a vocal performer in her own right who fills the *khazan*'s role for the Temple's services on the High Holy Days (*Rosh HaShana* and *Yom Kipur*). She is the only woman who sings in a ritual capacity on the *bima* [synagogue pulpit] in Ottawa.

No *khazan* **Necessary**

Besides Temple Israel, neither **Young Israel** (the other of the Orthodox synagogues) nor the Chavura or Reconstructionist congregations employs a professional *khazan*. Ritually this is possible because, liturgically speaking, a Jewish congregation can function without one.

In Judaism, there is a direct line of prayer between the individual and the Deity. The three obligational daily services can be validly said by a worshiper praying alone, without mediating clergy. Even the prescribed or ideal prayer situation—at least ten adults (a *minyan*) worshipping together—does not require a *khazan*. The participants informally appoint one of their number on an *ad hoc* basis to act in the capacity of *ba'al t'fila*[3]. The *ba'al t'fila* "leads" the service by beginning and ending each prayer aloud as everyone, including him, *davens*. (The Yiddish infinitive meaning "to pray" is *daven*. Jewish anglophones use *daven* in conversation as if it were English, so that, for instance, someone praying is "*davening*." The *ba'al t'fila* has to be a good "*davener*.")

The *ba'al t'fila* is not a cantor. He serves simply as the oral benchmark and reference point for the gathering to stay in synch, pacing the *daveners* so they proceed at the same rate. For some prayers, notably the benediction called the *kadish* that punctuates services at several points, he also provides the solo voice for a call-and-response interaction with the gathering. Likewise, he co-ordinates prayers such as the *Sh'mona Esrey* that are said once by all, more or less silently, then run through again with some parts said aloud by the *ba'al t'fila*, others chanted by the congregation in response, and yet others repeated by all silently.

The *ba'al t'fila*'s reading or chanting is of the most functional kind—pared down, even minimalist, just a degree above reading the prayers himself. He is not considered or construed by the congregation to be a *khazan*.

---

[3] *Ba'al* in Hebrew literally means "owner" but could be rendered "person responsible for"; *t'fila* means "prayer." The person responsible for reading the weekly Torah portion during the service is called the *ba'al koreh*, *koreh* meaning "reading." The plural of *ba'al t'fila* is *ba'aley t'fila*.

Representative of the People

The *khazan* takes the prayer service beyond the functional, basic run-through of prayers usually provided by the lay *ba'al t'fila*. He plays the role of *shli'akh tzibur*, "messenger of the gathering," a ritual ambassador from the congregation to God:

> When you get up on that *bima*, really, you're the *shli'akh tzibur*: you're supposed to be the empty vessel which transmits the prayers and innermost heartfelt feelings of the members of the congregation to God. When I'm on the stage with the Ottawa Symphony or the Opera Lyra, it's a completely different feeling. There you're performing. But here I really use the music as the medium to convey every single note and phrase of what the essence of the prayer is.[4]

The prayers of the individuals in the congregation take on added weight because they are delivered, enveloped in song, by the *khazan*:

> The role of the *khazan* is to add value to the meaning of the liturgy through the interpretation of the music, through linking the spirit of the prayer to the listener or to the participant. I believe the music is intended to involve the congregation in a more immediate way.

The "added value" that "involves the congregation in a more immediate way" is not only the music that is sung, but the emotion with which the *khazan* imbues every note he sings:

> The *Hineni* on the High Holy Days is the prayer *par excellence* of the cantor. In this prayer he says, "Here I'm standing before you. Please accept my prayers. I'm standing here as a *shli'akh tzibur*, and I'm the representative of these people. Please listen to my prayer, that I shouldn't stumble in the middle" and so on. Now, if you sing it with your heart and if you mean the words, people will feel it. And I know many, many times, a member of the congregation has come up after the service and told me, "Your *Hineni* today broke my heart."

In other words, there is a reflexive element to *khazanut*, whereby the *khazan* ACTS the prayers for the congregation so that the members feel the prayers in a way that they might not when they say them themselves, or when a simple *ba'al t'fila* chants them:

> The reason why the cantor is there is not because we want to pay somebody when somebody else can do the same job for nothing. You do that because you want this professionalism, you want someone to be up there and you want him to be somebody to sing in such a way that people really feel the prayer.

---

[4] Virtually all the quotes in this report are unattributed. There was a certain frankness in my conversations with the *khazanim* that I feel I should respect. To this end, I've made the quotes anonymous. I should also say that for readability's sake, the quotes have been quite heavily edited, though their meaning and intent have been scrupulously maintained. The taped interviews and their transcripts are stored in the archives of the Canadian Museum of Civilization.

The emotion with which a *khazan* is able to express a prayer may be dependent upon, but is not to be confused with, vocal technique. Says one *khazan* about recordings of *khazanut*:

> I listen to see if the *khazan* gives me a *krekhtz*: if he really moves me, if he touches my heart, I'll buy the record. I will listen to it because I feel I'm deriving something from it, it gives me a lift. And I'm not talking about the trills, I'm not talking about going to the high C.

The ability of the *khazan* to marry emotion and technique are part of the artistry of *khazanut*:

> I find in some cases that just in sheer timbre of the voice and the sheer beauty of how they phrase and so on, khazanut becomes an artistic experience as well as an emotional one. So even if you're not a religious person, if you're a spiritual one, the music has the means to move you in a much more potent way than just reading the words would.

Thus, as there are all levels of participation in prayer by the congregants, so the *khazan* functions simultaneously on many levels, expressing congregants' emotions that might already exist, intensifying emotions only partly felt, or inducing them outright. But the idea is that prayers that are heartfelt are more effective than those said by rote. This emotional component benefits not only the congregation, but the *khazan*:

> When you sing as a khazan, you're giving your heart. You're sharing your feelings with the people. And sometimes when a person—I mean, everybody has ups and downs in his life, not every day is the same: he's fighting one day with his wife, one day with his children. When he's feeling like this, and he believes in God and comes to shul [synagogue] and the khazan reaches his heart with peace—he goes home another person. He feels good today.
>
> And sometimes the khazan also has been having a hard time [laughs], and he davens and reaches out to God—God can change lives in a good way.
>
> When I come to shul, I'm concentrating to God, and I try to bring the people to do t'shuva [repentance]. But when I come to shul, I'm not trying to make a concert. I'm trying to daven. I try to do it b'ne'imut, with love, with a song.

Nusakh

Khazanim speak with reverence about the melodies they sing, invoking an ancient lineage:

> Some prayer melodies go back, like the *Kol Nidre*, 400 years, and if you look in the *Encyclopedia Judaica*, the version that's included there from the 5th century is the same version that we sing in the synagogue today. I mean, I get goose bumps when I think about that—that thousands of voices, millions of ears, have heard the same prayer over the millennium.

The term that *khazanim* employ in speaking about the melodies and families of melodies they use is *nusakh*. A *nusakh* is a mode, in the manner of the modes of the mediaeval Western church—Aeolean, Phrygian, Mixolydian—tonal scales from which melodies are fashioned. There are six basic *nus'kha'ot* (the plural) in Jewish cantorial music, used separately or in combination as the basis for the melodies of prayers on different occasions:

> *Nusakh* is a mode of singing: Friday night has its own *nusakh*, Saturday morning has its own *nusakh*, and Saturday afternoon has its own *nusakh*. Rosh HaShana has a *nusakh*, Yom Kipur has a *nusakh*, Sukot has a *nusakh*: each one has a *nusakh*, which is a mode.

The *Yishtabakh* mode, for instance, is the one heard on *Shabat*. It is the mode usually used to depict popular representations of European Jewish music: the song, "Sunrise, Sunset" in the Broadway musical, *Fiddler on the Roof*, is in *Yishtabakh* mode. Some occasions see a pairing or mixing of *nus'kha'ot*, but the principle of singing prayers according to the mode proper to the occasion is standard.

Each *nusakh* has a distinctive musical complexion—major, minor, modal—and characteristic motifs and successions of notes:

> *Nusakh* is a mode, style, way, or musical road that the cantor travels. Now, you can travel down Highway 16 or you can go on the 416, or you can go on 7 to get from Ottawa to Toronto. Your experience of all those three can be vastly different: one is going to be a scenic route, the other is just Whooom! right to the 401. But the bottom line is that each one has a distinctive character. So the *nusakh* primarily denotes what the nature of the service is.

Just as Christians might "get the Christmas spirit" on hearing carols in December, so singing a Jewish prayer in a particular *nusakh* summons up for the devout listener the context, the feeling of the occasion. In speaking about Sabbath songs newly composed by another *khazan*, one cantor says:

> When I hear these songs, you know, I feel like I'm at the Shabat table. I am there. I'm feel like I'm at the Shabat table by my parents. It's not simply a matter of their subject matter. These are tunes that he composed in the mood they're supposed to be in. If he can take me to the Shabat meal, to bring me to this mood, he's going to get in the right *nusakh*. You need a specialist in nusakh for that.

By the same token, as Christmas carols might feel out of place when heard, say, in July, so religious Jews are jarred when a prayer on a particular occasion is sung in the wrong *nusakh*. The different musical character of each *nusakh* is inextricably bound up with the feeling of the holiday or occasion with which it is associated:

> You cannot have on Friday night and Saturday morning the same mood. Because you don't feel the same on Friday night that you do on Saturday morning. And Saturday in the afternoon for Minkha it's also a different mood. And during the week you have a different mood. Rosh HaShana is a different mood, Yom Kipur is a different mood.

Nusakh styles come in several flavours, depending on their old world origins. There are *nus'kha'ot* Ashkenazic (East European/Russian/Germanic) and Sephardic (Spanish/Arab/Middle Eastern), and within those designations, regional variations:

Khazan:	The Germanic *nusakh* is much more modern than the others. It's also influenced by church music a little bit. In Germany, the *nusakh* is more the style of the famous cantor Landovsky, which was heavily influenced by the chorales which were brought into the synagogue in Germany. So it's mainly based on choral singing that is much more modern than the choirs in Eastern Europe would be.
ISP:	What do you mean by "modern"?
Khazan:	In the style, it's a modern style. It's based on operatics and on the local style of singing.

The *khazanim* have several *nusakh* styles in their respective repertoires, and favourites among them that they deploy according to their tastes and the needs of the service:

Khazan:	I like the Hungarian *nusakh* better. I'll give you an example.
ISP:	Hungarian's very special?
Khazan:	Yes, it's the real stuff. They have a lot of what nobody else has. This particular prayer talks about Noah. It's in three parts, when he went on the Ark and took in the animals, so you have to divide the melody into three parts—I mean the melody has to change three times. So: from here to here is one part, from here to here another part [from *zeh ha-yom* to *ashrey ish*] and then you come to *V'gam es Noakh b'ahava zakharta* ["and also Noah in love You remembered"]. So here you change the melody. [Sings.] Now with the flood, with the water. [Sings. He waves his hands quickly in front of him, right to left, right to left; the melody flows back and forth.]
ISP:	That's wonderful.
Khazan:	As I say, the Hungarians, they have it. I picked it up from old people, I was sitting with them every day....

Like their congregations, most of the *khazanim* in Ottawa are of Ashkenazic background and use Ashkenazic *nus'kha'ot*. Beth Shalom West's *khazan* Daniel Benlolo, born in Morocco and raised in Montreal, is the sole Sephardic *khazan* in Ottawa. On the *bima* he uses the Sephardic *nus'kha'ot* he grew up with, and Ashkenazic *nus'kha'ot* he learned during his training. He feels he has a certain flexibility in terms of repertoire and delivery:

| Benlolo: | Sephardic *khazanut* is so—it's not even *khazanut*, it's *piyutim* [poetic Jewish prayers composed in 9th-century Arab Spain ("*s'pharad*")]. It cannot be transcribed, because it covers such a wide range of octaves with eighth notes and sixteenth notes, and it slides and everything. So it cannot even be written down. And it certainly can't be played on a piano; it has to be played on a *kanun*, a 64-string instrument, there are so many little notes. That's why I can play with my music: I can sing an Ashkenazic piece—a Kussevitzky piece or a Rosenblatt piece,[5] and integrate a little bit of |

---

[5] Kussevitzky and Rosenblatt were the Carusos of *khazanut* in the first decades of the twentieth century. They are recorded and their music is transcribed and available to *khazanim*.

Sephardic nuance within it. And when you sing Spanish in an Ashkenazi *shul*—I'll let your imagination tell you the rest.

ISP: People like it.

Benlolo: They love it.

The other *khazanim* tease Cantor Benlolo about his crossover stylings. One time they did so using Yiddish, the language of Ashkenazic Jews, as a touchstone. After a local cantorial concert in which they sang a traditional East European Jewish song together, one was heard to quip as they left the stage, "You see, Daniel, Yiddish isn't so hard."

"I Make a Lot of Melodies Myself

Given Ottawa congregations' mostly Ashkenazic membership and cantors' Ashkenazic heritage and *nusakh*, one would expect that a worshipper could walk into any synagogue in Ottawa and hear substantially the same service as another. This turns out to be true of the overall "look and feel" of the services, and of many of its individual components. However, it is also true that a visiting worshipper will encounter a significant portion of the service that is different:

ISP: Is it the same everywhere? Is your *nusakh* the same as that of the others?

Khazan: The traditional *nusakh* is always more or less the same. The *Kol Nidre* is the same *Kol Nidre*, *Shabat* has more or less the same melodies—you find the same *nusakh* everywhere. In the whole world, wherever you go, it's the same tradition. On the other hand, the main dishes may be the same, but the side dishes you can change.

ISP: So what is a "side dish"?

Khazan: Let's say, *Lekha Dodi*: if you want to change the melody, why not? I like to use another melody for it every second *Shabat*. Or *Mim'kom'kha*, or *Shma Yisra'el*, or even *Adon Olam*, or *B'yom Ha-Shabat*, *Yis'm'khu*, you can change every second, every third *Shabat*. Like a side dish, you get bored every day if you eat potatoes.

ISP: I understand. So what are the "main dishes"?

Khazan: A main dish is the melody when you start the *Kadish* for *Shabat*, or the *Sh'mona Esrey*: it's always the same. [Sings.] Or the same for *Rosh HaShana-Yom Kipur*. *Kol Nidre* for sure, everybody in the whole world does it the same. [I confirm with the melody I know.] But let's say, *Yis'm'khu*: you can change that. I have at least 20 ways to sing that. And I make a lot of melodies myself.

ISP: Do you?

Khazan: Come on *Shabat*.

There are set musical pieces, then, in the Jewish prayer service, surrounded by prayers whose musical settings are more or less "up for grabs." There is a huge literature, both in print and on recordings, of music for these unset songs. The shelves of every Ottawa *khazan*'s library are lined with books and looseleaf binders of published, mimeographed, and xeroxed settings for them. The *khazanim* attend annual cantors' conventions and bring back more.

Another source of melodies for these unset pieces is Jewish popular music. In fact, finding melodies that will fit the words and the occasions and be attractive to one's synagogue members has been and remains something of a *khazan*'s sport. In the old days, the Jewish musical theatre repertoire was mined for tunes; now it is popular Israeli music. But choosing tunes involves applying careful criteria:

> You can bring modern melodies to the services, but when they're in the right mood and with the right key. That's not a *lateh* [patch]—you know, when we were kids and we had a hole, they would fix them with a any piece of material. Here there has to be a match.

Finding an appropriate tune for a prayer text has several dimensions:

1. It has to fit within the *nusakh* of the occasion on which the prayer is going to be said—Shabat, High Holy Days, and so on.

2. The melody has to fit the words without too much squeezing or pulling. Unlike Christian hymns, Jewish prayer texts are for the most part metrically irregular and non rhyming. To fit them into melodies of songs which are both, often means the prayers' phrases have to be rushed or words elongated so they "fit." It can be made to work, but one finds cases where the text has been made to lie uncomfortably on a procrustean bed of unsuitable melody.

3. The melody and the text have to match up in terms of "feel."

The ultimate source for new songs is the *khazan*'s own talent for improvisation. The *khazan*, like every individual worshipper in the traditional prayer service, has licence to improvise melodies for unset pieces:

> The difference between opera and *khazanut* is that opera—I have the music, I have the aria, if it's *Tosca* or *Rigoletto* or whatever, it has to be sung exactly like it's written. You can give more from your emotion, but the music is the music, you can't change anything. If it's top C, it has to be top C; you can't play games with it. Now, when we're talking about *khazanut*, *khazanut* is completely different. Every *khazan* has his own way and his own—actually what we have, we have like instructions. In *khazanut* it's called *nusakh*. But on the *nusakh*, every *khazan* can do his own music, his own interpretation.

Khazanim improvise on traditional melodies for the unset pieces, or on the public domain melodies written by the cantorial greats:

> Sometimes, we take melodies that are written already by Kussevitzky or Rosenblatt, famous *khazanim* that wrote pieces of music that are available for everyone. Now, how to interpret the music? That again is up to the cantor. He can follow exactly note by note, but then if he wants to do his own little *kvetching*, he can do it himself [laughs].

Or the melody can be improvised whole cloth, with notes and patterns from the *nusakh* as the raw materials. But the *khazan* has leeway to play, to depart from *nusakh* and return:

Khazan:	You can ad lib and sing whatever you can, however you want.
ISP:	Within that mode.
Khazan:	Within that mode, but you can get out of that mode; however, you have to come back in before you end that piece. Because you cannot finish in a different mode.
ISP:	Is it like a cadenza in a concerto, when the orchestra stops and the soloist performs a virtuoso passage?
Khazan:	Absolutely.
ISP:	He plays for two or three minutes, but at the end he has to come back in.
Khazan:	That's right. He cannot stop an octave higher or it really sounds like a break. But if he falls back in and "marries" back into the melody and the orchestra, then it sounds like it's part of it.

The improvisation can be purely of the moment, or it can be the seeds of new repertoire in that synagogue:

ISP:	Does anything ever solidify out of improvisation?
Khazan:	When you do something that you improvise and it sounds so beautiful, you say to yourself, "Wow, I can't believe I got that out."
ISP:	Right, but you can't write on *Shabat*, nobody's recording.
Khazan:	Yes, but what happens, if you do it, it marks you. And when it marks you, you can sing it again. And you do it over and over and over again, and you build on that tune, you build around it.
ISP:	So you can get it back.
Khazan:	Yes.

In some ways, attending a synagogue service led by a dynamic, talented *khazan* is akin to going to a jazz concert, or perhaps like seeing an ancient Greek drama as a member of the original audience: one knows the basic style or plot one is going to encounter, but the actual notes or words will be a surprise, and the spin applied by the artist on the traditional material might be a revelation. As with any artist, the creative process is a precarious one:

There are a lot of things that I improvise as I'm going along. But you have to be able to feel comfortable. There are days or weeks that you don't want to venture because you don't feel comfortable, you don't feel you've got it that day. And there are some days when you feel you can just sing anything and it'll work out. These are the days that you venture and explore. This is when the cantor is at his best, when he feels that at that moment, he can explore. When a cantor is able to explore—his voice, his music, talent, whatever it is—this is when you can really hear a cantor.

Then and Now

However traditional it remains in essence and on the surface, synagogue music in Ottawa (and the role of the *khazan* in performing it) is actually in constant flux. The fact of repertoire change can be taken for granted, but there are more profound changes that have taken place within one or two generations that have affected the music of Jewish synagogues.

One of the most visible changes has to do with the trend in Conservative, Reform, and alternate forms of Judaism towards widening the role of women in public religious performance. There is now a woman, Floralove Katz, acting as lay cantor of the Reform Temple Israel for the High Holy Days services. There is some tension ("bad vibes," says Ms. Katz) in situations where all the community's cantors, including Ms. Katz, appear together in public,[6] but Ms. Katz has received strong testimonials of support from her congregation. She tells of a woman she met last year between *Rosh HaShana* and *Yom Kipur*:

> Her eyes just filled up with tears and she said to me, "My father and grandfather were cantors in Vienna. My husband and I have been going to Temple Israel lately because of our children who have moved away from Orthodoxy and we want to be with them. When I heard there was going to be a woman cantor this year, I told my husband I didn't want to go. It was too much against tradition—but my husband prevailed on me, and you, more than anybody I've heard since leaving Vienna as a child, have captured the spirit of the tradition.

Lay cantor Katz, who has been *davening* for *Rosh HaShana* and *Yom Kipur* services at Temple Israel since 1992, comes to her role from a semi-orthodox upbringing in Montreal, an education in Hebrew and Yiddish, and experience as a performer of opera, klezmer, jazz, and folk music. She acquired her cantorial repertoire primarily from music supplied by the Rabbis at Temple Israel, supplemented by her own discoveries and suggestions from fellow lay cantors and members of the temple congregation. Ms. Katz makes no pretense of being a *khazan* either in training or performance, and she is mindful of the obligations she takes on as *shli'akh tzibur* for her congregation:

> What I was very concerned about in my first year serving as lay cantor was to offer the prayers great integrity through my complete focus on the prayers and how I brought the meaning of the words out through the music.

Like the professional *khazanim*, Ms. Katz wears a white robe during the High Holy Days. But she also wears a pearl-studded head covering made for her by her mother and grandmother:

> Every year when I get up on the *bima* and I have the honour to sing those prayers, which are so integral to my soul as a human being, as a Jew, as a woman, and as a member of a group that comes together to contemplate the previous year and how to progress in terms of ourselves and our social consciousness in the next year, the whole thing for me is a very overwhelming and awesome responsibility and experience.

---

6   In Orthodox Judaism, it is considered improper for adult males to hear the singing of a solo female voice; it is only in Conservative and Reform synagogues that one hears female cantors nowadays.

Other changes in Ottawa *khazanut* have to do with less controversial but just as revolutionary trends in Jewish life, particularly among Conservative Jews. At the heart of these changes is the general decline in *davening* skills. Fifty years ago, Ottawa synagogue goers, many of them first- or second-generation Canadians, were loud, vigorous, active *daveners*. They were intensely involved with the service, understood all the words, and actually said all the prayers. And just as hockey fans who themselves are players follow a star player's every move on the ice as if it were—if *only* it were—their own; so in a congregation of *daveners* the *khazan* performs vicariously for the congregants, with the talent, the voice, the repertoire, the ego, and the style to "do it right," as members look on and take pleasure in letting him do so. Thus in years gone by, the congregation gave the *khazan* all the time he wanted to perform:

> A cantor could improvise one piece—*Ahava Raba* before the *Shma*, say, or a *Kedusha*, that would take half an hour. He was the spiritual giver to the congregation. And they didn't mind staying until 2 o'clock on a *Shabbis*.

Old-style *daveners* may have been emotionally immersed in *davening* in a way that modern worshippers are not:

> When I came here in the early 1950s, we still had a lot of elderly people that had come from Europe and really knew how to *daven*. And they really *davened*. When it came to the High Holy Days, when it came to a prayer of *shma koleynu*, people were crying. When it came to the most solemn prayer we do, *U'n'taneh Tokef*, for the High Holy Days, *Rosh HaShana-Yom Kipur*, you sang "*tikateyvu*" and who shall live, who shall die, who shall be stoned—I mean, at that time, people really were crying, men and women. As the years passed away, the tears became smaller and smaller, and vanished completely.

As congregations seem more detached, the operatic vocal stylings of the *khazan* that one or two generations ago were synonymous with high emotion[7] may to some have gradually lost their impact. The trademark "sob" of the *khazan*'s voicings no longer tugs modern Jewish heartstrings the way it did 50 years ago:

> If you see that you wanted to show off with something, and they are sitting like *leymeleh goylem* [inanimate figures], they don't know the meaning, they don't follow you. You're going up and down and making *dreydlakh* [vocal ornaments] here and there, and it doesn't mean anything to them at all.

The result is that many cantors feel they no longer have the latitude to *daven* in the grand manner as they used to or were trained to do, that the performance of long, intensely emotional passages of pure musical emotion, flights of melodic fancy, and repetitions of highly ornamented phrases is an "indulgence" that few now are willing to allow them, or that no one listens to any more:

---

[7] Though opera was made fun of in popular culture at the time (in cartoons, for instance), the parodies betokened the public's familiarity with the form.

When I came here two years ago—you know Mr. Feinstein? He's 100 years old. I came here on *Yom Kipur*, and I sang the *sedra* of the *kohanim* that they used to worship at the Holy Temple. This is in the afternoon when everybody is tired and the *shul* is nearly empty and nobody's listening. And for the *kohanim*, this is something like the most important prayer of *Yom Kipur*. It goes like this: [Sings. It's very elaborate, with lots of "oy yoys."] And I'm thinking, "Why do I have to do it?" And I said, "No, here I am doing it for myself." When I finished *musaf*, Mr. Feinstein said to me, "*Khazan*, exactly like in Europe! All the '*oy yoy yoys*' exactly." That was the best compliment I ever got in my life. That shows that we don't have those things today.

Modern congregations by and large don't have patience for the old style *khazanut*, at least on the common Sabbath, when they demand to be out of the synagogue by noon or one o'clock:

Ottawans are not used to *davening* until 1 o'clock in the afternoon; not even till 12:30; God forbid, a
quarter after 12. You've got to be out of the main sanctuary by at least a quarter to 12; on *Shalosh Regalim*, that's another story, okay, 10-to-12, they'll forgive you. But 11:30 you've got to finish *Sim Shalom*, because there's announcements and everything. And this was a challenge for me. But I have to be accommodating, and find a way artistically and as a cantor to satisfy the needs of everyone.

Modern synagogue goers have places to go on Saturday afternoon, weekend activities to take part in, and sources for culture and entertainment that were not available to their counterparts two generations ago:

What did they have to do then? Did they have to run to turn on the TV for Seinfeld? THIS was the main thing. The cantor was the main entertainer in those days, and the people loved it, and listened. He was the soul, he was the *neshumeh*, of the people.

So *khazanim* are taking a new approach:

To me, today, if you want to function as a *khazan*, and you want to bring in the congregation to be WITH you, you have to teach them simple melodies that they can join in and feel part of. This is today's role of the *khazan*. In general you cannot be a performer today.

Khazanim are involving contemporary congregations in the service by bringing in attractive, group-accessible melodies and encouraging the worshippers to sing along:

We have to work so that people don't get bored. That's what I try to do on *Shabat*. I don't stretch out the melodies. Sing and finish: I don't have to sing too much. What I like is to have the congregation participate, to sing with me. Not to sing by myself. That's what I am trying to achieve.

Another approach is to make the music sung at traditional events more in keeping with current musical styles. It is obvious to the *khazanim* that the old approaches are not reaching people, particularly young people:

In Montreal I went to a wedding, and another *khazan* was doing the ceremony, and I was standing at the back of the synagogue and listening. And as I'm listening, I see that the guests aren't listening to the *khazan*. They have a feeling like, "You finish with your religious stuff; we want to have fun, to drink and dance and so on." And this bothered me. I said, "You know, actually, what is the *khatuna* [wedding]? The *khatuna* is the *khupa* [wedding canopy]. So why not give people the same picture, but with a modern frame? Not to take away from the picture, but just to bring people into the mood that they will be there. They are there physically, but they are not there emotionally."

So I had an opportunity to try something new. We had a wedding where three *khazanim* were participating. And I took the Seven Blessings, the *Sheva Brakhot*, and instead of doing them with the *khazanut*, I put them to a melody that we could do as a trio.

So: the *nusakh* is [sings:] *Barukh ata adoshem / Elokeynu melekh ha-olam*. This music is not related to people: they're not interested whatever. But I can take the same mood, the same *nusakh*, and do it like this: [sings].

The *khazanim* insist, however, that such changes be consistent with traditional *khazanut*:

> We have to present services to the community in a modern style that they will enjoy. But not to do away with the *nusakh*, because the *nusakh* is a very holy thing. This was made in the time of the holy Temple, the *beyt hamikdash*. So we have to take the same thing, but tailor it. Like you have a jacket, fashionable. But a jacket is a jacket.

Give and Take

If the *khazan* is a performer—and he is, whose job is to "sell" his "goods" with a beautiful voice and superb delivery—there is a fine line he walks between *shli'akh tzibur* and *maestro*:

> *Khazanim* are there not only to uplift ourselves but uplift everyone with us. On the other hand, we're big show offs: we have the unfortunate small arrogance to say, "You know what? I'm going to be able to move people." This arrogance helps us out. However, you have to be very careful and understand who you're standing in front of when you *daven*. It's a fine line. We have to be able to say, "I'm doing it to uplift these people, but at the same time, I'm not doing it for the people, I'm doing it for God. I want to do the best job I can, because God is in front of me."

There are other pressures. Ego and spiritual matters aside, the *khazan* is obliged to keep his "audience"—members of the congregation—happy to pay his salary, eager to return to services every week, and willing to renew their membership every year. So *khazanim* are constantly monitoring the congregational response to their performance, gleaning clues from how avidly the congregation sings, how quickly members pick up new melodies, or how readily they respond to call-and-answer songs:

> I know a song is catchy when everybody answers me. I say one line, the congregation says the line, then I repeat again. Then the congregation sings. And I come to this prayer here (*Ana adonay, hoshiya na*) [sings it], and the people answer me, and I know, it's going over.

Members of the congregation are not shy about directly expressing their approval or disapproval of the *khazan*'s choice of material:

ISP:	Does anybody come to you and say, "We don't like this melody"?
Khazan:	Sure.
ISP:	Do they come to you or do they go to the Rabbi?
Khazan:	No, no, they come to me. For instance, there's a lady who never came to *shul* except on the High Holy Days. She came to the *shul* six months ago when her niece got married. Now: when they put the Torah back in the Ark, I sing *Eytz Khayim Hi*. So on that occasion, I sang it to a different melody than usual. And she came up and said, "Why did you change the melody? I like the old melody. Why did you change it?" I changed it to: [he sings it]. No: she liked the old one. And I told her, "If you're such a critic, why don't you attend services more often?" She said, "I'll come next *Shabat*." I said, "Come! When you come, I'll sing the old one."
ISP:	[Laugh.]
Khazan:	So now when she comes on *Shabat*, I sing the old melody, and when she doesn't come—lots of times she's not here—I sing the other melody.
ISP:	A custom service.
Khazan:	Yes.

Eternal Prayers, Changing Melodies

Repertoire is always an issue between *khazan* and congregation. There are stories showing that each side represents at times the forces for change and innovation, and at other times tradition and "the way we've always done it." On the one hand, for example, the *khazan* often has a tendency towards musical exploration—trying out new melodies that he encounters at cantorial meetings or in the literature—an interest brought about, it should be said, not just by ongoing exposure to this new repertoire, but by the fact that he sings the old repertoire constantly and thinks "everyone" might enjoy a change:

> I started to bring in a little bit of a new flavour. You get tired of eating bread and butter every day, every day, every day. There's a world of music that I used to bring back from the conventions. I used to go every year when I was young, and I'd come back so inspired. I was going to turn the world upside down. But I learned the world doesn't go so fast.

Coming into a new synagogue is something of a repertoire minefield for a recently hired *khazan*. He must tread a narrow path between what he knows (and likes) and what the congregation is used to (and likes):

> Well, every synagogue has their tunes and they're married to these tunes, they want to keep these tunes and they don't want you to change them. The old timers are usually like that. But the new generation likes to have as many tunes as possible, change them as frequently as possible but come back to the old tunes.

Some cantors are quite circumspect on coming into a new congregation:

> When I came here, I was smart enough to sit down with the president and find out what the congregation wanted. So I started off on the right foot. I sang and the reaction was, "Oh, wonderful, he's fine." By nature, the congregation are traditionalists. I had to adapt in the beginning. Little by little, I introduced some congregational songs of my own. It

helped that I had a choir. The congregation picked the songs up, and the new melodies became part of the service.

Other *khazanim* might be more eager to strut their cantorial stuff their first time out:

ISP: Your first *Shabbis* here, did you hear melodies you hadn't heard before?

Khazan: Only in the *Kedusha* in *Musaf.* [Sings] *Na-a-ritzkha.* They started their melody right away, and I was thinking, "I have a beautiful melody." So when they finished, I started to sing mine. From then on, every time they sang it, I'd sing mine. Because I wanted to show them what *I* know. But now I don't mind their melody, because we sing the *Kedusha* together.

Many *khazanim* attempt to maintain a balance between old and new repertoires:

Khazan: I think the real art is to be able to introduce new tunes and to be able to keep the old tunes. You've got to be able to keep the old tunes, because if you don't, you're just someone who's coming and changing the landscape.

ISP: So you're talking about a patchwork quilt: you keep some things that are old over here but you change a little bit over there.

Khazan: You've got to work around what you have. You embroider what they already have set up for you.

The clashing of repertoires may be due less to the lure of the familiar or differences in taste than to diverse standards of what is appropriate. One cantor arrived to take up a position at a local synagogue and found the congregation using an unconventional, and to his ear, incongruous tune for *V'khol Ma'aminim* ["And All Believe"]:

Khazan: I listened to it and I said to myself, "Boy, it sounds so familiar to me." All of a sudden, it came to me. "Sure! It's a song from Jewish theatre, *Second Avenue.* It's called "*Oy, Malkaleh*" [sings:]

Oy, Malkaleh, oy, Malkaleh
Vi yikh hob dikh lib
Oy, da, da, da dum

So I'm hearing this: [sings the prayer to the same melody]. So I changed it. During the year we tried three different tunes to "*V'khol Ma'aminim.*" Congregational.

ISP: And what did you wind up with?

Khazan: [sings: slow, cantorial] But when I came, they were singing *Malkaleh.*

Sometimes the impetus to new or changing repertoire comes from the other direction:

It's not uncommon for someone in the congregation to come up to me and say, "You know, when I was a kid, I loved this setting," and I'll say, "Fine, can you get me the music? Let me have a look at it."

In selecting melodies for prayer services, most of the *khazanim* feel there is a line of decorum with regard to source and mood that must not be crossed:

I feel I have laws governing what I'm allowed to do, what I can do. I wouldn't sing *My Yiddishe Mameh* or something that doesn't fit. You have to do it with respect. It's hard, because I have to pick exactly the melody that fits.

Some *khazanim* feel a little freer than others in choosing melodies:

ISP: Are you still learning new melodies?
Khazan: Always.
ISP: From whom?
Khazan: Anything I can catch. Anything that comes my way.
ISP: We're not talking Top 40 records though.
Khazan: Anything. Anything that comes my way. I don't even know what to start from. Whatever is music—classical, rock, pop, anything.
ISP: So some might, say, might hear a theme from Mozart's symphony—
Khazan: Why not?
ISP: —or from a Gershwin operetta—
Khazan: Even better. You know Chris de Burgh? He's a pop singer from the same era as Paul Simon and Simon and Garfunkel and so on. He sang a song [he sings, ta da ta da.] Very famous song. And I started saying, "Wait, this is beautiful." [He sings the same tune, to Hebrew words:]

> Ra'u vanim et gevurato
> Shib'khu v'hodu lishmo
> Umalkhuto beratzon
> Kiblu aleyhem Moshe u'Vney Yisra'el—

Then I swing it, and then I make it more cantorial, and then you have a piece.

The problem with choosing familiar tunes is that, appropriate or not, contexts cross, and the sacred is undercut by the profane:

ISP: Is it better if the congregation doesn't recognize the melody?
Khazan: Much better. But a lot of times, they want to be pleasantly surprised and know the tune so they can join in and sing it. Sometimes when you do that, there are two thoughts that are going to go through a member's mind. One, "Can't the *khazan* find anything else but some regular tune to use?" Or two, "Oh, that's super—I know that too." And he sings it. So, you might attract or detract by singing something that's popular.

Whatever their source, the *khazan* often chooses melodies with congregational singing in mind, so they have to be both attractive and easy to catch on to:

Sometimes you cannot sing the piece in *shul* because it repeats a word sometimes three or four times, and sometimes that's not good for this generation. So you cut it off a little bit.

The *khazanim* usually introduce new melodies for prayers right from the *bima*, with no warning or preamble to the congregation. They watch for the reaction and see if the newcomer is going to fly:

You're going to find that most of the time when you introduce something new, people will not sing or even say the words. They'll just keep quiet and look—some with astonishment, some with a smile, maybe one or two will leave the room [laughs.] But usually, everybody accepts it. Now, if it's a very catchy tune, they'll greet it with open arms. But if it's not a catchy tune, it's a bit difficult, they're *kvetching* a little bit—it's too cantorial, it's long, whatever it is—then you lose them.

The congregation is not shy about giving their reactions directly:

ISP: Do they complain?
Khazan: They do.
ISP: Do they compliment?
Khazan: Definitely.
ISP: You hear it right after service?
Khazan: Oh, they'll let you know right after. And I prefer to hear it right after than hearing it by hearsay.

Sometimes a *khazan* will stand firm on a newly introduced tune, knowing that in the end the congregation will be won over:

And then, sometimes after the first year, some people came and said, "You know, Cantor, I'm not too in love with that new tune" [laughs]. I said, "Give it a chance. We can always discard it, throw it away. But give it a chance. You'll get used to it."

But because there is so much choice, and so many people's tastes and feelings involved, *khazanim* will often just go back and forth between old and new repertoires, making sure all musical interests are represented in the service:

About 10 years ago, I changed one *B'rosh HaShana*, so one day we'd sing one, and the next we'd sing another I'd picked up. [He sings a couple of lines.] Okay, it happens it's a nice, melodious melody, so they picked it up. So from then on, we'd sing the old one for the elderly who've been members there for 40 years, and this new one.

In a way, the *khazan* is a song plugger, trying out new items on his "customers," discarding what flops and incorporating what goes over:

Khazan: When I see a new song doesn't catch, when I feel I'm singing it by myself, I know it's no good. I didn't sell it.
ISP: So you give it two, three, four *Shabatot*.
Khazan: No. I can feel the first *Shabat* that it isn't going over. Or it's tough going on the second. I can feel it hasn't caught on.
ISP: So you'll drop it and get something else.
Khazan: Yes, right away. Take another one. Two years ago, I heard a nice *Adon Olam* and I decided to sing it on *erev Rosh HaShana-Yom Kipur*, because then they hear me cry and a cheerful *Adon Olam* at the end of the service lets them go home happy. So I did it with the choir, and they liked it very much. Everybody came up, "Oh, I like the *Adon Olam!*" I sang it again this year.

The dialogue between *khazan* and congregation is one of collaborators, and the process enriches the musical life of the worshippers:

I'm comfortable enough to change tunes now. With my congregation here, I can change tunes any time I want to, and still go back to the old tunes. Or introduce something new, and when somebody else *davens* when I'm not here, they still continue the same tunes I started. And they don't go back to their original tunes.

New Directions

Individually, the *khazanim* render many services to the community. For example, Cantor Aptowitzer, now retired, talked about a life of dedicated and varied service:

> Years ago, I was teaching day school, I was teaching afternoon school, I was teaching bar mitzvahs, I was leading the choir, and all the duties of a *khazan*, with funerals and *brisn* [circumcisions] and *pidyon ha-ben* [ceremony of Redemption of the First Born] and all these things. And then later on I became a *mohel* [circumciser].

But the *khazan*'s core function remains that of *shli'akh tzibur*. As a group, the *khazanim* feel themselves to be the representatives and guardians of an unbroken tradition that stretches back to the days of Solomon's temple in Jerusalem. But they see the need to keep pace with community tastes, to exercise flexibility in their repertoire and style, as long as they maintain their standards and the basic principles of their art:

> I believe that the *khazanim* have a responsibility to carry the Jewish tradition of the *nusakh* of the music. If you really want to be professional, you want to do the right thing, even if the congregation doesn't know what it is. It's not just to satisfy my congregants, so they will say, "You are a good cantor and we like you." We also have an obligation to educate people to maintain the tradition. But we can do it in a modern style, to incorporate modern "flavours" that will attract people. If you want to make services more attractive, don't take away from the *nusakh*, from the mood, the original. What you do is put more colours in it to make it more alive.

Ottawa *khazanim* regard their office as a foundation stone of Jewish religion, the heart of one of its most important institutions – the prayer service. Their identification with the community is deep, and their sense of responsibility to its continuity through religious practice, heartfelt.

Perhaps it should come as no surprise, therefore, that they are also beginning to extend their function as *shlikhay tzibur*, turning the role outward from their individual synagogues to the community, and from the local Jewish scene to a more cosmopolitan one. The *khazanim* rightly see their sound as iconic— representative of the Jewish community both to itself and to outsiders. They are broadening their role lately by appearing as a performing unit, a kind of "Five *Khazanim*" (a take on the currently popular Carreras-Domingo-Pavarotti "Three Tenors" collaboration). In the past year or so they have sung together at various local functions—the lighting of Channuka candles on Parliament Hill in the presence of the Prime Minister, a synagogue fund-raising concert in Nepean, the annual Jewish Burial Society dinner. To develop and promote these activities, they have formed the Ottawa Association of Cantors (there are counterparts in Toronto and Montreal), and at least one *khazan* has a gleam in his eye for a joint recording. In this era of globalization and the Internet, he feels it's time for the local Jewish community, through its *khazanut*, to make itself known to the wider Jewish world:

I have the picture of how it should look. Things have to pick up, things have to be more attractive, more busy, more doing. There are Jewish people here, a Jewish community, we have beautiful synagogues. We have to put Ottawa on the map.

GLOSSARY OF HEBREW AND YIDDISH TERMS

Adon Olam: the closing prayer of services. One of the favourite texts for cantorial adaptation and composition.

aliya: lit., "going up." The reading during services of the weekly portion of the Torah is divided into segments. Before and after each is read, a member of the congregation is called up to the **bima** to say blessings. This "going up" to bless the Torah segment is called an **aliya**.

Ana adonay hoshiya na: prayer for divine aid. Lit., "... God, help us."

Ashrey: the opening prayer in the morning service.

ba'aley t'fila: plural form of **ba'al t'fila**.

ba'al koreh: reader of the Torah during prayer services.

ba'al t'fila: member of gathering chosen informally to lead prayer services.

Barukh atah adoshem / Elokeynu melekh ha-olam: first line of many Hebrew blessings, lit., "Blessed art Thou, O Lord our God, ruler of the universe." Because in the interviews the blessing was uttered in a non-prayer setting, the Hebrew words referring to God are altered to the forms "**adoshem**" and "**elokeynu**."

beyt hamikdash: Solomon's Holy Temple in Jerusalem.

bima: pulpit, synagogue platform.

birkat ha-khodesh: blessing of the new month.

b'ne'imut: with pleasure, with love.

Borkhu et adonay ham'vorakh: first line of prayer, lit., "Bless God the blessed."

Borukh adonay ham'vorakh l'olam va'ed: Response to preceding line: "Bless God the blessed forever."

B'rosh HaShana: prayer, lit., "On the New Year"

B'yom Ha-Shabat: prayer, lit., "On the day of the Sabbath."

daven: lit., to pray (Yiddish). Anglicized to produce—
> **davened; davener; daveners; davening; davens**

dreydlakh: lit., "little tops" (Yiddish)

drosha: lit., "lesson."

erev: lit., "eve (of)."

Eytz Khayim Hi: prayer said on closing the Torah Ark during the Sabbath morning service, lit., "It is the tree of life."

Hineni: prayer said on **Rosh HaShana** that is usually taken as the **khazan**'s trademark prayer, since it is a petition to God to accept the worshipper's prayer, unworthy though he and it may be.

kadish: prayer of sanctification punctuating prayer services by being said at the end of various sections. Two instances are recited by mourners recently bereaved or on the anniversary of a family member's death (see **Yartzayt**).

kanun: Arab zither-like instrument with 64 strings.

Kedusha: prayer, part of the Shmona Esrey series of prayers.
khatuna: wedding
khazan: cantor, hence—
       khazanim — cantors
       khazanut — the cantorial art
khupa: wedding canopy
kohanim: priests
Kol Nidre: solemn prayer said on the eve of **Yom Kipur**, the Day of Atonement.
koreh: reading, as in **ba'al koreh**, "reader."
krekhtz: tug, catch
kvetching: complaining (Yiddish)
lateh: hole (Yiddish)
Le'dor Va Dor: prayer sung Sabbath morning
Lekha Dodi: prayer said to welcome the Sabbath on Friday evening
leymeleh goylem: inanimate figures (Yiddish)
Mageyn Avot: prayer, lit., "guardian of the fathers."
Malkaleh: little Malka (Yiddish - see **"Oy Malkaleh"**)
Mim'kom'kha: prayer, lit., "from Your place."
mim'kom'kha malkeynu sofia: line in prayer, lit., "from Your place you will appear."
minkha: the daily afternoon prayer service.
minyan: gathering of at least ten adults for prayer.
MiSheBeyrakh: prayer, lit., "He who blessed."
musaf: addition to the morning prayer service.
My Yiddisheh Mameh: sentimental 1920s pop song.
neshumeh: soul
nusakh: **khazanic** mode
nus'kha'ot: plural of **nusakh**
Oy Malkaleh: lit., "Oh, Little Malka," Yiddish theatre song
oy yoy yoys: The syllables "oy" and "yoy," particularly in sequence, express woe or distress in Hebrew and Yiddish.
piyutim: poetic Jewish prayers composed in 9th-century Arab Spain ("**s'pharad**").
Rosh HaShana: New Year
Rosh HaShana-Yom Kipur: New Year - Day of Atonement
rosh khodesh benshn: blessing the first of the new month
sedra: portion of the Torah
Shabat: Sabbath
Shabatot: Sabbaths
Shabbis: Sabbath (Yiddish pronunciation)
Shabbis M'vorkhim: the Sabbath on which the Torah portion **M'vorkhim** is said.
Shalosh Regalim: these are **Sukkot, Shavuot**, and **Peysakh**, the three major pilgrimage festivals when Israelites were obliged to bring sacrifices to the Temple in Jerusalem.
Sheva Brakhot: lit., Seven Blessings, said under the wedding canopy.
shli'akh tzibur: lit., "messenger of the gathering," the **khazan**'s role.
Shma Yisroel: "Hear O Israel," the prayer declaring allegiance to the one God of Israel.
Shma: see **Shma Yisroel**.
shma koleynu: lit., "hear our voices," part of a prayer.

Sh'monah Esrey: lit., Eighteen, a series of prayers forming the core of most prayer services.
shul: synagogue
Sidur: prayer book
Sim Shalom: prayer at the end of the *Shabat* morning service.
spharad: Spain (Heb.)
t'fila: lit., prayer (Heb.)
tikateyvu: Aramaic, "will be written," word from prayer said on Rosh HaShana expressing the belief that on that day God writes the names in His books of those who will live and those who will die in the coming year. On Yom Kipur, the books are sealed. The ten days between the two festivals are a chance for individuals to repent and have their fate rewritten.
t'shuva: repentence
U'n'taneh Tokef: solemn prayer said on Yom Kipur.
V'khol Ma'aminim: prayer, "And all believe."
Yitgadal v'yitkadash shmey raba: first line from the **Kadish** prayer (q.v.): "Glorified and sanctified be God's name."
Yom Kipur: the Day of Atonement
yortzayt: anniversary of a death

Miscellaneous Prayers or Phrases from Prayers:
Adoshem Malakh
Ahava Raba
Ashrey yoshvey beytekha od ye'hale'lukha sela
Ahava raba
Na-a-ritzkha
Shokheyn ad marom v'kadosh shmo
Tehilat adonay y'daber pi
Umalkhuto beratzon
V'anakhnu nevareykh ya me'ata ve'ad olam, haleluya
V'gam es Noakh b'ahava zakharta
Vi'vareykh kol basar sheym kodsho l'olam va'ed
Yakum Purkan
Yishtabakh
Yism'khu
Yism'khu b'malkhutkha

CANTOR ALBERT MAHON AND CANADA'S ANGLICAN PLAINSONG REVIVAL

by
Marcia Ostashewski

Introduction

Healey Willan (1880-1968) has been credited as one of the main figures in the plainsong revival that was at its height in Toronto around the middle of this century. As F.R.C. Clarke writes in his biography of Willan, the composer "had carried the fight nearly single-handed."[1] There is no disputing that Willan was a major promoter of this revival. However, crediting Willan as a single figure for the development of plainsong musical practices carries with it two basic problems. Firstly, not recognizing these musical traditions as collective cultural practices, which involve cantors, choristers and congregational singers, obscures the important roles played by others in the creation and revitalization of these practices. And secondly, it renders the traditions frozen in time and its cantors mere preservers of a musical practice. In this essay, I argue that musical traditions are created and re-created as a fundamental part of the way in which people carve a niche for themselves in a given community.

Some feel that cantillation is a tradition at risk---rapidly changing and possibly disappearing, that it is endangered, largely unrecorded and poorly documented. I counter this argument by focusing on the musical life of cantor Albert Mahon (b.1923), a cantor who sang under Willan's direction for nineteen years at St. Mary Magdalene's Anglican Church in Toronto. He continued to sing as a cantor in that church for nine years afterward, under subsequent musical directors. His changing role as a cantor suggests that, at least within this context, the tradition of cantillation is not dead nor static but alive and growing.

This cantillation tradition, like all traditions, wouldn't exist if it weren't for the collaborative efforts of many.[2] Such collaborative efforts usually entail negotiation and even conflict, between what is practised and what is considered traditional. As Christopher Waterman writes,

> Music is both a species of culture pattern and a mode of human action [...] While it would surely be a mistake to underestimate the "iron hold of culture upon the average individual" (Boas 1932:613), it is also clear that human behavior can never be the "mere execution of the

---

[1] 46, Clarke (1983).
[2] In his subtle recognition of the social ties that condition the performance practices of a symphony orchestra---musicians, instrument-makers, critics, arts councils, music educators---musician and social scientist Howard S. Becker (1982) recognizes the collective and cooperative character of musical production.

148

model" that guides it (Bourdieu 1977). Every realization of musical
norms in performance carries the potential for purposive or unconscious
change, every enactment of tradition opens tradition to transformation
(see, for example, Katz 1970).[3]

This essay explores the relationship between individual human agency and
collective effort in the music-making processes of the Anglican plainsong
cantillation tradition in its contemporary Canadian context. How did cantor Albert
Mahon participate in the tradition while at the same time exercise individual
agency? What did he do that had an impact on how the music was perceived by
everyone else?

To gain an understanding of these musical processes, I will examine the
context of this cantillation tradition that implicates the aesthetic and political
interests of composer Willan, the parishioners of St. Mary Magdalene's, and
cantor Albert Mahon. As we start a new millennium, we find ourselves facing
rapid cultural changes and the widespread deterministic idea that traditions and
cultures are dying away. By understanding the involvement of the many people in
this plainsong cantillation tradition and their individual contributions as part of
something that is growing and changing, it becomes obvious that this cantillation
tradition is not dying, but alive.

This report, too, is situated within its own ethnomusicological context; it is
part of current academic debates regarding issues of representation. Here I wish to
make reference to a book by Bernard Lortat-Jacob, *Sardinian Chronicles,* a series
of vignettes, portraits of individual music-makers and their families.[4] My essay
will attempt the successfulness of Lortat-Jacob's narrative style as well as a more
deliberate discussion and referencing of relevant academic thought.

*   *   *   *   *

The plainsong tradition that the Anglican Church drew upon during the
time of this revival is based on the Plainchant tradition so named in the 8th or 9th
century, and their original Latin texts. The English use of this music is traced to
the coming of Augustine to England in 597. The texts were later translated and
superimposed on their modal melodies for use in Anglican worship services. The
chief characteristic of plainsong, writes Willan, is its freedom of rhythm.[5]

Keith Hamlin, in his Master's thesis on Willan's contributions to the
plainsong tradition, outlines five characteristics of the composer's understanding
for the liturgical role of music. First, the music must not cause any delay or pause
in the liturgical action. Second, the music exists to support and enhance the sacred
texts and not to draw attention away from them. The music should fit to the
words, taking care to make certain the words are understandable when sung.

[3] 7-8, Waterman (1990).
[4] Lortat-Jacob, Bernard (1995). *Sardinian chronicles.* Chicago: University of Chicago Press.
[5] Willan (1963).

Third, liturgical music must be beautiful and refined. When asked to define this aesthetic, Willan replied,

> We all like beautiful things, and religion is a beautiful thing. Music properly used helps to make it more beautiful. People are looking for beauty everywhere, and in the Church particularly...[6]

Fourth, Willan believed liturgical music should be unique to its task, "essentially different from secular music, no matter how beautiful or magnificent this may be."[7] And fifth, the main goal of liturgical music is to encourage congregational participation.[8]

Ritual choir, Church of St.Mary Magdalene, Toronto, circa 1949. Albert Mahon shown front row, middle (third from left), with Dr.Healey Willan, front row, far right (fifth from left). Photo courtesy of Albert Mahon.

Albert Mahon has confirmed that Willan's adaptations of the chants and melodies made the texts clearer, the music easier to follow, and the declamatory rhythm more logical and sensible. Willan's adaptations and plainsong compositions affected more than just Mahon and the Ritual Choir that responded

---

[6] 99, Hamlin (1983). When I asked cantor Albert Mahon, in similar conversation, to define what he considered to be beautiful, he replied in much the same manner as Willan. Mahon said that the music must emphasize the meaning of the text and the natural rhythm of the words so that the words can be easily understood.

[7] 100, Hamlin (1983).

[8] 99-100, Hamlin (1983).

in services. A performance review published in the *Globe* newspaper substantiated Willan's influence on congregational singing. The following was written the day after the Gregorian Association in St. Mary Magdalene's Church held its fifth annual festival:

> ...interesting by-product of the close attention to liturgical quality the association has encouraged. That was that the congregation, especially the young churchmen in it, sang with accurate intonation, unaffected clear tone and diction worthy of a church rite.
>
> Many non-churchmen were in the congregation, which was not surprising in view of the fact that plainchant, particularly when adapted for the Anglican rite, involves the question of exact relation of sound and meaning...For the first time, the association made it possible to procure the order of service with music, which was immensely valuable in congregational participation, and following the religious and artistic intent. It was a music-reading set of worshippers.
>
> The fauxbourdons for the Magnificat and the Nunc Dimittis were written by Dr. Willan expressly for this service, and the gallery choir again showed itself a particularly understanding exponent of the Willan music.[9]

Twenty years later, in a newsletter published by the Gregorian Association of Canada, Albert Mahon quoted from a letter he received from a parishioner who heard Holy Week services performed by him and St. Mary Magdalene's Ritual Choir. In the letter, the parishioner had written how grateful he was that the cantor and choir performed in his church, how it enriched his religious and musical experience.[10]

The Composite Role of Cantor Albert Mahon

Albert Mahon's involvement in the plainsong tradition was not limited to singing during services. His main role as a cantor led him to make many other contributions, musical and non-musical, to the plainsong revival movement. He was a founding member and Musical Director of Canada's Gregorian Association, a central organization in the plainsong or plainchant revival.[11] As he wrote in a letter to Dr. Klymasz at the Canadian Museum of Civilization, "during my twenty-eight years as cantor at St. Mary Magdalene's the 'job' had evolved."[12]

In 1998 and again in 1999 I arranged to interview Mr. Mahon, with the hope of gaining a better understanding of his role in the Anglican Plainsong Revival in Toronto. We agreed that I would come speak with him in his home, where he keeps recordings, transcriptions and books from his days of being a

---

[9] Pearl McCarthy (1955)

[10] Mahon (1983).

[11] This organization was modelled after its English counterpart. See 50, Hamlin (1983).

[12] Written in a letter, dated 20 January 1998, to Dr. R. Klymasz at the Canadian Museum of Civilization.

cantor. When I entered his home in a spacious Yonge Street condominium complex in the northern part of Toronto, I was welcomed warmly and sincerely by both Albert and his wife Anne. We quickly went into Albert's office, where there was also a stereo set up and a comfy couch for me to sit on. Anne offered me a glass of water, which I gratefully took and drank while Albert played for me--- from his private recording collection, nowhere reproduced---an example of the music we would soon discuss. With their relaxed, kind and quiet manner, both Mr. and Mrs. Mahon also conveyed a sense of great seriousness for what was about to happen.

Mr. Mahon told me that his first experience with plainsong was during his childhood. "I joined the St. Alphege Church choir in South London at the age of seven. This was also where I performed my first solo, singing in the Passion of St. Matthew. During the time I spent with this choir, I learned music by rote. I learned that the words were of primary importance---the music was a vehicle for the language."

Since Mr. Mahon didn't seem very interested in continuing a discussion of personal history, I asked him how it was he came to sing at St. Mary Magdalene's in Toronto. "Well," he replied, "after I'd come home from the war, in 1945, I met my wife, Anne. We married three years later, in 1948. Three months after that, we immigrated to Canada. At this time, our parish priest in England was aware we were moving. He did some research, and recommended we attend St. Mary Magdalene's once we reached Toronto. He said it would be similar to our church in England, in terms of the music that was sung. We decided to stay at St. Mary Magdalene's after our first visit, because the parishioners and atmosphere were so welcoming and warm---though we did spend a few weeks afterward visiting other parishes." The Mahons soon befriended Malcolm Finch, who was a cantor in the parish. Within a few weeks of joining the parish, Albert was invited by Musical Director Willan to join the Ritual Choir and soon asked to become a cantor. This was the beginning of Mahon's twenty-eight-year tenure as cantor at St. Mary Magdalene's, the first nineteen of which were spent under the direction of Dr. Willan.

Mahon's basic role as a cantor was to lead plainsong during services. "I would begin by intoning the verse. Then the choir and congregation would follow. I had to be sure that my intonation was very clear so the melody would be easy to follow. I had to be sure to declamate clearly and sensibly, to follow the natural rhythm of the text." He repeated to me emphatically, "The words are of utmost importance."

Mahon took liberties in terms of stressing what he considered to be the most important words of the text. He said to me, "Of course, these words are self-evident. And these decisions also came about as a result of the many discussions and conversations with Dr. Willan." By making these choices, Mr. Mahon was emphasizing his own aesthetics and religious beliefs. Mahon's selective strategies, in this regard, had a significant effect on performance practices when one considers that only one verse was written directly underneath the melody in the service book. He had to fit the remaining verses to the melody. His interpretations were subsequently learned and reproduced by others within the parish.

Mahon's own directorial activities also played a considerable role in the revival of plainsong. Because the same music was repeated year after year, Mahon quickly became familiar with the music and texts. He gradually began to take on the job of rehearsing the Ritual Choir when Dr. Willan was absent. He also rehearsed the choir during the summers, when Dr. Willan was away from Toronto. (During the summers the Ritual Choir performed the entire Mass in plainsong.) Throughout the year, the choir would often go out together socially after rehearsals. They enjoyed many activities together, including regular evenings of madrigal singing.

Relating another directorial position he took upon himself, Mr. Mahon told me that, "At one point, Dr. Willan told me the nuns, who lived next to the Parish, asked him for some direction in their singing. Dr. Willan asked me to lead them in a few rehearsals since he was too busy at the time." Mr. Mahon explained that the Order of the Sisters of the Church had a convent on property neighbouring St. Mary Magdalene's.[13]

"And what was your response?" I asked.

"Well I did it, of course."

In addition to the above, Mr. Mahon's work as archivist and copyist was also significant. He worked long hours to help in the production of service books that were circulated for use amongst the choirs and congregation. He transcribed and planned music that was sung by the Ritual and Gregorian Association Choirs. He hand-copied music that Dr. Willan had tailored to specific services, then mimeographed copies for church members to use. "And in those days," said Mr. Mahon, "we didn't have these fancy, computerized xerox machines. I did it all, one by one, on an old mimeograph machine. Do you know what that is?" I assured him I knew with a nod of my head.

Because of his singing experience as cantor at St. Mary Magdalene's, Mahon soon became known as an expert in his field. In 1962, the newspaper of the American Guild of Organists, *The Diapason,* asked Mahon to review a book of plainsong notation. Mr. Mahon had little good to say of this particular

---

[13] The convent has since burned down; the land has been converted into a park named for Healey Willan.

adaptation of the chants.[14] "I don't really know why they asked me to write the thing, after all, I was no expert. But it was atrocious! I mean, I feel bad now--- which is why I don't like to talk about it, but it was a terrible book. The text didn't seem at all to fit with the music!" His experience with Dr. Willan's adaptations made Mahon critical of notation that did not fit the text well, confused the words, or was generally not easy for the congregation to read.

Mr. Mahon had an effect on Healey Willan as well. In the program for the service of Albert and Anne's recent fiftieth wedding anniversary celebration, Mr. Mahon wrote an anecdote of which many parishioners, choir and community members have heard a version.

> Early in 1963, Dr. Willan and I were having our customary discussion during the hour prior to Friday-night rehearsal. At one point, he opened his battered, brown attaché case and from it pulled out a manuscript, the Missa Brevis No. 14, which he slid along the desk towards me. "Well, here it is old man" he said, (and here, I think he used the word "last," but it could have been "latest one") "the last one." It indeed was the last mass he wrote.

> Dr. Willan then began opening his mail which had accumulated at the church during the past week. He obviously expected me to remark on the music, however, I was not about to make an idiot of myself with some asinine comment. Then I noticed that the manuscript showed only a number. I knew that he had given a name to all his masses written after number 6, so, cleverly avoiding any mention of the music, I said, "Doctor, you haven't given this one a name." "Mmmm...," he said, "you're right. I have not, have I?"

> After he had given the matter some thought he said, "You went to St. Alphege, didn't you?" And he reminisced about how he had taken an area rehearsal there, for affiliated choirs of the Gregorian Association, preparing for the annual festival service in St. Paul's Cathedral in 1910. And how, at that very service, he had met the man with whom, eleven years later, he would begin something momentous, at St. Mary Magdalene's in Toronto. That man was by then the vicar of the church, Fr. Hiscocks.

> He continued in that vein for some time. I had heard it all before, but I didn't mind. I found it fascinating, as always. He then came back to the matter at hand, "Mmmm...St. Alphege..." he murmured again. He reached out, pulled the manuscript back to him, took his fountain pen, and, across the cover, diagonally, he wrote the title, "St. Alphege." "There you are!" he said.

St. Alphege was, as I wrote earlier in this essay, the parish where Albert began to sing plainsong as a child. As Willan's biographer Clarke acknowledges, this dedication is a clear demonstration of Willan's respect for Mahon.[15]

---

[14] The book was written by Reverend Winfred Douglas, and published in 1952. *The Monastic Diurnal Noted*. Kenosha, Wisconsin: St. Mary's Convent.
[15] 227, Clarke (1983).

154

After Willan died, Giles Bryant held the position of Musical Director for seven years at St. Mary Magdalene's, and then a new Musical Director was hired. This new director's musical style was not appreciated by Albert and some other choir members. In fact, Albert felt the new musical style was in such great conflict with that of Willan that he eventually left the choir and St. Mary Magdalene's Parish. Albert bases his understanding of Willan's directorial intentions on a story Willan told him soon after they started working together. Willan told Albert that, when he became the Musical Director at St. Mary Magdalene's in 1921, two primary initiatives guided his work: that plainsong be accompanied so that the congregation would have an easier task in following along, and also that it be sung in English so that it would be intelligible and easily understood by the general congregation. Albert perceived several decisions made by the Musical Director to be incongruent with the intentions of Dr. Willan including the removal of organ accompaniment from plainsong singing in the church. Albert Mahon's job as cantor at St. Mary Magdalene's, never a paid position, ended over what amounts to a personal difference of opinion. Over the next several months, a consensus of dissatisfaction developed among many other choir members. Many of them eventually left the choir as well.

Mahon's important role in the plainsong revival, and the religious community it was part of, did not end with his appointment at St. Mary Magdalene's. For instance, in 1980 on the centenary of Willan's birth, Mahon became the Musical Director of the Gregorian Association and played a major part in the resurrection of its choir. In honour of the composer's centennial, the choir produced a recording of Willan's music.[16] Albert Mahon is credited as the producer of this recording. His leading role as an interventionist and facilitator is Mahon's primary contribution to Canada's Anglican plainsong cantillation tradition.

BIBLIOGRAPHY

Becker, Howard S. 1982. *Art Worlds*. Berkeley: University of California Press.
Clarke, F.R.C. 1983. *Healey Willan: Life and Music*. Toronto: University of Toronto Press.
Douglas, Rev. Winfred. 1952. *The Monastic Diurnal Noted*. Kenosha, Wisconsin: St. Mary's Convent.
Hamlin, Keith Allan. 1979. *The Plainsong of Healey Willan: A Study of Dr. Willan's Role in the Restoration of Plainsong to the Worship of the Anglican Church*. (master's thesis; University of Trinity College Toronto School of Theology, University of Toronto)

[16] For a full citation of this LP recording, see end.

Mahon, Albert. 1983. "Meditation of the Passion," in *Plainsong Notes: Newsletter of the Gregorian Association of Canada*. Mahon, K. (ed.). Number 2, March.

McCarthy, Pearl. 1955. "Plainchant Fine: Gregorian Association Advances Musical Art," in the *Globe*. (from a facsimile; complete citation not available)

Waterman, Christoper. 1990. *Juju: A Social History and Ethnography of an African Popular Music*. Chicago: University of Chicago Press.

Willan, Healey. 1963. "Plainsong: The Earliest Song of the Church," in *CanadianChurchman: The National Paper of the Anglican Church of Canada*. Vol. 90, No. 7 July-August.

INTERVIEWS

Albert Mahon (conducted by the author) 18 October 1999, 26 November 1998, 22 June 1998.

DISCOGRAPHY

Willan, Healey. [1977?]. *Healey Willan: a centennial celebration*. (Choir of the Gregorian Association of Canada; Giles Bryant, conductor; John Gartshore, organist; Albert Mahon, musical director.) Toronto: Anglican Book Centre. ABC-8002.

Albert and Anne Mahon on the occasion of their fiftieth wedding anniversary in Toronto. Photo courtesy of Albert Mahon.

At first I did not know what it was. At intervals the eight men in the chancel choir, or sometimes Dwyer alone, would utter what sounded like speech of a special eloquence, every word clearly to be heard, but observing a discipline that was musical, in that there was no hint of anything that was colloquial, but not like any music I had met with in my, by this time, fairly good acquaintance with music. My idea of church music at its highest was Bach, but Bach at his most reverent is still intended for performance. This music was addressed to God, not as performance, but as the most intimate and devout communication. It was a form of speech fit for the ear of the Highest.

Robertson Davies, *The Cunning Man* (1994)

Any man or boy may rise for his chant; anywhere from five to twenty individuals rise in succession. After a short speech of thanksgiving, the man chants to choral accompaniment as follows: a male chorus reiterates yells, sliding downward in scale; then it holds a tone and continues with a backround of sharp *heh-heh* to the singer's chanting. The women keep time with hand clapping. Two yells conclude the chant.

Gertrude P. Kurath, "Four Sacred Ceremonies"
from Six Nations Reserve, Ontario, 1968

INTRODUCTION TO THE PRECENTOR'S COMPANION[*]

I. THE EIGHT TONES

At the Mystical Supper, our Lord Jesus Christ and His disciples chanted psalms together, thus initiating Christian liturgical chant. By His own sublime example the Savior sanctified the exclusive use of vocal music (i.e., music without instrumental accompaniment) during the divine services. The holy apostles and their immediate followers made hymnody an indispensable aspect of Christian gatherings and worship services.

In his epistles to the Ephesians and Colossians (Eph. 5: 19; Col. 3: 16), the holy Apostle Paul urged Christians to find inspiration in the singing of psalms, hymns and spiritual songs. In the Acts of the Apostles it is related that when the Apostles Peter and John were released from prison, all the assembled Christians together, with one accord, sang the prayer of thanksgiving: "O Master, Thou art our God, Who hast made heaven and earth..." (Acts 4: 23-30).

Saint Ignatius the God-bearer, the disciple of the holy evangelist John the Theologian, introduced antiphonal singing to the churches of Antioch.

The musical practice of the early centuries of Christianity, according to the testimony of writers of that period (Philo [1st cent.] and Tertullian [2nd cent.] resulted in different forms of execution and a definite type of liturgical singing which, by the 3rd century, had already begun to crystallize into eight tones. The early Christians chanted either all together, congregationally, or in individual groups, when, for example, the singing of the men alternated with that of the women. Sometimes a single chanter sang alone, or responsorially with the people. The 4th century was a time of intense musical activity as a result of the appearance of the various heresies. To combat these, the holy fathers - Basil the Great (329-379), John Chrysostom (347-407), Ephraim the Syrian (+373), Athanasius the Great (296-373) and Ambrose of Milan (373-397) - used hymnody as one of the most powerful means of influencing the people against the heretics. Canon 15 of the Council of Laodicea (364), concerning the introduction of chanters and readers as persons responsible for the divine services, was enacted at this time. In this period chanting according to a system of eight tones had not yet taken on a definitive form, but the existence of tones by the end of the 4th century is beyond

---

[*] Excerpted with permission from Isaac Lambertsen's translation from Russian, "The Forewords & Introduction to the Third Edition of *The Church Singer's Companion"* [*Sputnik psalomshchnika*, 3rd ed., St. Petersburg, 1916], New York, 1994.

doubt, since Saint Pambo (+399) mentions them in a discussion with one of his disciples.

A more definite arrangement of singing according to tones (or modes) was made in the 5th century, although it had not yet achieved wide currency and did not have a set number of tones. Paul of Nitria, who lived early in the 5th century, mentions that the churches of Alexandria and Constantinople chanted using tones (or modes), without, however, indicating the number of tones. Saint Anatolius, Patriarch of Constantinople (+458), already composed the resurrectional stichera known as Anatolian, to eight definite tones. His contemporary, Saint Romanus the Melodist, composed kontakia and oikoi in eight tones. James, Bishop of Edessa (+710), also composed hymns for Palm Sunday in eight tones. The ultimate regulation of the tonal chanting of the Eastern Church took place in the 8th century, thanks to the labors of the great hymnographer Saint John of Damascus, who collected the hymnodic material produced by past ecclesiastical hymnographers and created from it an orderly, musically based system of eight tones, which became known as the Octoechos. The Octoechos was accepted and entered the practice of all the Eastern Churches as the fundamental law of liturgical chanting, uniting the Churches and providing stability and definition to church hymnody. The 10th century was a time during which the eight-tone system of the Eastern Church flourished. The chanting of the Byzantine Greeks was particularly glorious. It is not without reason that tradition has preserved the words of our forefathers, the emissaries of the holy Prince Vladimir, who, after they had listened to the divine services in Constantinople's Church of the Holy Wisdom, said: "When we were in the church of the Greeks, we knew not whether we were in heaven or on earth." After the baptism of the holy Prince Vladimir of Russia, equal of the apostles, the Russian people were converted to the Orthodox Christian Faith by the Church of Constantinople, and together with the Faith they also received the music used in the Byzantine Church, i.e., the eight-tone system of chanting which had been devised by Saint John of Damascus and which he expressed by means of non-linear symbols, or neumes. Russian church singers first learned chanting in eight tones under the direction of Greek and Bulgarian chanters who had come to Russia; but afterwards they formed their own Russian schools of chant, which produced well-trained chanters. Among the chanters' schools those of Novgorod were from of old the most famous. The resolution of the Russian Council of Vladimir (1274) that "laymen neither read the epistle, nor chant the prokeimenon, nor enter the sanctuary," but that these things be done by specially ordained persons, indicates that at that time the Church of Russia was experiencing no particular lack of trained singers. Before long, the chanters of the Church of Russia had mastered the whole body of liturgical music and were displaying an independent creativity. By the 11th century, our forefathers had not only produced their own church music compositions, following the same monodic form in which hymnody was transmitted to us from the East, but even their own non-linear notational system, the Znamenny or hook-notation. Stichera composed by Russian hymnographers for Russian saints - Theodosius of the Caves (+1095), the holy Princes Boris and Gleb (+1072), and the commemoration of the Translation of the Relics of Saint Nicholas to Bari (1087) - may be found in the most ancient notated books, and in the perfection of the technique of the shaping of the Znamenny melodies in no way differ from the models created by the Greek masters.

II. THE CHANT SYSTEM

The original chant of the Church of Russia, preserved in manuscripts dating from as early as the 11th and 12th centuries, is known as the **"Great Znamenny Chant."** This name was derived from the non-linear neumes which are used to express it in its original, monodic form. In its artfulness and the well-balanced technical disposition of its melodies (which are composed of characteristic motifs and long, set phrases, corresponding to the text of the hymns), the Znamenny Chant is the most developed, the most polished of the chant systems. It is quite expansive, yet not so much that it hides and obscures the meaning of the text; it is remarkably pliant in its turns of melodic phrase, yet is at the same time elevated and majestic. The main and essential characteristic of the Great Znamenny Chant is its total dispassion and even a certain severity which imparts to it a beauty which is particularly exalted and spiritually inspired. The complex melodic patterns of the chant refined by centuries of religious thought are woven in smooth modulations, almost lacelike in their rare proportion and expressive beauty. The Znamenny Chant produces the same powerful impression in both choral settings and monodic, unison chanting. It is the most extensive as regards the number of hymns set to it. These include stichera for all eight tones (for "Lord, I have cried...", the aposticha, litia, the evangelical stichera, etc.), heirmoi, troparia, megalynaria, and many other hymns from the Octoechos and elsewhere. From the 11th through the 17th centuries there were, in practice, no other chant systems besides the Znamenny. Thus, over the course of nearly seven hundred years, the melodies of the Great Znamenny Chant were the only chants which adorned the Russian Orthodox kliros. At the end of the 16th century, the Great Znamenny Chant underwent modification and simplification. This modification and simplification of the chant took place independently in both the north and the south of Russia. In the north, the abbreviated form of the Znamenny Chant became known as the **"Little Znamenny Chant,"** while in the south it became known as the **Kievan**. The difference between the Little Znamenny Chant and the Kievan lies, in the first place, in that the former, which developed in the north, is outwardly bland, colorless and melancholy, whereas the latter, which developed in the south, is clear, expressive and melodic; and, in the second place, in that the vocal phrasings of the Kievan Chant are structurally distinguished more by decisive and bold movements than the phrases of the Little Znamenny Chant, which are rich neither in original movements or tonal content; and in the third place, in that the number of hymns set to the Kievan Chant is quite extensive, while those of the Little Znamenny Chant are few in number ("Virgin Theotokos, rejoice...", "To thee, the champion leader...", "O Lord of hosts, be with us...", et al.). The advantages of the Kievan Chant were the reason why it completely eclipsed the Little Znamenny Chant and became the chant form most widely utilized. Hymns chanted to Kievan Chant melodies include many from the Octoechos ("Lord, I have cried...", "God is the Lord...", the prokeimena, heirmoi, etc.) and from other sources ("Glory...The only-begotten...", "Blessed is the man...", "O gladsome Light...", the megalynaria, "Behold, the Bridegroom...", "Let all human flesh keep silent...", "Thy bridal-chamber...", "A mercy of peace...", et al.). In Kievan Chant, the latter have a characteristic peculiarity: words are repeated, and in many cases their melodies exhibit a symmetrical rhythm which bears witness to the influence of Western music from Galicia and Poland. In the second half of the 17th century, other chant systems, originating in the Christian lands of Bulgaria and Greece, joined the Znamenny and Kievan chants.

One must not confuse the **Greek Chant** with the ancient Byzantine eight tones which were absorbed by the Russians after their conversion to Christianity and which, after adaptation to the Russian ear, developed into the Great Znamenny Chant. The Greek Chant developed in Greece after the fall of the Byzantine Empire (conquered by the Turks in 1453), and was brought to Russia in part by itinerant Greek chanters, and in part through the Greek notated books obtained by Patriarch Niken (1652-1666). It is well known that Tsar Alexis Mikhailovich (1645-1676), in order that his own royal choir might learn Greek chanting, wrote to Greece for the Greek deacon Meletius, which is why Greek Chant was at first sometimes referred to as the "Meletian Version." Greek Chant is distinguished by its triumphal liveliness and freshness of melody, which express a joyful religious sensibility. The melodies of the Greek Chant are light, mobile and easily accessible, although they do not follow melodic phrases strictly.

Greek Chant is used when we sing hymns from the Octoechos ("God is the Lord...", heirmoi) and from elsewhere ("Bless the Lord, O my soul...", the hierarchal "It is truly meet...", "All creation rejoiceth in thee...", the rapid "Christ is risen...", "Let my prayer be set forth..." et al.). The Greek Chant melodies for the singing of the resurrectional troparia from the Octoechos serve as the model for the singing of all troparia and kontakia.

The **Bulgarian Chant** was borrowed by the Church of Russia at about the same time as it borrowed the Greek Chant. It was originally brought into Russia by singers of the brotherhoods of southwestern Russia in the mid-17th century. Later, other manuscripts were obtained from Bulgaria when Patriarch Nikon was conducting his correction of the liturgical books. In their magnificence, their smooth and undulating movement and abundance of sounds, the melodies of the Bulgarian Chant have much in common with the melodies of the Great Znamenny Chant. The essential difference between these chant forms lies, in the first place, in the fact that the melodies of the Bulgarian Chant have a very limited number of melodic phrases, which are repeated interchangeably with literal precision, while in the Great Znamenny Chant a multiplicity of phrases is continually varied, adapting themselves to the text; and in the second place, in that the melodies of the Bulgarian Chant lack the austerity of the Great Znamenny Chant. The mood of the melodies of the Bulgarian Chant is either sad and solemn ("The noble Joseph...") or joyous and solemn ("Today the Virgin..."). In artistic dignity, the Bulgarian Chant surpasses both the Kievan and Greek Chants. At the present time, there exist printed settings of Bulgarian Chant for the following hymns: "Now the powers of heaven..." (in Tone I), "It is truly meet..." (in Tone I), "Today the Virgin..." (in Tone III), "Having fallen asleep in the flesh..." (in Tone III), "The noble Joseph..." (in Tone II), and "Thee Who dost clothe the heavens..." (in Tone V). In the older anthologies "God is the Lord..." in the eight tones and "Come, let us bless the ever-memorable Joseph..." have been preserved. At the present time, we would have non conception of this chant form were it not for these hymns.

A simplified and abbreviated form of the Kievan, Greek and Bulgarian Chants is known as the Usual Chant *[Obikhod]*. There exist three main forms of the Usual Chant: 1) the Kievan, or South Russian version, which was printed in the anthology of the priest Ablamsky; 2) the Petrograd, or Court version, arranged for four voices in the anthologies of Alexis L'vov and Nicholas Bakhemetev; and 3) the Muscovite version, printed in *The Cycle of Church Hymns Sung According to the Chant of the Diocese of Moscow*. The ordinary Moscow Chant, which is set forth in the three parts of *The Cycle* (All-night Vigil, the Irmologion, and the Lenten Triodion), was set down and published in quadratic (square) notation in the late 19th century by the Society of Lovers of Church Music, founded by Bishop Ambrose, then a vicar-bishop of the Diocese of Moscow, subsequently Archbishop of Kharkov. Each locality has its own ordinary local chant containing particular local variants. Lately, ordinary local chants written down by various individuals have begun to appear in printed editions. Among those who have collected local chants are Raisky in the Ufa Province, Konevsky in the Nizhegorodsky Province, Zinoviev in the Yaroslavl' Province, and others.

III. THE SHORTCOMINGS OF KLIROS CHANTING

The original form of Russian church singing was monodic. This is testified to not only by historical information, but also by all surviving ancient church manuscripts notated for singing, which only contain music for a single voice. Polyphonic choral singing, also known as "part-singing," was introduced to the kliros of the Church of Russia only in the 17th century, when the Russian ecclesiastical authorities, basing themselves on the fact that the Church's typicon gives no indication with regard to any particular characteristic of liturgical singing, requiring only that it be "orderly and melodious," and that the Church Universal, during the reign of Emperor Justinian (527-565), blessed the use in the Church of the Holy Wisdom of all Orthodox Christian chants, wherever they existed, addressed to the Eastern patriarchs the question of introducing polyphonic choral singing into kliros practice; and in 1668, they received official letters from the patriarchs permitting this.

At the present time, we are permitted, when chanting the liturgical services of the Russian Orthodox Church, to sing not only polyphonic settings of ancient chants, but also the free religious compositions of Russian composers, with the indispensable condition, however, that their compositions not depart from the particular type of liturgical hymnody created by the Orthodox Church, the characteristics of which are: seriousness, sincerity, restraint, modesty, inner fervour and intimacy.

The passion for choral singing which, from the time of the influx of Italian composers into Russia (Araja, Galuppi, Sarti, et al.), achieved particular maturity and brilliance, shifted basic Russian Church music to a secondary position, and it gradually began to be forgotten, the first position being occupied by Italianate compositions which often not only lacked anything in common with the established form of liturgical singing, but no longer corresponded even externally with the texts of the hymns, which were quite mechanically bent to fit the music, with unnecessary repetition of individual words. Such peculiarities were characteristic not only of the Italian maestros, who neither understood nor wished to understand the meaning of the Slavonic sacred texts, but also of the compositions of their Russian disciples, who imitated their teachers in every respect and through their activity created the period known as the "Era of the Concerto" (1736-1825). Representatives of the "Era of the Concerto" were profoundly ignorant of fundamental Russian church singing, and occupied themselves exclusively with the writing and performance of their own free compositions during the divine services. The abnormality of the direction taken in church music was very well understood by the Russian composer Dmitri Bortnyansky (1725-1828), who, contrary to the prevailing Italianate trend, turned again to the forgotten ancient chants and occupied himself with providing choral settings for them. Yet in his compositions even Bortnyansky did not entirely renounce the deeply rooted Italian tendency. After Bortnyansky, history provided us with a whole series of Slavic Russian composers who labored successfully to adapt the fundamental Russian church singing for choral performance. By their compositions, Turchaninov, L'vov, Glinka, Potulov, L'vovsky, Smolensky and others gradually cleansed choral liturgical singing of the alien "Italianate part-singing" of the "Era of the Concerto."

A full cleansing of church singing from foreign part-singing has, however, not been achieved even to the present day, since the taste for the pseudo-church music which was artificially planted in Russia by Italians has put down even deeper roots than one might have assumed. The literature dealing with church music which has been published up to this day is distinguished, in the majority of cases, by an unforgivable lack of principle and the complete lack of any churchly spirit, in consequence of which the masses of the people, nurtured on it, have ultimately lost the ability to understand and value proper Russian church singing. Despite the rapid growth of the number of church choirs, the perfection of church singing is noticeable only in the excellence of vocal technique; the attempt at specialization in the province of ecclesiastical art is completely lacking even among those who lead the chanting on kliros. It is now quite common to encounter choir directors and precentors who adhere to any course in chant because they have a very vague understanding of the ancient chants of the Church.

While he was still archbishop in Pskov, His Eminence, Archbishop Arsenius of Novgorod & Starorussk, a well-known lover of good order and majesty in the Church, turned his attention to the chaos which had infected the church kliros and summoned the teachers of church singing in Pskov to attend a conference. In Novgorod, two such conferences were organized - in 1911 and 1913. In a speech addressed to the teachers of church music at the First Novgorod Conference, His Eminence outlined the contemporary state of church singing in the following vivid colors:

"At the present time, in the majority of cases, church singing is presented by precentors who have received the poorest training. The usual contingent of candidates for the position of precentor are individuals expelled from seminaries 'for poor performance, boisterous conduct, or for exceeding the age limitation'. They most often view their task from the point of view of a job which earns them a piece of bread. And because there is a lack of suitable candidates for precentors' positions, they are often filled by these unworthy men. It would be better for the Church and the clergy, whenever there is no worthy candidate for the precentor's position, to make do with a volunteer singer. I repeat: within the diocese, as regards the precentors, the task of chanting is, generally speaking, being performed by untrained persons.

"For this reason, there are places where amateurs are replacing the precentors. I must ask that, more often than not, they are guided by love for their task. They want to satisfy the demands of the people, who want to listen to choral singing in their churches. I think that you know this type of amateur very well. Often expelled from seminaries themselves, they organize their own choirs and become masters of the kliros. They hold themselves in high esteem and sometimes refuse to consider the entirely appropriate desires of the priest in regard to the singing. They are not satisfied with simple melodies, but try to keep up with the city choirs, sharing scores with them. Their idea is to see how much they can get away with in church. The hymns which they perform, though perhaps well harmonized, have so ruined the taste of the people that it is painful and sad even to speak of it.

"What is the result of the fact that church singing is presented by such untrained precentors and these amateur choir directors?

"Church singing, from the musical and, more importantly, from the liturgical point of view, does not satisfy the most modest requirements. These distorters of church singing do not understand that church singing is an integral part of the divine service, that in it the soul pours itself out, entreating, glorifying and giving thanks to God.

"They think of one thing only - producing an effect. They are in church to make an effect by means of their own artistic (but in actuality, illiterate) music. For them it is absolutely necessary to perform complicated pieces. They will not sing anything "simple", but only the abstruse. They leave what is "simple" for the left kliros to sing, or to an old chanter, as though it were (in their ignorant opinion) lacking in any significance.

"In this the objective of the divine services, which consists of teaching the Faith and making the people steadfast in the Faith, is forgotten. This objective is attained by singing the stichera and other church hymns, which are the precious treasure of our divine services and their spiritual adornment. Take the Octoechos and the Triodia, and examine all the stichera which form part of the services for the main feasts and the commemorations of the sacred events from the history of Christianity, and you will see that this is a rich treasure bequeathed to us by the Greek Church through its great hierarchs, the preservers of its dogmas and traditions, the artistic creators of its liturgical rites. The people love to sing, read and listen to them, because from them the soul of the people draws forth the teaching of the principal dogmas of the Christian Faith! In the early centuries of Christianity, these hymns served as the principal arsenal in the struggle against the false teachings of the heretics, who also used the singing of hymns and songs at their prayer meetings as a way of spreading their doctrines among the people. Can we in our times neglect these powerful means in the task of spreading the Faith and repelling all manner of sectarian assaults? Yet we see just such a neglect in the persons of all the amateur choir directors, who consider themselves called to perform all manner of polyphonic compositions, ignoring what is truly edifying and salvific. They do not consider it necessary to be corrected by the Church's typicon, and each makes up whatever order of service strikes his fancy. Unfortunately, such an ignorant choir director considers it his absolute right to dominate the kliros.

"We have forgotten the very basis of church singing - the eight tones. Do we need to be told how gradually the distinct character of the hymnody of the Christian Church was worked out? When Christianity was only beginning to spread, freedom with regard to church singing was dominant in the Church. In various places one could hear, on a par with purely Christian chants, those borrowed from the Jews and pagans. This diversity in church hymnody ended with Saint John of Damascus, who introduced the eight tones of the Church. And we, who have received this inheritance from the holy father, must cherish it. Moreover, we have forgotten the beauty of the Znamenny, Bulgarian and Greek chants, which have been handed down to us.

"The supreme ecclesiastical authority, in the person of the Most Holy Synod, and individual diocesan bishops, have, since early in the 19th century, opposed and striven in vain against this decline in church singing. However, the measures taken by the Most Holy Synod to drive from the churches the "concerto"- style of music which is alien to the divine services have not achieved their goal. Church singing continues its constant decline. The decline in church singing in Russia is mirrored by the analogous decline in iconography. There was a time when the painting of icons of the Savior, the Mother of God and the saints was approached with prayer and fasting, when the iconographers did not look upon their work as a mere profession. Thus, the iconography of churches of the 12th- 16th centuries has a special character. It is true that in the figures painted in that time there is no refinement or strict adherence to the laws of proportion, yet they have one advantage which infinitely elevates ancient iconography above that which is practiced today: they bear the seal of holiness. Why do we now, during a time of return to the lost ideal of iconography, seek out ancient icons in all the churches? Why do we value the Church of the Holy Wisdom, the Church of the

Savior on Nereditsy? Because the art they contain belongs to an era when they looked upon iconography as a spiritual struggle, a holy work.

"Beginning with the 17th century, when we directed our gaze toward the West, we began to change in every aspect. When foreign influences among us intensified, our entire style of life was altered: our art changed, as did our liturgical singing. At the time of the introduction of Christianity among us, a hymnody was heard in our churches which was felt by the heart: a sincere, and therefore edifying hymnody. With the intensification of foreign influences, artistry became the objective, as it were, in liturgical hymnody. The singers who sing in church - to their shame - think only of showing off their complicated vocal acrobatics. Little by little, they have lost any taste for the ancient chants such as the Znamenny, etc. And traces of this hymnody have ultimately been preserved only in certain ancient monasteries - not in the singing of the monastery choirs, but in old books notated with neumes. We have forgotten that singing is a holy work. We have forgotten that in the time of our forebears the singers did not stand with their backs to the icons.

"Thus, in the end the same thing happened with singing that happened with iconography. Instead of the stern visages of the Cathedral of the Holy Wisdom and the Nereditsky Church of the Savior, the faces of the saints are painted in an entirely different manner. One even sees icons of the Mother of God on which she is depicted with a plunging neckline! There are those who paint or commission icons depicting their paramours. Arakcheev, for example, had an icon on which was depicted the notorious Nastasia Minkina. And in singing also we have forgotten the wonderful Znamenny, Bulgarian and Greek chants. Church singers imagine themselves to be artists: they have begun to think that they are rendering a service to the Lord with a singing that is foreign to the character of our liturgy; they conduct themselves as lords of the kliros; they have forgotten the very elementary truth that those who stand on kliros must, first and foremost, be men of prayer, and not artists. The more risqué and illiterate the harmony used to set certain church hymns, the greater the ecstasy to which such singers are moved. Instead of employing strict harmonies to set, for example, the Cherubic Hymn, they set it to vulgar melodies. They are prepared to introduce into liturgical hymnody the music of any romance suitable for performance in a music hall; they are prepared to make of the kliros a stage. And this at the very moment when the sacred ministers are preparing to perform the Christian Mystery of the Eucharist. Is this not shameful and sinful of us? And we take not the least thought of what responsibility we will have to bear for this profanation of the divine services by our singing.

"Recently in Russian society an interest has arisen in archaeology and, in particular, in the ancient Russian church chant. Russian society is beginning to understand that only a culture based on the firm foundation of the past is durable. You know that schools now exist and are being opened where the ancient chants are studied. The Synodal School in Moscow is just such a school. Composers are studying examples of ancient Russian chant with interest.

"Yet each of us must also labor on his own to inspire interest in this new trend in the province of liturgical music. In the task of regulating church singing I am still unable to count on the present precentors and amateur choir directors, for the reasons outlined above. And in the matter of the restoration of a strictly ecclesiastical manner of singing I am able to rely on the seminaries only when the instructors themselves are imbued with a consciousness of the importance of church singing and, without limiting themselves to classic modes of instruction, will guide their students directly with hymnody in church, and will not present them with the tastes they have developed on their own. Classical instruction must find a suitable liturgical application. The school which I opened in autumn of this year in the old Likhudovsk Building, where singing will be accorded the most serious attention, must serve the task of the rebirth of a strictly ecclesiastical music. I call you also to serve this task.

"The objective of the present Conference lies in the selection of certain uniform liturgical chants from among the vast body of church music which is contained in the notated Synodal liturgical books - the Teaching Anthology, the Octoechos, the Irmologion, the Triodia and Festal Anthology - which contain the most ancient chants - the Znamenny, Kievan, Greek and Bulgarian. The necessity of this is occasioned by the lack of such uniformity in the chants of the churches of the Diocese of Novgorod in connection with the sad state of church music in it. The chant most usually employed constitutes a distortion of the melodies included in these notated books or a traditional fabrication by singers of what has been handed down by ear from one chanter to another. Moreover, in these notated books, published in various years, the same chants are sometimes set forth differently. Hence, there is considerable variation in the performance of church hymns. Such a phenomenon, since it does not correspond to the orderliness of the divine services of the Church, must be eliminated. From the vast body of church music we must select and verify those chants which are most suitable for use in church, and the knowledge and study of them should be made obligatory for all precentors and those studying in church schools.

"Furthermore, the harmonizations of the chants of the Church are too diverse and at times so rife with the self-inventiveness and illiterate creativity of unknowledgeable harmonizers that it is difficult to recognize the basic melody of a given chant. In view of the obligation of educating church choirs, especially those formed of students, it is necessary to point out those settings in which the melody of a chant is most simply and clearly preserved.

"I will not speak to you at any length about the importance of achieving the proposed objective in connection with the significance, on the one hand, of the ancient chant of the Church, and on the other hand, of its sorry state among us. You know, of course, why it is necessary to cherish our ancient church singing. It is the expression of the spirit of our people, who were nurtured and grew under the influence of the Church, which was their tutor, their solicitous mother. But if the Church exercised a religious and moral influence upon the people, the people also brought much of their natural wealth and gifts into the bosom of the Orthodox Church in the form of melodies which expressed the depth and power of their religious sensibilities and the character of their soul in general. These melodies - some simple and elevated, austere and important; some gentle, moving and compunctionate - the people give with a pure heart to their mother, the Church, as their highest possession. This is why these native sounds are dear to them, for they were carefully thought out, felt and experienced by them. They speak volumes to the Russian man: of the past, of the present, and of what awaits us in the future; in them beat the highest, most noble of impulses, holy feelings of love for the Faith, for the Tsar and our native land. This is why it is essential to cherish these national melodies as monuments of the hymnodic creativity of the religious people. Unfortunately, we do not cherish them. Thus, true church hymnody is forgotten, and a new one, alien to the spirit of our people, is devised. Care for the preservation and restoration of ancient church hymnody is one of the principal concerns of those to whom the interests of Church and nation are dear. With this goal in mind, I have convoked the present Conference, which must work out ways for the suitable presentation of church singing in church and secondary schools. You must transmit this true church singing by teaching it to your students. The Conference must show that it need never happen in church that when a clergyman announces the prokimenon in Tone IV or VII, the kliros sings the text of the prokimenon on a single note or chord. In church it is never appropriate to say one thing and do another. In selecting hymns for the divine services, the members of the Conference must give priority to melodic singing over harmonic: the latter pleases, yet does not express a prayerful mood. Church music must be strictly prayerful. Have you noticed that during melodic singing a prayerful silence is, at it were, audible in church? This is not so during harmonic singing, especially when the harmonies are illiterate. When harmonized pieces are sung, each person standing in church follows one or another vocal part, or what the conductor does, etc. But the kliros is not a stage for actors. In church everything must be holy.

"And so, with the help of God, labor now to realize the goals of this first Conference in the Diocese of Novgorod. May the Lord bless you."

I was born in Montreal, Quebec on August 11th, 1977. I lived in Montreal for 12 years before my family moved to Greece for the next two years, but it wasn't until we relocated to Belleville, Ontario, that Byzantine Chant entered my life.

It was the doing of Rev. Father Nicholaos Andreou, who, when he heard me trying to sing along at the altar during a service, offered to take my brother and me under his tutelage. Needless to say, once my mother heard of his offer, there was little to be done about our fate for the next two years. We studied for at least one hour a day, and practiced with Pater for at least 2-3 hours a week. We soon moved to the psaltirion where we chanted almost on our own for vespers and for the Sunday Orthros. This went on for two years when I left for Bishop's University in Lennoxville, Quebec, to pursue an art of a different sort, namely, football ...

Due to the fact that I recently came back to Montreal for the summer, I am now studying with my original teacher's brother, Matheos Andreou, who is the protopsalti at Agiou Georgiou on Côte-St-Catherine Street in Montreal.

Pavlos Papadakis, Nov. 17,1997 (from the internet)

RUBRICS FOR THE CHANT OF THE MASS^{**}

I.   When the Priest goes towards the altar, the cantors begin the Introit. On Ferias and Simples the Intonation is to be sung by one cantor as far as the sign*: on other Feasts and Sundays, there should be two cantors: but on Solemn Feasts there should be four, if as many as four are available. The Choir continues until the Psalm. The first part of the Verse of the Psalm as far as the asterisk, and the /V. *Gloria Patri* are sung by the cantors, the full choir taking up the rest of the verse. Afterwards, the Introit as far as the Psalm is repeated by the full choir.

II.   When the Antiphon is over, the choir sings the *Kyrie eleison* thrice, the *Christe eleison* thrice, and again the *Kyrie eleison* thrice, alternately with the cantors, or with the other half of the choir. But the last *Kyrie eleison* is divided into two or three parts, marked by a single or double asterisk. If there be only two parts, and hence only a single asterisk, the first part is sung by the cantors or by the first half of the choir, the second part by the full choir. If there are three parts, the first being marked by the simple asterisk, and the second by the double one, then, the first part is sung by the same side as in the former case: but the second part, which repeats the melody of the first part, is sung by the other half of the choir: and the third part is by both sides together. Sometimes there are even five parts: then the manner of dividing the alternations in the chanting is marked by the single or double dividing sign being several times inserted; what has been said above sufficiently explains the execution.

III.   The priest alone in a clear voice gives the Intonation of the *Gloria in excelsis Deo*, and then *El in terra pax hominibus*, etc., is continued by the choir divided into two parts, which answer each other, or else the full choir sings in alternation with the precentors. Then follows the response of the choir to the *Dominus vobiscum*.

IV.   After the Epistle or Lesson one or two cantors give the Intonation of the Responsory, which is called the Gradual, as far as the sign*, and all, or at any rate the cantors chosen, conclude the chant with due care. Two sing the Verse of the Gradual, and, after the final asterisk, the full choir finishes it; or else, if the responsorial method is preferred, the full choir repeats the first part of the Responsory after the Verse is finished by the cantors or cantor.

---

^{**} Excerpted from *The Liber Usualis* edited by the Benedictines of Solesmes, Tournai (Belgium), 1934, pages xv and xvj [sic].

If *Alleluia, Alleluia*, is to be said with the Verse, the first *Alleluia* is sung by one or two voices as far as the asterisk*: and then the choir repeats the *Alleluia*, continuing with the neum or jubilus which prolongs the syllable *a*. The cantors next sing the Verse, which is finished by the full choir, as before, beginning at the asterisk. When the Verse is finished, the cantor or cantors repeat the *Alleluia*, and the full choir sings only the closing neum.

After Septuagesima, the *Alleluia* and the following Verse are left out, and the Tract is sung, its Versicles being chanted alternately by the two sides of the choir answering each other, or else by the cantors and the full choir.

In Paschal Time, the Gradual is omitted and in its place the *Alleluia, Alleluia* is sung with its Verse as above. Then one *Alleluia* immediately follows, which must be begun by one or two cantors until the neum is reached, when it is not repeated, but finished by the full choir. The Verse and one *Alleluia* are sung at the end, in the manner above described.

The Sequences are sung alternately, either by the cantors and the choir, and or else by the alternate sides of the choir.

V.   When the Gospel is finished, the priest gives the Intonation of the *Credo*, (if it is to be sung), the choir continuing with the *Patrem Omnipotentem*, the rest, according to custom, being sung either in full choir or alternately.

VI.   The Offertory is begun by one, two or four cantors, in the same way as the Introit, and is finished by the full choir.

VII.   When the Preface is finished, the choir goes on with the *Sanctus* etc., but exclusive of *Benedictus qui venit*. Then only is the Elevation of the Blessed Sacrament. Meanwhile the choir is silent and adores with the rest. After the Elevation the choir sings *Benedictus*.

VIII. After the Response at the *Pax Domini*, the *Agnus Dei* is sung thrice: either by the full choir, the Intonation being given by one, two or four cantors each time: or alternately, but in such a way as to have the *Dona nobis pacem*, or the word *sempiternam* in the Mass of the Dead, sung by the full choir.

After the Communion, the full choir sings the Antiphon which is thus named, the Intonation being sung by one, two or four cantors as in the case of the Introit.

IX.   The priest or the deacon sings the *Ite Missa est*, or the *Benedicamus Domino*, and the choir answers with the *Deo gratias* in the same tone.

In the Mass of the Dead, the choir answers *Amen* to the *Requiescant in pace*.

THE CANTORIAL TRADITION IN CANADA: A BIBLIOGRAPHY

by
Robert B. Klymasz

Introductory Note

This listing is meant to highlight various aspects of Canada's cantorial traditions and generally bypasses related materials published abroad. As such, it is non-exhaustive and ignores the numerous incidental references to cantors scattered throughout a wide range of printed genres. The following classificatory scheme is used to tag individual entries, as appropriate, by using alphabetic letters inserted to the left of each entry:

> C = Comparative, general
> F = French Canadian tradition
> Gr = Greek tradition
> Gg = Gregorian tradition
> J = Judaic tradition
> M = Islamic tradition
> R = Russian tradition
> U = Ukrainian tradition.

The listing ends with an appendix devoted to non-print materials.

Materials in languages other than English or French are noted accordingly. Cyrillic has been transliterated in keeping with a modified version of the international scholarly system. In most caes, copies/originals for unpublished or obscure materials listed below are housed by the CMC's research archives division where they are availabe for consultation by appoinment.

"Appeal for Information Concerning Church Cantors," *Beacon Ukrainian Rite Bimonthly* (Toronto), 34:1, p.23. One response (from Stan Chepyha, U   Saskatoon, Sask.:letter dated March 9,1998) on file.

Bellan, Matt. "Israeli Cantor [David "Dudu" Fisher] Moves Audience to Tears at Negev Gala Concert," *The Jewish Post and News* (Winnipeg, Man.), June J   24, 1998 (vol.12, no. 42), pp.1, 12. With b/w photos.

Bilovus, Josyf. "Nevtorornyj djak. Humoreska z seljans'koho zhyttja," *Tochylo* (Winnipeg), 2 (1935):65-66. A short, humorous scene about a village U   cantor in the Old Country. In Ukrainian.

Borysyk, Mykhailo. *Diak uchytelem. Ditocha komediika na odnu diiu* [=The cantor as teacher. A little comedy for children in one act]. Winnipeg: "Promin'", 1927. 24 pages. (This item is in the card catalogue of the Library of the Ukrainian Cultural and Educational Centre, Winnipeg. However, efforts
U   have failed to locate a copy of this work.) In Ukrainian.

Brearley, Denis. [exhibition catalogue:] *The Publishing of Russian Orthodox Church Music 1700 to the Present.* Prepared for the Eleventh Annual Russian Orthodox Church Musicians' Conference. Ottawa, 1997. Especially item no. 21 (partially reproduced in this publication:
R   "Introduction to the Precentor's Companion").

Breckenridge, Joan. "Tight Funds Put Squeeze on Cantors," in *The Globe and Mail* (Toronto), Sat. September 14, 1996, p. A6. With 1 b/w photo. (See
J   entry under rudacheck, below.)

Buyachok, M. "Dauphin [Manitoba] Deanery Holds Successful Cantor School," *Progress - Ukrainian Catholic News* (Winnipeg), Nov.23, 1997 (no. 22/1893), p. 13. With group photo. "Over 50 participants gathered from
U   such areas as..."

Bzdel, Gerard. "Fr. John Sianchuk Conducts Cantor School," *Progress - Ukrainian Catholic News* (Winnipeg), Sept. 14, 1997 (no. 17/1888), p. 3. With group
U   photo. See entry below under Sianchuk.

"Cantors' Institute Bibliography, compiled 1983, revised 1984"(Toronto?), 2 pp. With 36 itemized entries and 10 addresses "from which books may
U   possibly be obtained."

Calendrier pour les chantres pour l'année 1827. Saint Philippe, Quebec, 1826.
F   34 pages.

"Les chantres et bedeaux sous le régime français", *Le bulletin des recherches
F   historiques* (Quebec), vol.46 (1940):1, pp.121-122.

Corbin, S. "Cantor in Christian Liturgy", in *New Catholic Encyclopedia* 3 (New
C   York, etc., 1967), p. 71 With bibliography.

"Djakivs'ki kursy," *Nasha kul'tura* (Winnipeg), no. 189, 1953, column 32. In
      Ukrainian. The course for cantors, lasting three months, was scheduled to
U   begin Jan.15, 1954.

Djakivs'kyj kurs: zbirnyk cerkovnyx pisen' [=Cantors' course: collection of
      church songs]. Winnipeg: Ukrajins'ka hreko-pravoslavna cerkva v Kanadi,
U   1954. 46 pages. In Ukrainian.

"Djaky kolys' a nynji," in *Iljustrovanyj kaljendar kozaka Harasyma CHornoxljiba*
      (Winnipeg), 1921, pp. 132-138. A discussion about cantors "then and
U   now." In Ukrainian.

"Djaky v Kanadji," in *Iljustrovanyj kaljendar kanadyjs'koho rusyna* (Winnipeg),
      1916, pp. 18-19. The cantor as an important figure in the life of the
U   community. Need for musical training. In Ukrainian.

Elbaz, André E. *Sépharim d'hier et de demain: Trois autobiographies*
      d'immigrants juifs marocains au Canada. Ottawa: Canadian Museum of
      Civilization, 1988. Especially the second chapter/interview with Makhlouf
J   Pérez (Toronto), pp. 114-153.

Feldman, Anna. "Yiddish Songs of the Jewish Farm Colonists in Saskatchewan,
      1917-1939." Master's thesis, Carleton University, Ottawa, Ont., 1983. 2
J   vols. iv+259 pages, music, 1 sound cassette. Passim.

Galadza, Petro. "Vaha i znachennja djakivs'kyx kursiv" [=The importance and
      meaning of cantors' courses], in same volume cited under Romanyshyn in
U   this bibliography, pp. 857-858. In Ukrainian.

Graner, Ronald E., Jewish cantor, Toronto. Dossier of materials on his career and
      activities as a cantor and promotor of the works of composer David
J   Nowakowsky, 1848-1921. Materials received at CMC March 1998.

Gregorian Association (Canada). *Fifth Annual Festival 1955, Order of Service,*
      Toronto, Gg 1955. With music designated for "cantor."

Heller, Charles. *Encore.* 2 vols. Toronto, Toronto Council of Hazzanim, 1983-
      1988. 45+70 pages. Music. Duets and trios with piano accompaniment

176

J   arranged by C. Heller.

_____, ed. *A Testament of Song: Z'MIROT, NIGGUNIM AND SONGS Recalled from Family Tradition.* Toronto: Beth Emeth Bais Yehuda Synagogue, 1990. Three items in this collection (song item nos.16, 28 and 57), all religious, are identified as "Sung by Cantor Harry Federman."

J   Music, texts (with English translations), explanatory notes.

Hrycyna, JE. "Hotujtesja do djakivs'kyx kursiv," in *Vira j kul'tura* (Winnipeg), no. 10, 1954, pp. 28-30. Concerns a training course for cantors. Outline of

U   program of studies and comments on the dire need for qualified cantors.

Huk, John. "Ukrainian Cantors and Church Elders" in his *Strangers in the Land:*

U   *The Ukrainian Presence in Cape Breton.* [Sydney, N.S.1980?], pp. 39-41.

Ilarion, Mytropolyt. "Kantyljacija" [=Cantillation", in his *Biblijni studiji* [=Biblical studies], Winnipeg: "Nasha kul'tura,"1963, pp. 87-89. In

J   Ukrainian.

Kazymyra, Bohdan. "Slidamy Ispovidnyka Iepyskopa Nykyty Budky: Pravyla Ukrajins'ko-katolyc'koji cerkvy v Kanadi" [=In the steps of Bishop Nykyta Budka: rules for the Ukrainian Catholic Church in Canada], in Oleh B.Gerus et al. eds., *The Ukrainian Experience in Canada: Reflections,* Winnipeg: The Ukrainian Academy of Arts and Sciences, 1994, pages 173-197. The Bishop's "rules" were originally published in Winnipeg in 1915 and with reference to cantors (*djaky*) offered guidelines regarding pay

U   (p. 181), and emphasized their musical/liturgical significance (pp. 186-187).

Klymasz, Robert B. "The Cantillation Reseach Project: A Brief Statement and

C   Report," Hull, Que., CMC, April 9, 1998. Unpublished document, 1 page.

Kirshenblatt-Gimblett, Barbara. Her collection of narratives recorded in Toronto among Yiddish informants 1968-1969 includes at least three items of interest. See CMC archival finding no. KG-B-20 (collector's tape

J   nos:1968:27 [folder 210/12]; 1969:25; and 1969:38).

Kolias, Nina K. "Cantors and Chanters of St. Demetrius Church [Calgary], 1957-

Gr   1995," in *The Greeks in Alberta 1903-1995,* Calgary, Alberta, 1996, p. 93.

Koshyc', Oleksander. "Pylyp Overkovych Oleksandrovs'kyj" in his *Spohady* [=Memoirs] part 1 (Winnipeg, 1947), pages 96-108. The renowned composer-conductor offers a rare portrait of a village *djak* and the cantorial
U   tradition in old Ukraine. In Ukrainian.

Kowalchuk, Morris. "The Role of the Cantor." Hazelridge, Manitoba. Unpublished document (4 pages, typed) with covering letter received
U   January 21, 1998.

Kudlyk, Teodor, I. "Uspishne zakinchennja djakivs'koho kursu" [=A successful closing of cantors' courses], in same volume cited under Romanyshyn in
U   this bibliography, pp. 862-864. In Ukrainian.

Kurath, Gertrude Pokosch. "Four Sacred Ceremonies" and "Men's Individual Chants or Adonwe," *Dance and Song Rituals of Six Nations Reserve,*
C   *Ontario*, Ottawa: National Museum of Canada, 1968, pp. 77-78.

Lavriv Oleksa. "Blahorodnyj djak" [The Noble Cantor], in *Tochylo* (Winnipeg),
U   3(1937):45-49. A fictional narrative. In Ukrainian.

Lepkyj, Bohdan. "Opovidannja djaka" [A Cantor's Tale], in *Kaljendar "Holosu*
U   *Spasytelja"* (Yorkton, Sask.), 1945, pp.149-152. In Ukrainian.

Makuch, Andrij. *Hlus' Church: A Narrative History of the Ukrainian Catholic Church at Buczacz, Alberta.* Edmonton:Alberta Culture & Multiculturalism, Historical Resources Division, 1989 (Historic Sites Service, Occasional Paper No. 19). Especially p.17 ("The Diak" as
U   assistant) and pp. 116-118 (activity schedule for "The Diak").

McIntyre, Paul. *Black Pentecostal Music in Windsor.* Ottawa: National Museums
C   of Canada, 1976. Especially pp. 30-31, 50, 58-59, 65-67, 72, 88.

Noy, Dov. [CMC archival collection, file nos.: NOY-B-76 to 90, passim.:synopses, in English, of folkloric materials recorded on audio-cassettes among Ontario informants, 1972-73]. See also Noy's "Classification of the Yiddish (East-European) Joke" with "Alphabetical Index," 4 typescript
J   pages (CMC archival finding no.: NOY-A-1.3).

Papadakis, Pavlos. *Brief Bio of Pavlos Papadakis* [on-line], 5 paragraphs.
    Available: http://www. Owned. org/~pavlos/bio.html [1997, November
Gr   17].

Peacock, Kenneth. *Songs of the Doukhobors*. Ottawa: National Museums of
C   Canada, 1970. Especially p. 15 ("There is no conductor.").

Petrivs'kyj, M[yxajlo] (1897-1982). *Djakouchytel' v shkoli. Komedija v odnij diji.*
    Z zhyttja shkoljatriv tak-zvanoji "djakovchytel's'koji shkoly" v Kanadi j
    Ameryci. Winnipeg, 1927, 22 pages. In Ukrainian. A humorous stage-play
    on student life in immigrant schools in Canada and America where the
U   teachers were cantors.

Quereshi, Regula. Section on "Religious Music" in her "Ethnomusicological
    Research Among Canadian Communities of Arab and East Indian Origin,"
    Ethnomusicology 16(1972):3, p. 390.
C, M

Radkevych, Jaropolk. "Dekan, dyjakon, i djak" [Deacon, subdeacon, and cantor],
    in *Postup* (Winnipeg, Man.), vol.37, no.38 (Oct.1,1995), p. 4. In Ukrainian.
U   the three positions are clarified and distinguished from one another.

Robertson, Gary (Janow/Elma, Manitoba). Unpublished archival correspondence
    and varia, including letter dated November 6, 1997 ("Yes I ended up as
U   church [sic] diak as there was no one else to do the job"...).

Roccasalvo, Joan L. *The Plainchant Tradition of Southwestern Rus'*. Boulder:
    East European Monographs, 1986. Especially p.17 ("Education: Rusin
    Bishops, Clergy and Cantors"), and p. 154, n. 61 ("The position of cantor
    among Rusins continues to be highly esteemed. Approximately ninety
C, U   percent of the Divine Liturgy is sung and led by the cantor").

Romanyshyn, Petro. "Djakivs'ka shkola v Vinnipezi" [=Cantors' school in
    Winnipeg], in Pavlo Sencja, ed., *Svityl'nyk istyny: dzherela do istoriji*
    Ukrajins'koji bohoslovs'koji akademiji u L'vovi 1928-1929-1944. Znahody
    jiji 50-litn'oho juvileju, vol.3, Toronto (etc.), 1983, pp.858-859. In
U   Ukrainian.

"Rozvij ukrajins'koji kul'tury", in *JUvilejnyj kaljendar ukrajins'koji rodyny na 1941 rik -richnyk II* (Mundare, Alberta), pp. 63-65. Cantor training schools ("djakivs'ki shkoly") were held in Mundare in 1939 and in 1940. In
U   Ukrainian.

Rubin, Ruth, folksong collector. CMC archival finding no./folder: RU-B-7 (1 to 16); first song item in this folder is identified as a Chassidic song ("Der rebele, der gabele") recorded by Rubin from Mr.Zachar in Montreal, October 1955. Audio tape no. RU7; with musical and text transcriptions,
J   and translation into English.

[Rudachek, Eugene.] "Squeeze on the Cantorate," *Progress - Ukrainian Catholic News* (Winnipeg), Oct. 13, 1996 (No.33-34/1786), p. 3. The writing of this piece by a Ukrainian Catholic priest was spurred by an article on the Jewish cantorate published about a month earlier in *The Globe and Mail.* (See
U, C   entry above under Breckenridge, Joan.)

Sagasz, Volodymyr. "Djakivstvo i cerkovnyj xor," in Kazymyra, Bohdan et al. comps and eds., *Spil'nym zusylljam i napolehlyvoju praceju: Juvilejna knyha*...[etc.]; (added title-page in English: Conviction, Dedication, Effort: Jubilee Book, 1925-1975, Saint Basil the Great Ukrainian Catholic Parish), Regina,Sask., 1975), pp. 228-236 (includes section, "Djakivs'ka biblioteka..."). In Ukrainian. Followed by abridged version in English
U   ("Cantors and Church Choir"), pp. 237-238.

Scheffel, David. *In the Shadow of Antichrist: The Old Believers of Alberta.* Peterborough, Ont.: Broadview Press, 1991. Especially "Symbols of
R   Orthodoxy: The Church," pp. 131-137.

Shepherd, Harvey. "150 Cantors to Compare Notes: Montreal Convention, Concert and Record Launch to Celebrate Declining Tradition," in *The*
J   *Gazette* (Montreal), Sat. June 14, 1997, p. J7. With 1 b/w photo.

Sheptyc'kyj, Andrej. "Do djakiv" [=To the cantors] in *Pys'ma-poslannja mytropolyta Andreja (Z chasiv bol'shevyc'koji okupaciji)* [=Letters-epistles of Metropolitan Andrej (during the Bolshevik occupation)]. Yorkton, Sask.:Lohos, 1961 (=offprint,Biblioteka Lohosu, tom 24), p. 6.
U   (This letter-epistle is dated December 1939.) In Ukrainian.

Slobin, Mark. *Chosen Voices: The Story of the American Cantorate*. Urbana:
J   University of Illinois Press, 1989, xxv+318 pages.

Sokulski, John. "My Vocation," *Progress - Ukrainian Catholic News* (Winnipeg),
U   May 11, 1997, p. 4.

Steinberg, Ben. "Cantors," *Encyclopedia of Music in Canada*, Toronto:
        University of Toronto Press, 1992 (2nd ed.), pp. 656-656 For French
        version see his "Chantres juifs," *Encyclopédie de la musique au Canada*
J   (1993), pp. 1725-1727.

Stiassny, M.J. "Cantor in Synagogue Service," in *New Catholic Encyclopedia* 3
J   (New York, etc., 1967). p.72. With bibliography and 1 b/w. illus.

Sulte, Benjamin. "Cinq maîtres-chantres," *Trois-rivières d'autrefois* (2nd series),
F   Montreal) vol. 19 (1932), pp. 74-77. Article is dated 1887 at end.

Swan, Alfred. J. "The Makers of the *Znamenny* Chant," in his *Russian Music and
        Its Sources in Chant and Folk-song*, New York: W.W.Norton & Co., 1973,
R   p. 39-44.

"Toronto Cantorial Fund" [on-line], 1 page re this "professional fellowship of
        cantors." Available: http://www.feduja.org/commserv/organize/0177.stm
J   [1997, November 14].

"Toronto Council of Hazzanim (Cantors)" = entry no.1846 with "organizational
        profile" and other data in *Associations Canada: An Encyclopedic Directory
J   / Un répertoire encyclopédique 1997/98,* p. 1146.

Tracz, Orysia. Unpublished typescript received by CMC/CCFCS as a contract
        report, March 1997, on Winnipeg's tradition of Ukrainian cantors. The
        report is composed of 4 parts: "Family Tradition (remembered by Rev.John
        Sianchuk [see next entry], son of Stefan Sianchuk."), 6 pages; "Steven
        Pasternak - diak...[etc.]", 1 page; "Diak"(a synopsis of entries found in three
        Ukrainian encyclopedias), 3 pages; and "John Role [?]. Lecture-
        introduction (from audiotape of lecture), Cantor School 1985, Winnipeg",
U   6 pages.

Ukrainian Catholic Cantor School, Winnipeg, 1998. Rev. John Sianchuk, instructor. Set of U instructional materials including 16 booklets and 15 audio-cassettes.

Zhukovsky, A. "Precentor (*diak*)," *Encyclopedia of Ukraine,* vol. IV.University of
U   Toronto Press, 1993, pp. 182-183.

Zvereva, S.G. "O xore gosudarevyx pevchix d'jakov v XVI v." [="On the choir of tsar's singing diaks in the XVIth century"] in the Academy of Sciences of the USSR, *Pamjatniki kul'tury, novye otkrytija... ezhegodnik 1987* [="Monuments of Culture, new discoveries" yearbook for 1987], Moscow,
R   1988, pages. 125-130. In Russian.

APPENDIX: NON-PRINT MATERIALS

Bodnarchuk, Paul/Pavlo. [A set of 5 audio-cassettes, briefly annotated, featuring liturgical singing performed by Bodnarchuk at 97 years of age.] Melfort, Sask.: privately recorded, 1989. Housed in Library, St.Andrew's College,
U   Winnipeg.

[Compact disc:] *L'art des diacres de l'église russe / The Art of the Deacon in the Russian Church, Live from the Moscow Festival February 1993.* Germany: CDM ("Le chant du monde"), 1994. 19 items (73.30) ("Excerpts from the First International Festival... held in Moscow in February 1993"). With accompanying booklet and brief essay (3 pages) by André Lischke ("L'art des diacres de l'église orthodoxe") followed by English and German
R   translations.

[Long-playing disc recording:] *Vespers. St. Vladimir's Ukrainian Orthodox Cathedral Choir* [Toronto, about 1990?]. Jacketed set of two 12 inch long-playing records, 4 sides, 33 1/3 r.p.m.. With explanatory notes by G. Ferenciw. Cantor identified as J.[Ivan] Radkewych. Text in English and
U   Ukrainian. Label no. SCV1003.

[Video-cassette:] Interview with Daniel Benlolo, cantor with Beth Shalom Synagogue Ottawa; *Shalom Ottawa,* Ms. Jackie Collier, program host and
J   interviewer, Dec.8, 1997. Rogers Community TV Production (Ottawa).

The principle role of the muezzin in Islam is to invite people to prayers. Normally, this call is practiced where Moslems are concentrated. The invitation is made in a loud voice in such a manner that it is heard by all Moslems. Presently and with the advance of technology, the Azzan in most Islamic societies is pre-taped on cassettes that are played at the times of prayers. [...] Consequently, the muezzins are not needed. Moreover, most of the mosques in Canada and specifically in Montreal, where we may count around 20 mosques, have no minarets; and therefore Azzan is not performed.

[Also,] loud public announcements are in general considered as disturbing to others which makes it unlikely that Azzan be accepted. [...] What do you expect from the non-Moslem communities when they hear Azzan or screaming from the top of a tower!

There are no active muezzins in Canada.

> Ali Daher (Montreal),
> letter dated December 18, 1997

ABOUT THE AUTHORS

Carmelle Bégin is an ethnomusicologist and serves as the Chief of the Cultural Studies Division, Canadian Museum of Civilization, Hull, Quebec.

Claudette Berthiaume-Zavada is an ethnomusicologist whose research has focused on many aspects of traditional Ukrainian music. She has conducted much of her work in association with the University of Montreal's *Laboratoire de Recherche sur les Musiques du Monde* (Music Faculty).

Michael Owen Jones is Professor of History and Folklore and Director of the Center for the Study of Comparative Folklore and Mythology, University of California, Los Angeles.

Robert B. Klymasz is Curator, East European Programme, Cultural Studies Division, Canadian Museum of Civilization, Hull, Quebec.

Natalie Kononenko is an Associate Professor in the Department of Slavic Languages and Literatures, University of Virginia (Charlottesville) and has written widely on the topic of Ukrainian minstrelsy and allied phenomena.

Isaac E. Lambertsen serves as Reader with the Russian Orthodox Church Abroad in New York City.

Bohdan Medwidsky is a Professor in Slavic Studies at the University of Alberta (Edmonton) where he was instrumental in the founding of a programme in Ukrainian folklore studies.

Marcia Ostashewski is completing a Ph.D. in ethnomusicology at York University. Her research focuses on music and dance in Ukrainian communities both here and abroad.

I. Sheldon Posen is a writer, researcher and consulting folklorist based in Ottawa. As a youngster in the 1950s, he spent many Saturday mornings *davening* on the *bima* for Beth Shalom Synagogue's Junior Congregation in Toronto.

Anne-Marie Poulin is a specialist focusing on the ethnology of Francophone communities in North America. She lives in Sainte-Foy, Quebec.

LIST OF ILLUSTRATIONS